Missouri Folklore Society Journal

Special Iss

Black Mu
in the Black Press:

An Anthology of Essays
from the Heartland

Volumes 35-36
2013-14

Missouri Folklore Society Journal

(Volumes 35-36, 2013-14)

Special Issue

Black Music in the Black Press:

An Anthology of Essays from the Heartland

by

Marc Rice

General Editors
Dr. Jim Vandergriff (Ret.)
Dr. Donna Jurich
University of Arizona

Missouri Folklore Society
P. O. Box 1757
Columbia, MO 65205

This issue of the *Missouri Folklore Society Journal* was published by Naciketas Press, 715 E. McPherson, Kirksville, Missouri, 63501

ISSN: 0731-2946; ISBN: 978-1-936135-64-6 (1-936135-64-7)

Library of Congress Control Number: 2018964470

The *Missouri Folklore Society Journal* is indexed in:

The *Hathi Trust Digital Library*: Vols. 4-24, 26; 1982-2002, 2004. This library essentially acts as an online keyword indexing tool; only allows users to search by keyword and only within one year of the journal at a time. The result is a list of page numbers where the search words appear. No abstracts or full-text incl. (Available free at http://catalog.hathitrust.org/Search/Advanced).

The *MLA International Bibliography*: Vols. 1-26, 1979-2004. Searchable by keyword, author, and journal title. The result is a list of article citations; it does not include abstracts or full-text.

RILM Abstracts of Music Literature: Vols. 13-14, 20; 1991-92, 1998. Searchable by keyword, author, and journal title. Indexes only selected articles about music that appear in these volumes only. Most of the entries have an abstract. There is no full-text.

A list of major articles in every issue of the journal also appears on the Society's web page. Go to *http://missourifolkloresociety.truman.edu/MFS-Jcnts.html*.

Notice to library subscribers and catalogers:
Though the cover date on this volume is 2013-2014, the volume was actually published in 2018.

The Society's board is working to produce enough issues to catch up with the journal's publishing schedule as quickly as possible.

Contents

Introduction

When future scholars examine the news media of the early 21st century, they will better understand the events that have shaped our world. But, quite possibly, they will also trace the transition from print to online distribution, the instantaneous mass communication afforded by the internet, and the fact that almost all of our media outlets have some sort of bias. In addition to tracing sequences of historical developments, tomorrow's scholars of news media will gain some understanding of the hopes, dreams, tensions, and conflicts that shape our own world. They will recognize the ideological divides of our times, not just through the events, by also by the ways in which these events were reported and discussed.

And so it was with the media of the past. We can read printed media to trace the march of historical events, but we can also take our research further, gaining an understanding of the relationships between newspaper owners, editors, writers, and audience. And while history books may be mostly written by the people in power of a society, material for a more comprehensive study of history is often left by those at the margins of society as well. In the United States, immigrants, Jews, and African Americans had their own media outlets, particularly newspapers, expressing their opinions, hopes, and dreams in a country that was often openly hostile to them.

This book is an anthology of selected writings on popular music that appeared in African American newspapers active in the Midwest from the 1880s to the Great Depression. These selections often reveal new information about historical events, genres or performers, and perhaps that is important. But the pieces also illustrate some of the emotional issues that shaped black life at that time. In them, we can see the rise of black progressivism among African Americans in this part of the country, their pride in achievement, and their economic concerns. The cultural norms and class tensions that were a part of black society are also revealed. A historian is by default an outsider, and as a white scholar looking at African American history, these writings have taught me a great deal about my country, its people, and the music that I love.

The journey of this book began with a phone call. In 1994 I was a Ph.D. student of musicology at the University of Louisville, in the process of shaping the ideas for my dissertation, which would examine the audience reception of 1920s jazz. I was particularly interested in the territory bands of the Mid and Southwest, being inspired by the research of Frank Driggs.[1] Having read Gunther Schuller's *Early Jazz*[2] I took an interest in bandleader Alphonso Trent. The Trent band had made a few recordings which Schuller analyzed, and they sounded very polished and well-rehearsed. I read a brief biography of Trent and learned that his hometown was Fort Smith, Arkansas and that he died in 1959. Somehow the thought occurred to me of calling Fort Smith 411 to see if there were any Trents still living there. The operator gave me a list of six, the first of which was Essie Mae Trent. I proceeded to dial the number.

"Hello, my name is Marc Rice. I am studying jazz history, and I'm looking for any relatives of Alphonso Trent, who was a bandleader in the 1920s and 1930s."

"Oh, hello dear. I'm Mrs. Alphonso Trent."

Essie Mae, Mrs. Alphonso Trent, had survived her husband by 35 years. History was now speaking to me personally. We talked informally for a bit, she wanted to know why I was interested in her husband, and I told her that I would come to visit the following week. I had studied ethnographic interviewing in one of my classes, so I had prepared questions before the trip. I would not have the use for any of them. Five minutes into our discussion Mrs. Trent had changed everything that I thought I understood about the African American experience.

I grew up in a white suburb of Cincinnati in the 1960s and 70s, when there were white neighborhoods and black neighborhoods, and white music and black music. I didn't know anything about the black people who lived in Avondale and Over-the-Rhine, but as a kid, I knew I liked the Jackson 5 much better than the Carpenters, rock music much more than country, and later, jazz much more than Beethoven. Although I had a Catholic education in a post-Martin Luther King world, black people were still presented to me as being all poor and disadvantaged. And I thought that all media, including television, radio, and our two newspapers, the *Cincinnati Post* and the *Cincinnati Enquirer*, reached and represented all

---

[1]Driggs, Franklin S., "Kansas City and the Southwest," in *Jazz: New Perspectives on the History of Jazz by Twelve of the World's Foremost Jazz Critics and Scholars*, ed. Nat Hentoff and Albert J. McCarthy. (New York: Da Capo Press, 1959)

[2]Schuller, Gunther, *Early Jazz: Its Roots and Musical Development.* (New York: Oxford University Press, 1986)

people equally.

Mrs. Trent disabused me of many of these last notions. She told me that Alphonso's orchestra played for the middle and upper classes, both black and white. She told me that she was a debutante, and met him when his band played a ball organized by her family. I sort of knew what a debutante was; those were the rich white girls whose dances and coming out parties were announced in the *Enquirer*. She told me that her husband's band only played in hotels, ballrooms, and steamships. She told me that when the Great Depression led to the band's breakup, she and Alphonso moved to Deadwood, South Dakota, where they made more money entertaining people who had come there to mine for gold. And that when they returned to settle in Fort Smith, they invested in real estate, purchasing most of the houses on their street, which she still owned. Finally, she instructed me to see her husband's grave marker, which was the largest on either side of the town's segregated cemetery.

My interview with Mrs. Trent was my first indication that the territory bands did not just play in bars, dives, cabarets, and jook joints. She taught me that African Americans, like white Americans, like pretty much every culture in the world, have a class structure and that the territory bands made the vast majority of their money performing for the middle and upper classes, both black and white. I continued to gain a better understanding of these issues with the tutelage of Dr. Yvonne Jones, a professor of African American Anthropology at the University of Louisville, and one of the most important members of my dissertation committee. Professor Jones taught me about the black newspapers, what they represented, and how to use them in my research.

Focusing my dissertation studies on Kansas City jazz, and the Bennie Moten Orchestra, in particular, I started to examine the *Kansas City Call* in the mid-1990s. Founded in 1919 by Chester A. Franklin, the *Call* provided a counterpoint to the city's white-dominated newspaper the *Star*, which reported no information on black sports, politics, life, or entertainment. Reading the two newspapers together, the cultural division between whites and blacks becomes stark. The *Call*, as did all African American newspapers, fulfilled a critical need among its readers for representation and inspiration. Again, new worlds were opened to me.

This book is the culmination of twenty years spent collecting and reading material on music in the black press. It is intended to further understanding, to engender discussion, to teach, to be used. I've kept my voice to a minimum, striving to provide context for the material and to enable the original authors to speak once again. They had much to say about their world, and we have much to learn from them.

The concept of this book has been made possible by digital technology. When I began in this field, old editions of newspapers were on microfilm. One went to a library or archive with a stack of dimes, put the microfilm into the reader, and read through each issue with the hope of discovery. Having found something significant, the researcher needed to decide if it could be written down in a notebook, or required a printout, which would cost 10 cents.

The age of digitization has opened up new possibilities for the acquisition and study of archival material such as newspapers. Instead of putting a dime into a microfilm reading machine for one photocopy of one page, researchers can now make pdf files for free, enabling the quick gathering and organization of vast amounts of material. Instead of traveling to a library to use a microfilm, now many of the black newspapers have been digitized and can be read online. The ability to collect, organize, and analyze material has moved forward at hyper speed and is fundamentally changing all fields of archival research, including the creation of this anthology.

With so much material made available because of digitization, I had to create boundaries to shape a research focus. I chose the Midwest because that is where I'm from, and where I live now, because the Midwest was a destination for many southern African American migrants who reshaped the region's cultural landscape, and because there is still more to learn about the region's contribution to African American music. I chose to focus on secular music; an equally large work would be needed to examine sacred music in the black press. The book begins with an article from 1888, when the first wave of postbellum migrants had settled in Kansas and Indiana after the end of Reconstruction, starting newspapers in the process. It ends with the Great Depression, which transformed life for all, especially African Americans and the musicians who entertained them.

The first four chapters draw material from a wide range of sources. They each cover a decade, from the 1880s to the 1910s. During this period there were dozens, if not a few hundred, black newspapers in the country. The essays of the first chapter reveal the establishment of musical communities in the Midwest in the aftermath of the first migration. The essays of the second chapter illustrate what newspaper editors and their readers had to say about minstrelsy and "coon" songs. The third chapter focuses on the creation and the spreading popularity of ragtime. The essays of the fourth chapter concern the further dissemination of ragtime, the evolution of jazz, and the impact of World War I on black music in the Midwest.

By the 1920s larger presses emerged, including the *Kansas City Call*, the *Chicago Defender*, the *Pittsburgh Courier*, and the *New York Amsterdam*, with which the newspapers from smaller towns could not compete. Thus for this period, I've chosen to make a case study of the Midwest's two largest black newspapers, the *Call*, and the *Defender*, the subject of the book's final four chapters. Chapters 5 and 6 provide examples of the *Call*'s musical coverage, specifically the jazz life of Kansas City and the black middle and upper classes which supported it. Chapter 7 focuses on The Stroll, Chicago's State Street collection of cabarets where New Orleans rhythms met the corruption of Prohibition. Chapter 8 is a selection of the writings of Chicago musician/composer/bandleader Dave Peyton, which reveals the challenges of life for musicians at that time.

There is much more to be gained from reading and researching the historical black press. The newsmen and women wrote about politics and civil rights issues, religion, sports, social organization, issues relating to women, and a plethora of other topics that await our investigation. And the topics that are represented in this book are far from completely exhausted. I chose material for detail, and to create a linear narrative, but, in the end, only a fraction of what there is to be found has made it into this work.

Acknowledgments

Going into this book are the hundreds of teachers, students, librarians, historians, and family members who shaped my thinking and the choices that I have made. Professor Stephen Goacher introduced me to jazz during my undergraduate days at Northern Kentucky University. His patience with me and his love of the music continue to inspire. Dr. Greg Smith at the New England Conservatory also showed patience and taught me what jazz research was all about. Mark Tucker's class on Duke Ellington at Columbia University was a revelation. At the University of Louisville, Dr. Jean Christensen and Dr. Yvonne Jones did not simply instruct me, they changed my career and my life.

At Truman State University I've been blessed with many supportive colleagues. Drs. Jay Bulen and Jesse Krebs in the Music Department, in particular, inspired me to write this book for our students. Neal Delmonico, Bob Mielke, and Cole Woodcox read early samples of my work and provided valuable feedback. Lori Allen at Pickler Library did amazing work in tracking down the microfilm. Adam Davis was very supportive of the work, encouraging me to submit it, and working on the editing of it. And ultimately, I am grateful to the University as a whole for the sabbatical I received in the fall of 2015 enabling the completion of this book.

And now for my family. This book is dedicated to my dad, Jay Rice, who supported me and whose spirit is still with me now. It is dedicated to my mom Mary Sue, and my brothers John and Tim. It is dedicated to my stepson Al, who makes my heart sing. It is dedicated to our three dogs and four cats, all of whom watched me write it.

And finally, this book and my life are dedicated to my wife, the musicologist Laura Pita. My love, my partner, and my inspiration. *Te quiero mucho, mi amor.*

Chapter 1:
Music and the African American Exodus, 1879-1890

This study begins in the 1880s when the first wave of African American migration from the South to the Midwest sparked the rapid growth of several black communities large enough to sustain a newspaper, and in some cases more than one newspaper, in states such as Kansas and Indiana. This mass movement began when the end of Reconstruction in 1877 led to the swift persecution of blacks in the Deep South, eliminating their possibility of living as equal citizens in control of their own destiny. In groups of dozens, hundreds, and thousands black people left the Jim Crow laws, political disenfranchisement and violence of Alabama, Louisiana, Georgia, and Mississippi. Thousands of migrants, following activist/organizers such as Henry Adams from Louisiana and Benjamin "Pap" Singleton from Tennessee, referred to themselves as "Exodusters," akin to those who took up the journey with Moses in the desert. Their path of escape was the Mississippi River, which took them to the western gateway of St. Louis. From here many went west across the former slave state of Missouri to arrive in Kansas, where they joined pre-existing communities or established their own. In North Carolina, another group of black politicians and activists, disenfranchised after the pro-Confederate Democrat party took control of the state government, seriously considered a mass- movement to Liberia, before deciding upon central Indiana as a more reasonable place of refuge. In one 30 day period in 1879, 6,000 people left North Carolina to settle

1

near Indianapolis.[1]

By the late 1880s Kansas, the goal of many Exodusters, had by far the most African American newspapers of any state in the country. Between 1875-1890, there were at least 14 weeklies in circulation, and the most fruitful for material pertaining to music and other arts were the *Nicodemus Cyclone*, which published from 1887-1889, and the *Leavenworth Advocate*, published from 1888-1891. In Indiana, 1888 saw the first edition of the *Indianapolis Freeman*, whose motto was "An equal chance and fair play," and had by far the most in-depth and detailed coverage of black music and theatrical performances in the final decades of the 19th century. Ohio's *Cleveland Gazette* began in 1883 and ran until 1945, and covered not just events in Cleveland, but also in Cincinnati and on the East Coast.

Essays from the Exodus

The first two documents, written three months apart in 1879-1880, are editorial essays from the most widely distributed newspapers in Kansas and Indiana at the time. Both writers were already established in their respective towns and were thus observing large groups of people from the South suddenly entering their community. Both acknowledge the travesties of white rule in the South and the reasons for quitting the region. The Kansan writer seems to be encouraging the newcomers, with whom he finds kinship by referring to them as "our people," to try other states, while the Indianan writer observes that the new arrivals are experienced farmers, much needed in an undeveloped state:

---

[1] The scholarship regarding the black migration to Kansas begins with the work of Nell Irving Painter, whose 1977 book *Exodusters: Black Migration to Kansas after Reconstruction* (NY: W.W. Norton, 1998) is the first comprehensive examination of the group, their leaders, and the issues that they faced. Also important for the study of the Exodusters is Painter's article "Millenarian Aspects of the Exodus to Kansas of 1879," in the *Journal of Social History* (Spring, 1976): 331-338. Lisa M. Frehill's article "Occupational Segmentation in Kansas and Nebraska, 1890-1900," in *Great Plains Research* (Autumn, 1996): 213-244 details the economic impact of the resultant population growth during and after the black migration. Bryan M. Jack's work *The St. Louis African American Community and the Exodusters* (Columbia: University of Missouri Press, 2008) examines the impact of black migration during this time in the city that served as the departure point for the West. And Frenise A. Logan's essay "The Movement of Negros from North Carolina, 1876-1894," in *The North Carolina Historical Review* (January 1956): 45-65 details the loss of political power for the state's African Americans, and the decision of their leaders to forego migration to Liberia, settling instead in Indiana.

Plain Talk

... We favor the exodus. We have several reasons for favoring it. We are in favor and would be glad to welcome every colored man from the South to the growing West. We think some good might derive from a move to get some of our people from the South to go elsewhere than Kansas: not that this State is too crowded, but because other Western states hold out as great inducements to the new-comer as Kansas.

Another and a prominent reason why we favor the exodus is because affairs in the South have undergone such a change, that it is simply impossible for the colored man to remain there with any degree of safety to either life or property; because he is not allowed to exercise the rights guaranteed by the laws of the very State in which he resides; because he is cheated, robbed and even murdered by his professed best friends; because he has no redress for wrongs before the courts of his native State, and in fact is not looked upon by the chivalrous Southern as constituting a part of the body politic; because he is not allowed representation in the councils of his State, when it "is generally known" that the colored voters are in the majority.

If a fair and honest election could be held, the States of Mississippi, Louisiana, Georgia and South Carolina would roll up rousing Republican majorities; but as matters now stand, the shotgun Democrats have captured the State governments, and are prepared to hold them.

Yes, we favor the exodus, first, last and all the time.

Source: *Herald of Kansas* (Topeka), February 6, 1880, 2.

The Exodus

Last Saturday a car load of immigrants from North Carolina passed through the city en route for Greencastle.[2] A reporter of *The Leader* visited and interviewed them at the union depot. They are all farmers from the vicinity of Goldsborough. They are a fine looking set of men, of more than average intelligence. They have no desire to locate

---

[2]Greencastle is about 40 miles west of Indianapolis.

in the cities but wish to get into the country where they can find employment with the prospect of being able in a short time to purchase homes. They all tell the same story of the fraud, persecution and brutal treatment to which they are subjected in the South. No candid man who talks with these people and mingles with them can believe any of the stories of colonization so industriously circulated by Democratic papers and politicians. These people are not the paupers and riff-raff of the Southern cities. They are the industrious farmers and laborers from the country–the very bone and sinew of the land. Many of them have money and property at home. One of the immigrants above mentioned had about two hundred and fifty dollars and others sums varying from twenty-five to a hundred and fifty.

Indiana needs such men to develop her resources, and it is strange that men of pretended intelligence will allow a blind prejudice to put them in opposition to a movement that must tend greatly to the material wealth and prosperity of the State. These people leave the South because they are defrauded and robbed of their honest earnings, denied their political rights, and otherwise brutally used by the semi-barbarous whites of the South. They come to Indiana because they can find employment with honest employers, and human treatment in civilized communities. Let them come, and let all good citizens lend a helping hand to the honest effort these poor people are making to better their condition and make a future for their children.

Source: *Indianapolis Leader*, November 29, 1879, 1.

Exodusters Making Music

The largest African American population in Kansas, both before and after the arrival of the Exodusters, was in Topeka and the surrounding area. By 1880 there was already an established black community, with a church and social hierarchy. This review illustrates the presence of Euro-American popular music within this, and most northern black communities, especially in connection with churches and schools. The performers here were amateurs from the local music club; the concert must have been the cultural highlight of the week for the community, and the performances themselves were hit-and-miss:

THAT CONCERT
Union Hall Was Crowded to Overflowing
It Was Not as Good as Expected
THIS IS THE PREVAILING SENTIMENT

The attendance at Union Hall last night to witness the musical and dramatical [sic] entertainment given by the Topeka Musical Club, for the benefit of the Second Baptist Church was very large, and the concert first-class with very few exceptions.

The opening Chorus by the company Music Sweet Music was rendered in good style, but [the] piano playing was of an inferior quality.

Mr. H.W. Dillard, in his specialties, brought down the house, and likewise the indignation of the majority of the audience.

Miss Mary F. Herr then sang a solo "Mona May" which we are unable to tell anything about, as it was in such a low tone of voice.

The duet "The Old Oaken Bucket," by Messrs. H.H. DeShattio and John Wheeler, was rendered in a style that would have did [sic] credit to older singers, and elicited continued applause from the audience. Their voices were clear, and every word of the duet could be distinctly heard in every part of the hall.

Miss Mollie Martin, of Lawrence, then sang a Solo and Chorus "When 'Tis Moonlight," which was heartily received, and many were the complements heard during the evening in reference to the sweet voice of Miss Martin. The lateness of the hour prevents the notice that Miss Martin deserves. She certainly could, with a little more practice, become a singer of no small caliber.

The Solo "In Happy Moments," by Miss M.V. Price did not fail to accord to her the appreciation and applause of the entire audience and had Miss Price's voice been louder, her effort would have been all the better. However, Miss

Price's singing compares favorably with that of anyone in the concert.

Miss Mary A. Thompson rendered the Solo "When the Birds Have Gone to Sleep," with fine effect, but the "pianer" [sic] playing during this piece was simply ridiculous, and the audience could readily see the effect it had on the singer.

"The Little Pathway Mid the Daisies" by Mr. James Miller, or Lawrence, was good and highly appreciated. Mr. Miller has a good voice, but he sings entirely too low to be heard in such a place as Union Hall.

Miss Mollie Martin of Lawrence in the Solo and Chorus "Somebody's Coming" convinced all that she could sing, and when she had finished singing the applause was deafening. Miss Martin's sister performed on the piano during the singing of the piece.

The Herald may be a little prejudiced, but the singing of the Lawrence ladies was far superior to any of the Topeka talent in the concert, with but one exception, and that was Miss Mary Price, who we are compelled to give the credit of being a first-class singer. However, it is hardly fair to make special mention of singer's talent, as it has a tendency to create a prejudice.

The solo and chorus by Miss Willie Martin, of Lawrence, was probably good, but the writer failed to hear just what she was singing ...

Source: *Herald of Kansas* (Topeka), May 28, 1880, 2.

The town of Nicodemus, Kansas was founded in 1877 by a small group of former slaves from Kentucky wishing to create the first all-black community in the isolated northwest part of the state. For the first two years, the population increased, reaching 800 by 1880. But by mid- decade, it was on the decline, beset by poor harvests and the opposition of nearby white communities. In 1888, there was a campaign by the citizens to attract more people and a railroad, and the *Nicodemus Cyclone* was central to this effort.

The two advertisements below appeared in the *Cyclone* from January to May 1888. Lyon & Healy at this time specialized in cornets and string instruments; eventually, they would become important harp manufacturers. They were the Chicago branch of the Oliver Ditson publishing company.[3]

---

[3]Lyon & Healy, Oxford Music Online, accessed September 13, 2015.

The only black newspapers where this organization regularly purchased ad space in 1888 were the *Chicago Dailey Inter Ocean,* and for these few months, the *Cyclone.* The ad buy suggests the possibility that the *Cyclone* had a further reach than just the few hundred citizens of Nicodemus. Probably representatives from the town took it on trains to the larger cities of the region in their attempt to attract new settlers. In any case, the ad does reveal that there was a market for music books of all types among the region's African American community, even as many were in the process of establishing new homes. The subsequent ad, "Are You a Music Teacher," from the same company, appeared later in the year in the *Leavenworth Advocate.*[4]

The Musical 1888.

As the musical New Year heaves in sight, we greet it with the "sound of Cornet," (or any other musical instrument, for all of which Oliver Ditson & Co. provide the very best Instruction Books.)

With the New Year many New Pupils will commence to learn the Piano; to them and their teachers we commend

RICHARDSON'S NEW METHOD
FOR THE PIANOFORTE,

a peerless book, which has held the lead for many years, and, unaffected by th appearance of other undoubtedly excellent instructors, still sells like a new book. Price $3.

CHILDREN'S DIADEM [30 cts., $5 per doz.] is filled with happy and beautiful Sunday School Songs, and is one of the best of its class. The newest book.

UNITED VOICES [50 c's., $4.80 per doz.] furnishes abundance of the best School Songs for a whole year. The newest book.

Books that sell everywhere and all the time:

College Songs 50 cts., War Songs 50 cts., Jubilee and Plantation Songs 30 cts., Minstrel Songs, new and old, $2, Good Old Songs we used to Sing $1.

KINKEL'S COPY BOOK [75 cts.] with the Elements and Exercises to be written, is a useful book for teachers and scholars.

Any Book Mailed for the Retail Price.

LYON & HEALY, Chicago.
OLIVER DITSON & CO., Boston.

ARE YOU A MUSIC TEACHER?

The best tools make the best work. The best instruction books make the best scholars. The best teachers use Ditson & Co.'s Instructors.

The following books sell largely, and all the time:

Richardson's New Method for the Pianoforte. ($3) N. E. Conservatory Method for the Pianoforte. ($3) Mason & Hoadley's System for Beginners, (on Piano) $3, and Mason's System of Technical Exercises $2.50. Bellak's Analytical Method for Piano, (for beginners) $1, and Winner's Ideal Method, (for beginners) 50 cts.

EVERY MUSIC TEACHER needs a full set of Ditson & Co.'s great Catalogues, describing fully the largest stock in America. An investment which pays well is a subscription to Ditson & Co.'s Monthly Musical Record, ($1) which describes intelligently every new music book as it is issued, and every new piece of music; prints excellent lessons, pieces and songs, discusses theories, and gives a condensed "Record" of the world's music.

SCHOOL MUSIC TEACHERS are invited to examine and use the newest of our successful School Music Books; Song Manual (Bk. 1, 30 cts. or $3 per doz. Bk. 2, 40 cts; or $4.20 per doz. Bk. 3, 50 cts or $4.80 per doz.) by L. O. Emerson. Thoroughly good and interesting graded course. Also Song Harmony, (60 cts. or $6 per doz.) by L. O. Emerson to be used in High Schools or for Adult Singing Classes.

LYON & HEALY, Chicago.
OLIVER DITSON & CO., Boston.

Souces: *Nicodemus Cyclone,* January 27, 1888, p. 1 and *Leavenworth Advocate,* October 10, 1888, 4.

Minstrelsy in Kansas

During the last decades of the 19th-century minstrel shows employing black, not white, performers were one of the most popular forms of en-

---

[4]For more on the town of Nicodemus, see Nell Irvin Painter's book *Exodusters* pp. 149-154, and Kenneth Marvin Hamilton, *Black Towns and Profit: Promotion and Development in the Trans- Appalachian West, 1877-1915* (Urbana: University of Illinois Press, 1991).

tertainment among African American audiences. These shows presented the audience with a conflict: while the singers, musicians, and comedians perpetuated offensive stereotypes, they also demonstrated good musicianship, dancing skills, and sharp comedic timing. Many black newspapers featured an entertainment section, where columnists reported on the travels and reception of the minstrel troupes, and promoters bought advertising space for shows. Reviews of the shows that appeared in the Midwest were usually quite positive, remarking both on the skill of the performers, and the community's interest in their progress and desire to see them succeed:

> ... **Harvey's genuine colored minstrels, composed of Leavenworth talent, which took the road a few weeks ago are meeting with success far beyond their expectations. At Valley Falls last week they played to a large audience, and people who seen [sic] them, says they are the best minstrel party that ever visited that town. Next Thursday night they will play at the Crawford. They go from here to Wyandotte where they play next Friday night ...**

Source: *Nicodemus Cyclone,* January 27. 1888, 1.

> **McCabe & Young's Operatic Minstrels was greeted at Chickering Hall by a crowded house last night, and is beyond all reasonable doubt, the finest and most complete Minstrel organization that has visited this city for many years. McCabe and Young are a whole party by themselves; and old Ben Hunn a party-and-a-half. We hope you return boys, as it is a rare treat.**

Source: *Leavenworth Advocate,* September 8, 1888, 2.

On the other hand, as Abbott and Seroff make clear, one of the primary goals of the newspaper owners was to agitate for civil rights, to demand respect from whites, and to encourage their black readership to act in ways that would garner respect.[5] Indeed essays appearing in these newspapers were a part of the beginning of the fight against racial oppression that would lead to the NAACP, the Urban League, the work of DuBois and many others, and ultimately the Civil Rights movement of the 1950s and 60s.

---

[5]Lynn Abbott and Doug Seroff, *Out of Sight: The Rise of African American Popular Music, 1889-1895* (Oxford, MS: University Press of Mississippi, 2009): xxi.

And thus there was conflict, for often the owners/editors of black newspapers saw European culture, including the arts, as the ultimate demonstration of a refinement that would bring respect to their readership. And certainly, light classical music was a mainstay of the concert halls and schools of any black community. But for entertainment, for dancing, and for after hours, many in the community turned to the syncopated rhythms, the blues-inflected melodies, and the dark humor of African American musical expression. And in the decades after Emancipation, new generations of black entertainers were re-appropriating their artistic heritage.

These next two excerpts illustrate the point. First is a review of a performance of "East Lynne," a British romantic novel-turned-play popular in the mid-19th century both in Europe and the U.S. The review points out that the actors were from Leavenworth, many had never acted before, yet they organized the production to provide "a higher order of entertainments and amusements." The reviewer liked the show, but was frustrated with the lack of attendance, in the final sentences questioning the tastes of his readership with the harshest language used to refer to the popular minstrel shows:

The young ladies and gentlemen of talent in this city have organized for the purpose of giving us a higher order of entertainments and amusements to take the place of the common festivals. The production of "East Lynne" this week, which was well rendered by the company, considering the time they had to prepare for the exhibition and the disadvantages under which they labored; many of them never appeared before an audience in the capacity of actors and actresses, they certainly did well. It is hoped that this will not be their last effort to entertain the public. We have but one complaint to offer, and that is not in connection with the performance, but the slim attendance. The Conservatory of Music, where the performance was given, should have been filled to its utmost capacity by our people instead of being sparsely filled as it was. We wonder when our people will learn to appreciate and endorse the good that is in the Race? When will they learn to encourage and applaud the laudable undertaking of our cultured young ladies and gentlemen? Had it been a white man's "nigger" show, apeing and deriding colored people, making all manner of sport of them, the house would have been filled to overflowing with colored people to listen to the ridicule of themselves, by white men blacked playing "nigger."

Source: *Leavenworth Advocate*, September 7, 1889, 2.

In contrast to this damning essay, less than a year later an advertisement appeared in the same paper for a visit to Crawford's Grand Opera House in Leavenworth by one of the most popular African American minstrel shows, "Cleveland's Colossal Colored Carnival Minstrels." The list of attractions included a parade, which was "truly grand and gorgeous," gladiators, and "Correct Representations of Native Africa." Whether or not James Bland was actually "the Highest Salaried Colored Artist in the World" cannot be ascertained, but indeed he was famous as a versatile performer. He had left the Howard University law school to become a minstrel performer in 1876 and was known in particular for his songs "Oh Dem Golden Slippers" and "Carry me back to old Virginny," as well as his acting and acrobatic stunts.[6]

CRAWFORD'S GRAND OPERA HOUSE
"BIG BLACK BOOM." WEDNESDAY NIGHT, AUG. 6TH.
W. S. CLEVELAND'S COLOSSAL COLORED CARNIVAL MINSTRELS

W. S. Cleveland—Solo owner and manager of The Big Mouth Comedian, TOM McINTOSH, The Highest Salaried Colored Artist in the World, Jas. A. Bland, Billy Farrell, Will Eldridge, Doc Sayles, The Four Brewer Bros. Geo. Thichner, Eaton & Willims, Grant & Williams, Smart & Taylor, Sans Souci Quartette, Twilight Quartette, The Great Javelin, Mons. LeVard, Jas. Wilson, Cicero Reed and 49 other colored minstrel notables. The March of the Mozambique Gladiators, An Original and Unique Novelty, with Correct Representations of the Native Africa. The Grandly Realistic, Classic First Part Spectacle, the Toreadors unequaled in its display. The truly grand and gorgeous parade takes place every day at noon. Don't miss this grand display.

H.W. Semon———————————————-Manager
Chas. Holton———————————————-Gen'l Agent.

Scale of prices as usual. Reserved seats may be secured at the Palace Drug Store three days in advance. Secure seats and avoid the jam.

Source: *Leavenworth Advocate*, August 2, 1890, 3.

---

[6]"James A. Bland," Oxford Music Online, accessed September 23, 2015.

The following week a different kind of minstrel show came to Leavenworth. Primrose and West were whites who had begun their career
as blackface minstrels. But in 1881 they encountered a British minstrel
troupe touring the U.S. which featured not African American caricature
but European-style entertainment. In response, Primrose and West had
completely abandoned blackface, in favor of ballet, orchestral music, and
drama featuring fox hunting and lawn tennis.[7] Although they were white
performers, the Leavenworth Advocate found much to admire in their
more tasteful presentation:

CRAWFORD'S OPERA HOUSE

F.C. DAVIS,————————————————Manager
Thursday, Aug. 14
Appearance of America's
Favorites Primrose and West's
Minstrels
50 Great Artists 50

Presenting a novel entertainment. See, the March of the
Imperials, Log Cabin Neighbors, The mystifying Crema-
tion, A Horrible Night and the Beautiful Monti Cristo. First
Part Grand street parade of this stupendous organization
at 12 noon on the day of the performance. Advance sale
open Aug. 12th at the Palace Drugstore.

Source: *Leavenworth Advocate*, August 9, 1890, 3.

Minstrelsy in Ohio

The Cleveland Gazette was another black Midwest newspaper with a
strong political stance and detailed coverage of musical events. Kenneth
Kusmer's comprehensive study of African Americans in Cleveland illustrates the pattern of black population growth during the 1880s, and the
same push and pull factors of Southern racism and greater opportunity in
the industrialized North seen in Kansas and Indiana. In fact, according

---

[7]Robert C. Toll, *Blacking Up: The Minstrel Show in Nineteenth-Century America* (NY: Oxford
University Press, 1977): 152-54.

to Kusmer, the black population in Cleveland grew from 1,300 in 1870 to 3,000 in 1890. He also finds that Cleveland's African Americans had a higher economic status than in most cities, and faced a lower level of prejudice. And Kusmer also discusses Harry C. Smith, one of the several black entrepreneurs, and his newspaper *The Cleveland Gazette*, which Smith used as a vehicle for his opinions on segregation, discrimination, and racial prejudice.[8]

In December 1883 a week-long minstrel festival took place in Cincinnati. Although issues of the *Cincinnati Afro-American* of the time are no longer extant, the event was also covered by the *Cleveland Gazette*. In this sample, an announcement of the event that first appeared in the *Afro-American* and was later published by the *Gazette*, the writer, and presumably at least some of his readership, are enthusiastic about the festival. There are phrases such as "wonderful undertaking," and the description of the scenery seems to hope for a realistic depiction of black life, as opposed to that presented by white minstrel shows.

This example sites many characters, some obscure but others important to the history of minstrelsy, especially in the Midwest. George Ward Nichols was a Colonel in the Union army, serving under John C. Fremont in Missouri, and later with Sherman during the Atlanta campaign. He was the first to write about the exploits of Wild Bill Hickok in an article for *Harpers*, and later wrote a book on Sherman's March. He ultimately settled in Cincinnati, where he founded the College of Music and served as its first president.[9] In this role, he must have served on the Board of Directors for Cincinnati's Music Hall, which was completed in 1878. It was, and continues to be, the city's premier space for classical music performance, and the home of the Cincinnati Symphony Orchestra.

The Frohman brothers were important promoters of minstrel shows. One of their most successful endeavors was the purchase in 1881 of the small African-American troupe Callender's Consolidated Colored Minstrels. Through investing in sets and costumes, and a merger with another black troupe, the Frohman brothers developed the Callender's group to such an extent as to control the market for black minstrelsy.[10]

Several minstrel performers are mentioned, the most famous being Billy Kersands. Kersands was known for his large mouth, which he used while playing up racial stereotypes, to great comedic effect in his songs and skits. Although he based his career on caricature roles of slow- witted

[8]Kenneth Kusmer, *A Ghetto Takes Shape: Black Cleveland 1870-1930* (Urbana: University of Illinois Press, 1976).

[9]J. G. Rosa. "George Ward Nichols and the Legend of Wild Bill Hickok," in *Arizona and the West* (summer, 1977): 135-162.

[10]Robert C. Toll. *Blacking Up*, p. 204.

blacks with exaggerated features, he was very popular with both white and African American audiences. In this show, he performed a duet with George Ward Nichols, a send-up of the balcony scene from *Romeo and Juliet.* Presumably, Kersands played Romeo, as the over-sexed male was one of his stock characters.[11]

THE GREAT MINSTREL FESTIVAL

From the [Cincinnati] Afro-American[12]

George Ward Nichols has at last withdrawn his opposition to the introduction of colored minstrel talent on the stage of Music Hall during the Great Minstrel Festival which will be given at our magnificent Cincinnati Music Hall, commencing December 31, and lasting the entire week.

This wonderful undertaking was originated by those imperial theatrical managers, the Frohman Brothers, and our own popular and noted R.E. Miles, of this city. The plans to make this one of the greatest events of the year are in the hands of such eminent and capable men that the prospects are favorable indeed for the realization of the highest interpretations of the minstrel's art. Almost an army of talent has been engaged and will appear during the week in characteristic renditions. The comedian, the vocalist, the artistic clog dancer and the impersonator, each and all have been engaged. A grand orchestra band of over a hundred performers have been engaged and will appear during the week.

The most magnificent and realistic features of the scenic art will be brought into requisition in order to present perfect and real-life scenes and incidents of the colored race of all parts of the country. [emphasis mine]

Professor Charles Singer, an old and favorite Cincinnati man, has charge of the Festival, as leader of the orchestra and grand choruses. An interview with Prof. Singer elicited the following facts: The famous Lion Choir, of Chicago, will be on hand and form one of the leading attractions of the Festival. The jolly and funny comedian and end man, Billy Kersands, together with his Mammoth Cave

---

[11]For more on the popularity of Kersands among black audiences, see Toll, *Blacking Up*, pp. 256-262.

[12]*The Cincinnati Afro-American* was first published in 1882. The end of its run is unknown.

grin, will appear.[13] The noted Billy Banks, Billy Green, Bob Mack and Pete Devoneau and others will be here. The colored Campanini, Wallace King, undoubtedly the sweetest-toned tenor in America, will also appear. Charles E. Bentley, the Cincinnati representative tenor-vocalist, will also be in the Festival, as also will be the Hyer sisters. Prof. Singer, who has had an experience of a number of years as leader of Callender's Colored Minstrels, will have charge of the music of the Festival and is now in the city superintending the work that is being pushed forward rapidly to a successful finish. George Ward Nichols and Billy Kersands are rehearsing the balcony scene from "Roam O Julie Yet" for the Minstrel Festival.

Mr. Gustave Frohman, who has had many years of experience with colored people as the manager of colored minstrel companies, says that he has found that quite a large number of them possess eminent talent and ability. He said also, that inasmuch as they had but few opportunities of displaying their talents that he had determined to afford them as many chances as he possibly could. Besides the great Minstrel Festival, which originated with his brother and himself, and in which only colored people will appear, that he has purposed to establish a Colored Opera Company, believing that this, like his other ventures, will prove successful ... .

Source: *Cleveland Gazette*, December 22, 1883, 2.

The major minstrel shows did not often come to Cleveland, as they focused on touring the east coast and the south. Sawyer's Minstrels were a short-lived organization, led by one of the few African American promoters of the time A. D. Sawyer. Cleveland in 1885 was not a territory controlled by one of the big companies. Although famous names did not often appear in Cleveland, the *Gazette* also reported on other types of musical events in town, including minstrel-type shows organized by local performers:

Sawyer's Minstrels proved a veritable Mascotte[14] to the People's Theater last week and packed the house every matinee and evening. Miss Frankie Brown, in her solos,

---

[13]Mammoth Cave National Park is in central Kentucky, 190 miles south of Cincinnati.

[14]The term "Mascotte" may very well refer to a popular opera by that name, composed by Edmond Audran, which had debuted five years earlier.

cannot be excelled. The sweetness of her voice is indeed remarkable, and her numbers upon the program were gems indeed. Hunn, Sayles, and in fact every one of the company are artists in their specialties. Without a doubt Mr. Sawyer will have continued success, because he merits it, having given this city the best minstrel show ever brought here. He visits Canton, Toledo, et al., before going into the West ...

Source: *Cleveland Gazette*, April 18, 1885, 2.

The Cleveland Patriarchie held a successful entertainment last Wednesday evening at Haleyon Hall. The Patriarchie, under command of Captain L. W. Wallace, gave one of their excellent drills. Messrs. J. Fairfax, R. Decker, E. Vaughn and Joseph Brown contested for a watch, the first named winning it, each having respectively 450, 53, 91, and 83 votes. After an enjoyable hop to Bush's orchestra, all wended their weary limbs homeward. January 1, 1885. The Misses Buckingham, Blakely, and Brown, comparative strangers, present at this entertainment, created sad havoc with many a dude's heart ...[15]

Source: *Cleveland Gazette*, December 3, 1885, 4.

AMUSEMENTS
MANAGER B. C. HART'S BENEFIT

On Sunday evening, June 6, Manager Hart takes a farewell benefit at the Academy of Music. This will be the last night of the Academy under the present management, and when Manager Hart announces a benefit the public is sure to get something new and novel in the shape of an evening's entertainment. A colossal minstrel first part will start the programme, with Manager Hart and John N. Norton, of the Press, on the ends. Among the many novelties of the evening will be a grand shaving contest for the championship, and for a purse. One hundred different people will take part during the long and varied programme promised for the evening, and we are safe in saying nothing in the history of amusements will equal this night's performance.

---

[15]The Cleveland Patriarchie were a drill team.

Source: *Cleveland Gazette*, May 29, 1886, 2.

The *Gazette* also featured musical news from upstate New York, the Great Lakes region, and south to Louisville, but only if the event had some political or cultural implication:

> **During a recent engagement of the Kersands-Hicks Minstrel Company at Louisville, Mr. Hicks one of the proprietors of the company, stood down at the theater door and steered the colored people into the gallery of the theater. The colored people of Louisville are greatly incensed thereat and have written the names of Kersands and Hicks on their revenge books.[16]**

Source: *Cleveland Gazette*, July 25, 1885, 1.

Syracuse

> **... The concert and festival which took place at the A.M.E. Zion Church February 6 was largely attended and a financial success. The boys deserve much credit for their effort. Instead of a concert, it was a minstrel, under the management of Rufus Watson. He and Frank Wagner are pretty clever minstrels. Augustus Collins as the Professor was a great hit, and Browny Collins carried the audience by storm in his swell song, "The Hebrew Dude."[17] With all due respect to the parties concerned, we suggest that the next similar performance be taken to some hall instead of the church, as it is not the proper place for burnt cork and Ethiopian songs and jokes ...**

Source: *Cleveland Gazette*, February 14, 1885, 1.

The Detroit Excursion, Et.

The Cleveland Patriarachie made a fine appearance at the Past Grand Masters Council in Detroit last week. The entertainment at Casino Rink was rendered largely by Clevelanders, addresses being made by Messrs. W.O. Bowles

---

[16] As Toll writes, Kersands's popularity was such that he could challenge segregated seating, with repercussions of a boycott of his shows. *Blacking Up*, p.256.

[17] During this time, the phrase "dude" was slang for a man with a stylish sense of fashion.

and W.T. Anderson, of this city. The musical part of the entertainment was given by the Washington family, of this city, a programme of which appears elsewhere. We are sorry to learn, through the columns of the *Plain Dealer*, that one of the participants disgusted the Detroit thinking people by the rendition of a trashy song. We coincide with our contemporary in that such selections are admissible in minstrel and variety shows, but should have no place on a programme prepared for the entertainment of ladies and gentlemen. Such taste does not show a spirit of progression, especially when shown in our young people, and we should show no approval, but decline being entertained in any such manner. What we want and need, is brain food. If we can't have it we will refuse chaff, and fast.

Source: *Cleveland Gazette*, July 2, 1887, 3.

Minstrelsy in the *Indianapolis Freeman*

As Abbott and Seroff make clear, the *Indianapolis Freeman*, an African American weekly, was one of the most important resources for information about black entertainment from the 1890s to the early 1920s. It was the first "Nationally Illustrated Colored Newspaper," it did indeed have a national distribution, and it ran a column relating the activities of tours and ensembles from the East Coast to the Midwest. It was also run, after 1892, by George L. Knox, an ex-slave with progressive ideas.[18] Indeed, every issue has something to say about either entertainment, African American racial uplift, or other related topics. I've included just a few examples to provide the research a sense of what the *Freeman* has to offer.

This is an announcement for the first performance of a group organized in Topeka and featured a parade with a drum major drill. The writer for the *Indianapolis Freeman* praises the performance and wishes for their success:

Johnson & Wilson's refined and original minstrels were greeted by a large audience at Music Hall, Topeka, Kan., on the 25th inst [abbreviation for *instante mense*, or the current month. This must refer to the previous month of April]. The performance was a very creditable one, many original and unique features of minstrelsy being introduced which elicited much applause from the highly appreciative and

---

[18]Abbott and Seroff, *Out of Sight*, pp. xii-xiii.

large audience. This company was organized in this city
by Messrs. Ed. Johnson and Joseph Wilson, both possess-
ing considerable talent for the stage, and will doubtless,
should they continue, gain quite a reputation. The most
stirring features of the performance are the Drum Major's
drill, of six artists headed by C. Moss, Captain, which exhibits considerable skill, and the soloists, Messrs. D. W.
Dillard and A. Ray, the latter exhibits more than ordinary
ability as a guitar and mandolin soloist. The company only
needs financial backing to ensure success. The company
is under the direct management of Mr. Edward Johnson.
The *Freeman* wishes them success.

Source: *Indianapolis Freeman*, May 11, 1889, 2.

Of course, the *Freeman* supplied information, advertisements, and reviews of performances occurring in the Midwest, including Indianapolis,
and, as was seen in the previous example, Kansas. Here is just one example. McCabe & Young were among the most popular minstrel troupes of
the late 1880s. Their typical tour took them through the Midwest, down
south, and finally for a run in Cuba. Note the reference in this progressive newspaper to phrases such as "gentleman," "artists," "genteel in appearance," and "free of that coarseness characteristic of such companies."
Clearly, unlike previous white performers playing in blackface, the writers
of the *Freeman* approved of this troupe's portrayal of African Americans:

The McCabe & Young Minstrels

The lovers of refined minstrelsy were given a grand treat
by this famous and excellent organization of burnt cork
artists last Monday and Tuesday evenings. The street parade was elegant, tony, and particularly attractive. The
performances were new, unique and enjoyable, being free
of that coarseness characteristic of such companies. The
gentlemen composing the company were not only artists
in their special lines but were genteel in appearance and
deportment. There is no better combination on the road
than the McCabe & Young Minstrels. They will visit the
South and then go to Cuba.

Source: *Indianapolis Freeman*, November 1, 1890, 2.

Writings in the *Freeman* about African American troupes such as Mc-
Cabe & Young focused not just on the appeal of their performances, but

also on the opportunities for racial uplift and respectability that talented black performers provided. Especially noted in the newspaper were instances when these troupes challenged segregated seating practices at the risk of limiting their earning potential. Note here both McCabe & Young's stance on segregated seating, and the *Freeman*'s call for other troupes, included those working in the North and West, to adopt similar practices:

> **McKabe [sic] and Young's combination played to appreciative audience at St. Augustine, Fla., Jan. 28 and 29. The troupe is first class in every particular. Messrs. McKabe and Young deserve great credit for refusing to yield to the urgent request of some of the white citizens who urged them not to reserve any of the parquetted seats for colored people, as it would hurt them financially, for the white people would not patronize them. The committee making the request was plainly told: "We will take the risk of financial loss, as we value our principle. Any colored lady or gentleman will have the equal right of any white lady or gentleman at our performances in this or any other city." These are the kind of managers needed in a number of squeamish northern cities.**

Source: *Indianapolis Freeman*, February 6, 1889, 4.

With its wide distribution, the *Freeman* also brought news of doings on the east coast to its readership in other parts of the country. This piece is typical of the entertainment column which appeared in the newspaper at that time. I've chosen its inclusion as an example of the variety of artists and the details of their travels discussed in the newspaper, including the musical career of Frederick Douglass's grandson:

> **The fall season has opened up but not as brilliantly as was anticipated. I suppose, owing to the very bad weather we are having, people not desiring to run the great risks. Yet among the white actors, there is a big boom. The Theodore Drury Colored Opera Company opens in New York on the 10th and 11th insts. About the 1st of November, they will start on a tour west for twenty-four weeks if business will permit.**

Sam Lucas, wife and son, signed a few days ago with the Boston Pavillion U.T.C. company.

Will H. Peirce, the tenor soloist, is at present residing in Baltimore.

The Morris Quartette, of Providence, will give a concert at Blackstone Hall in that city, on the 5th inst. At which time Miss Ednorah Nahar, elocutionist of Boston; Madam Waring, soprano, of Washington/ Mater Joseph Douglass, violinist, of Washington, will make their first appearance in Providence.

Master Joseph Douglass is the grandson of Hon. Frederick Douglass, and is at present a pupil at the Boston Conservatory of Music.

Artists, please send their routes for publication. Queries concerning the stage will be answered not by mail, but through these columns.

The McGibney family are playing the West to good business.

Nearly all the colored minstrel companies are playing the West.

A.D. Sawyer, formerly of Hicks & Sawyer has started a minstrel troupe which will be playing the Long Island circuit for a short while, and then probably start west.

Ray Wilson, the well-known comedian, is spending a few days in Providence.

Source: *Indianapolis Freeman*, October 12, 1889, 5.

Confronting Minstrelsy

By the late 1880s, the African American press was becoming a forum through which writers could agitate for civil rights and contemplate the place of blacks in American society. The final two examples in this chapter introduce writers who saw music as a component of this struggle. The first is a fiery commentary on segregated seating in the South, and a call for action. The second is more nuanced. In the author's view, whites hold two concepts of the African American. In one view they are held up by philanthropists (i.e. well-meaning whites) as "high above his merits," whose minstrel songs extoll their virtues; in another view, they are "considered scarcely above the brute creation." The author feels that neither view is correct, and calls for a deeper examination of African Americans and their progress in the United States in order to understand and address the "Race Problem:"

The Baptist Pioneer[19] **has opened a holy war against Afro-Americans patronizing institutions that belittle their manhood and at the same time make such base discrimination. It cites the fact of minstrel troupes coming south and advertising themselves all white to cater to bourbon prejudices. The theaters have a little pen for "colored people only." Into this, the** *Pioneer* **complains, numbers of Afro-Americans go to hear these minstrel troupes belittle them in the most degrading and obscene manner. The coarser and more obscure and low the take off the better the bourbon attendance. It is time Afro-Americans had acquired some pride and self-esteem. "The Negro pens" in the corner of Southern theaters should be left empty. Jim Crow cars should be left for white ruffians. There is nothing like touching a man's pocket to bring him to his senses. Our race journals should keep this "doctrine" as a standing "ad" warning Afro-Americans away from such places.**

Source:*Detroit Plain Dealer*, October 3, 1890, 4.

The Race Problem

Mr. Editor: –It is an old aphorism that "the dripping of water will wear away stone." That this is true even the most casual observer will admit, and so it goes without

---

[19] *The Baptist Pioneer* was published in Selma, AL by the Board of Trustees of the Alabama Baptist Normal and Theological School.

saying. We are led to this reflection because of the agitation now going on both in the public Press and the Forum, concerning that part of God's humanity, commonly called the Negro. This species of creation has certainly sounded a greater commotion in the world at large, especially in the Western Hemisphere, than any other class of human being. By some ardent philanthropist, the Negro has been lauded high above his real merits: by others, he has been considered scarcely above the brute creation. On the one hand history, both sacred and profane, is perused with all diligence, to show forth the Negro as Par Excellence; while even the masses have been invoked and the song of the minstrel has been heard extolling him as of the special ones of the many races of men through whom, not only is the fatherland to be regenerated, enlightened and even Christianized, but that he eventually will stretch out his hands to God with all that, that may imply; again, there are those who will not accept the doctrine of the brotherhood of man, save the Negro be excluded from the category, and if accepted at all it is that he is of a very low and inferior type of humanity, and fit only to be A SERVANT OF SERVANTS TO HIS BRETHREN. In our opinion both estimates of the Negro are faulty. The first sees him through the eye of philanthropy, through history and with the stamp of his Maker upon his brow; the other observes him with a bondage of 240 years as a heritage—all the noble aspiration smothered and stifled, the moral eye scared and blotted almost out, while they, themselves, have enjoyed the advantages that the toil and the blood of the Negro has purchased for them. If any one thing in the history of the world is most conspicuous, it is the growth and development of the races of mankind. From the keeper of paradise to the shepherd watching their flock by night, we can discern through the long centuries intervening, the slow but sure strides of mankind toward a better, higher, nobler, existence. Among all the various races of men of whom history gives any account, from Herodotus, the father of history, who by-the-by assures us the ancient Egyptians were a people of dark skin and kinky hair, and that the shepherd kings who subdued Egypt in the times of "the Pharaoh" were the descendants of Cush who was of the lineage of Ham...from Herodotus to the introduction of African slavery upon this continent, the Negro was found trying to climb upward and onward as if to reach even unto the throne of God itself. But it is not our purpose at this time to give a historical dissertation of the Negro or any other race of men. We simply desire to look at, ponder, and offer a few thoughts relative to the American Negro as he is, and to proffer what to us seems a reasonable, an easy, and a just solution of what is termed the "Race Problem." From the small nucleus of 20 blacks who landed at Jamestown, Virginia in 1620, they have increased in less than three centuries to more than seven millions of souls: a brief synopsis of his [The African American's] career from the first importation up to the late Civil War will lead to a deduction which we believe will solve the "Race Problem," and give rest and stability to the government, and at the same time be a measure of even and exact justice to this over-cared for class of our population.

Wm. D. Kelly

Source: *Leavenworth Advocate*, January 18, 1890, 2.

Chapter 2:
Cakewalks and Coon Songs in the Black Press, 1890-1900

By the 1890s three new genres began to appear with frequency in the black press of the Midwest: the Cakewalk, the Coon Song, and Ragtime. Minstrelsy continued, but newspaper editors, focusing on racial uplift, now called for songs, dances, and skits which were less demeaning to and more representative of African American culture. Events sponsored by black social organizations often featured skits in which amateurs imitated the professional performers touring the region. And the black population of the region continued to expand, leading to an increase in the number of newspapers and readership, as well as differences of opinion regarding the role of popular music in the black community.

As the first wave of African American migration continued in the wake of the end of Reconstruction, the black population continued to increase in the Midwest, and new arrivals spread out into the rural areas. This population growth led to a rise in the number of African American newspapers, as this comparison demonstrates:

Number of African American Newspapers

1880-1889	1890-1900
Kansas 12	Kansas 29
Indiana 2	Indiana 3
Illinois 1	Illinois 4
Michigan 1	Michigan 2

Ohio 2	Ohio 3
Nebraska 0	Nebraska 3
Iowa 0	Iowa 3
Missouri 0	Missouri 0

While all Midwest states except for Ohio and Missouri saw a rise in publications, the black press had the largest growth in Kansas and the nearby states of Nebraska and Iowa, as the Exodusters, and those who followed them from Mississippi, Alabama, Louisiana, and Texas, began to disperse. The lack of African American newspapers in Missouri at this time is at least partly due to its legacy as the only slave state in the Midwest, and the site of brutal racial hostility before, during, and after the Civil War. Also, these numbers only represent the total number of newspapers that existed during the decade. It was a risky business, and newspapers were constantly folding, to be replaced by new publications in other towns.

As the comparison shows, there were at a minimum 47 African American newspapers active in the Midwest during the 1890s. A few featured extensive coverage of musical events in the region. The *Indianapolis Freeman* continued to offer details of national events pertaining to black music, especially theatrical music. The *Topeka Plaindealer* emerged in 1899, owned and edited by Will Harris, who held a progressive political stance and a strong view of anything derogatory of African American culture, including music. The *Illinois Recorder* was a particularly progressive newspaper, supporting the Republican Party, and advertising itself as a vehicle for the Afro-American League, an organization dedicated to racial solidarity.[1]

This chapter begins with an essay by the composer William Marion Cook, illustrating for the reader the challenges faced by black musicians during the decade. The 1890s witnessed the rise of the "coon song," which, as will be shown, was popular among both white and African American audiences. In these essays the term "ragtime" was applied not only to piano music but also as a general description of the new, syncopated rhythms that accompanied "coon songs" and other minstrel tunes of the decade.

Cook was an African American composer who had trained with Antonin Dvorak. He is best known for a style, especially present in his theater music, that incorporated traditional African American songs as melodic and harmonic inspiration. One of his best- known works, *Clorindy, or The Origins of the Cakewalk*, was done in collaboration with poet and novelist Paul Laurence Dunbar and was the first Broadway musical production with an all-black cast.[2] An interesting feature of this essay is that, although the

---

[1]Emma Lou Thornbrough. "The National Afro-American League, 1887-1908," *The Journal of Southern History* (November 1961): 494-512.

[2]Thomas Riis. "Will Marion Cook." *Grove Music Online*, accessed September 1, 2015.

songs "All Coons," and "The New Bully" contain racially derogatory lyrics, Cook's main complaints are purely musical. Indeed,Cook chastises Ernest Hogan, the author of "All Coons," but not for the song's notorious lyrics. Ernest Hogan starred in the initial production of *Clorindy*, and the final song of the show, "Darktown is Out Tonight," features the line "Warm coons a-prancin,' swell coons a-dancing." Cook's issue with Hogan's song is its reliance on the melodic and harmonic language of Italian opera composers instead of on the "beautiful song of the black slave," and he feels that the ragtime syncopation present in these songs will be "extremely short-lived."

MUSIC OF THE NEGRO

Prof. Will M. Cook Writes of its Past, Present, and Future

The charm of the Slave Songs lay in their Pathos, and from their Melodies will be Developed Music Which Will be Truly American

Has the Negro degenerated musically? What else will account for such ephemeral clap-trap compositions as "The New Bully, "A Hot time in the Old Town," "All Coons Look Alike to Me," etc?[3] "There'll be a Hot Time in the Old Town Tonight" was composed the same year by Theodore Metz and Joe Hayden. "All Coons Look Alike to Me," by Ernest Hogan was one of the most popular, and most controversial songs of the 1890s, and will be discussed further in this chapter. All three songs featured a syncopated piano accompaniment, with accents on the 2nd and 4th beats of the measure. [/footnote] Were not musicians, after listening to such soul-stirring melodies as "Steal Away," "Swing Low, Sweet Chariot," etc. led to believe that from this despised race had sprung a fountain of lyric genius destined to overflow and refresh the entire tone world? The critics overjoyed at finding evidences of musical genius in this strange and unexpected quarter, studied carefully the beautiful song of the black slave, and eagerly await some masterpiece of tonal beauty the heralding of which had been so clearly heard. They were disappointed. The melodies

---

[3]According to Steve Sulliavan there were six versions of a song using the phrase "New Bully" and based upon a tune sung by black stevadores working the Mississippi River near St. Louis that was published between 1895-96. The most popular version was composed by Charles E. Trevathan. Steve Sullivan, *Encyclopedia of Great Popular Song Recordings* Vol 1 (Plymoth, UK:The Scarcrow Press, 2013): 813.

of the slave have sunk into the rubbish of the popular "coon" song. Rags, they are called and ragged indeed, they are in construction and finish. Why is this? Has the Negro, in laying aside the chains which bound him down to a miserable servitude, laid aside also the genius which brought forth precious songs—songs which crept into your heart, and as the pain, and mystery, and hopelessness became unbearable, caused you too to cry, "O Lord, how long?"...

The charm and attractiveness of the slave songs lay in their individuality and pathos. In a certain sense the Negroes of today have lost these characteristics from their music. They have heard too much, they have too quickly and too thoroughly absorbed the beautiful in other music...

"All Coons Look Alike to Me," divested of its "rags," also proves that some Negro, having heard strains from Lucia or Traviata, was attempting to make all songs sound alike to him, barring a slight poverty of dress. Thus he has momentarily thrown aside his original, peculiar, melodic and harmonic effects for the more conventional ones of the Italian...

The "rag" accompaniment, about which so much has been written, and so many views have been advanced, until a very simple problem has been turned and twisted into a very difficult one, is nothing more or less than a constant, even bass chord accompaniment in the left hand against a charming and syncopated thematic development in the right. ...

The "rag' is unscientific and unmusical, and has nothing to recommend it except its odd rhythm. It will be extremely short-lived. Already its popularity has begun to decline, and in a few years "rag time" will be a thing of the past ...

Source: *Illinois Record* [Springfield], May 3, 1898, 1.

The *Illinois Record,* in which this essay appeared, was one of the most progressive newspapers in the Midwest during the 1890s. The choice to publish the essay was a reflection of the *Recorder*'s editorial policy of encouraging racial uplift among its readership. These issues will be an important theme in the selections for this chapter, for in the 1890s new types of rhythms, dances, and songs did indeed shape black entertainment culture, but often they came loaded with derogatory racial stereotypes that, in the minds of several newspaper editors, impeded the racial equality and uplift at the center of their mission.

Racial Consciousness and the Cakewalk

The cakewalk phenomenon swept through the Midwest in the late 1880s, introduced initially by minstrel shows. In early 1892 a large cakewalk dance was held at Madison Square Garden, inspiring similar events in Chicago and Cincinnati. By the late 1890s dances, parties and other social gatherings were a feature of black entertainment even in the smaller towns of the Midwest. The cakewalk featured couples dancing in a line to a syncopated 2/4 rhythm, and if done for a ball or dance, the couples were judged and prizes were awarded. However, as Baldwin has shown, in minstrel shows, postcards, early motion pictures and published sheet music, the cakewalks were presented with derogatory imagery, which seems to the 21st-century audience prohibitively offensive.[4] And yet, as the following essays reveal, cakewalks were held in black theaters, halls, and even churches, for entertainment, for organizing the community, and even for charity events. And in the Bloomington, Illinois event, participants even danced to coon songs:

> **The colored people of Chicago will have a grand jubilee meeting and ball in Greenbaum's Hall on the evening of Nov. 20. The entire colored population is expected to turn out. A "cake-walk" will be a prominent feature of the evening's entertainment. Zachariah Daniels is master of ceremonies.**

Source: *Chicago Daily Inter Ocean*, November 10, 1888, 7.

> **Carthage, Ill. May 10—Special Telegram**

> **A merchant's carnival has been held in this city at the Opera House for two days past. Over sixty ladies, elegantly dressed and bearing banners advertising different business firms paraded in military evolutions. The entertainment closed this evening with a cake-walk and a reception.**

Source: *Chicago Daily Inter Ocean*, May 11, 1889, 2.

---

[4]Brooke Baldwin. "The Cakewalk: A Study in Stereotype and Reality," *Journal of Social History* (Winter, 1981): 205-218.

THE CAKE WALK NEXT WEEK

Many Couples Say They Will Contest for the Handsome Prizes

Applications for a position in Tuesday night's cake walk at Battery D came thick and fast last night, when Arthur G. Cambridge, the dramatic agent, received the walkers at his office and entered them as contestants.

Over twenty-five colored men called, and each averred that he could hold his own in such a contest, and that he would have for a partner a young woman, who could do the same. Once of the first to call and express his intention of competing for the prizes was W.E. Fomer, known as "Sporting Billy."

W.A. Brady, who is conducting this cake walk, says he wants to have it patronized by the leading society people, as that at Madison Square Garden, New York, was.[5] He is now in the East arranging other like contests, but a letter from him received by his business manager yesterday says that no pains should be spared to make the affair a first-class one.

Among the walkers will be, in all probability, Luke Blackburn, Ike Pulley, and Polo Jim, who were awarded the prizes at the Madison Square Garden cake-walk. Mr. Brady has received a telegram from them, saying that they will surely be on hand to give the Chicago walkers a hard time to win.

Luke Blackburn is an old-time cake-walker. He originated the cake-walker's trust some time ago, which monopolistic corporation was composed of half a dozen of the best cake-walkers in the East. Between them they soon managed to get a corner on all the cakes offered at cake-walks.

"Tige" Smith, the door-keeper at the Haymarket Theater, and a well-known colored man, will be master of ceremonies.

---

[5]The previous week, on February 17, 1892, a "Grand Cakewalk" was held in Madison Square Garden, a successful event which triggered other large cakewalk affairs throughout the county, such as this one in Chicago. Seroff and Abbot, *Out of Sight*, pp. 205-206.

The prizes for the women will be a $300 upright piano, a fur cape, and a toilet set; for the men, a gold watch, a gold-headed cane, and a silver watch. The awards will be made by six gentlemen to be hereafter selected.

"Do you know what constitutes a successful cake-walker?" asked Mr. Brady's business manager yesterday, after he had finished taking the names of various young and athletic-looking colored men, who had called to say that they would enter the contest.

"He must be, of the whole party, the Chesterfield in manner, the Beau Brummel in dress, and the [Evander] Berry Wall in style.[6]

Source: *Chicago Daily Inter Ocean*, February 25, 1892, 5.

THE WHITE ROSE CLUB

The White Rose club promises the pleasure seekers of Leavenworth a treat in the way of a masquerade cakewalk at the Independent Baptist church February 5. The ladies have promised to spare no pains in making this one of the grandest socials given in the history of the church. Masks strictly first class. Cast of characters: Cinderella, Red Riding-hood, Gypsy Queen, Mrs. Sitting Bull, Mohamadean King, and others too numerous to mention. Everyone is invited to participate in the masquerade. Forget hard times; come and spend an evening of pleasure. The grand promenade will take place promptly at 11 o'clock, led by Mr. Daisy Harris, who wears the belt as our leading figure on the floor. Don't forget the date, February 5.[7]

---

[6]Evander Berry Wall was a New York socialite known for his extravagant fashion style. His nickname was "King of the Dudes," and in fact, the phrase "dude" was used to designate a stylish young man at this time.

[7]This passage is interesting for a few reasons. First, none of the characters to be portrayed are African American stereotypes, which was one of the issues condemned by certain members of the black press. And Daisy Harris, a native of Leavenworth teamed with "Doc" Brown of Kansas City to create a popular dance rivalry that was followed by people in the region (Abott and Seroff, Out of Sight, pp. 209-210).

Source: *Leavenworth Herald,* January 19, 1895, 3.

THEY WERE ANXIOUS

Negro Cake Walkers Could not Restrain Enthusiasm

Twenty-third Regiment Band Gives a Successful Program in Auditorium

The Auditorium was comfortably filled last night to hear the grand concert which had been advertised by the Twenty-third Regiment band. The cake-walk was the feature of the evening to some, and the entertainment was of such a diversified nature that all were more than pleased.

After many band and vocal numbers came Charles Caldwell, of Oskaloosa [Iowa], and Joe Curry, of Topeka, two clever boxers who went a six round go. Curry showed better form while Caldwell was very clever and shifty.

During all this time the excitement among the cakewalkers behind the scenes was accumulating. Expectation stood on stilts. No program had been arranged and there was a great deal of misapprehension as to just when they should appear.

"Ah must limbah my motors," said one of the contestants for the cake and he immediately proceeded to go through a series of evolutions that would surely have won the cake had the judges seen him.

Here, the cake walker ceased peeking through the crack in the door and announced:

"We's next."

This produced a small sized cyclone behind the scenes and there was a lively scramble for places.

If it had not been for the timely appearance of the master of ceremonies the show might have been thrown into confusion at their point because the first couple was ready to push open the door and begin the contest. But it was all a false alarm. The time had not come and the couple who had been interrupted in their love making over in the corner hastened back and sitting on a small table took up the thread where it had been so unceremoniously dropped.

After many musical numbers the time at last came, and to the lively strains of "A Georgia Camp Meeting" they all went out, led by the prompter, Alice Murdock. The cake walk was executed in a truly professional manner, and won much applause...

Source: *Topeka Weekly Capital*, November 2, 1900, 1.

Bloomington [Illinois] Cake Walk

The much advertised cake walk occurred last Wednesday amid great enthusiasm, and the speculation as to the probably winner reminded one of an American Derby.

The event took place on the public square and was under the auspices of the Annual June Festival, given by the citizens. ... Each couple was attired in full dress costume and made a fine appearance. Excitement developed into a fever heart when a tip came down the line that a combination had been formed to shut out Gus Smith of Jacksonville, and Bradford of Springfield, the two strangers, but through the efforts of the four veterans from this neck of the woods.... the combination was broken and the word went out that merit alone would decide the contest.

The square was lavishly decorated in honor of the event and when all was in readiness the band struck up the favorite and popular air, "My Coal Black Lady," to the music of which the seven couples stepped off with a grace that made the would be cake walkers who were not in the affair turn green with envy...

For two hours and a half the battle raged fierce and furious. Dixon and McCray were the first to be declared out of the race. Then followed Crawford. They all went some, and when the band played "All Coons Look Alike to Me" and "I am Tire of Living on Pork and Beans," the stuff was off...

Source: *Illinois Record*, June 4, 1898. 1.

While many of their readers organized and participated in cakewalk dances, and some newspapers reviewed these events favorably, other publications took a stance against the cakewalk and its ridiculous spectacle of black stereotypes. Some of the strongest essays against cakewalk amusements came from the *Topeka Plaindealer*, which began publishing in January 1899:

It is reported that the president [William McKinley] was entertained, while visiting in the South, by a cakewalk given by the Negro servants of the Sans Souci clubhouse. If the barbaric South Carolinians had given a lynching bee in honor of His Excellency, with some of the "bloodthirsty" Negroes as chief actors, we might hope for a protest against the treatment of Negroes in the South. There will be a paragraph on the efficacy of the cakewalk as a civilizer, in Mr. McKinley's message to the next Congress. Just watch for it!

Source: *Topeka Plaindealer*, March 31, 1899, 2.

A large number of our influential race papers are waging war on "ragtime music" and "coon songs" now so popular. If they will add to their list of condemned practices the vile and disgusting "cakewalk," equally as much a fad, and not allow a single issue leave the press without a strong denunciation of these dual evils, they [cakewalks] will become unpopular. There is nothing elevating or ennobling in the "coon song: and "rag-time music," and everything about the "cakewalk" is positively degrading.

Source: *Topeka Plaindealer*, July 28, 1899, 2.

The Negro and City Hall Dedication

The Commercial Club of the city of Topeka, in arranging for the dedication exercises of the new city hall, have invited the Negroes of the city of Topeka to participate in the above-mentioned affair, and to prepare to entertain the public one night, at least, during the period of self-gratulation [sic] incident to the occasion. The invitation extended is nothing more than just recognition of an important fact in the city's body politic, but the implied suggestion as to what should constitute the entertainment presented is an insult to our intelligence and a positive affront to the self-respecting element of our people.

The predominant characteristic of the representative Negro is no longer to play the ape and the monkey, and we look with positive disfavor upon the part we are asked to play in an event which will mark an epoch in the city's commercial and material greatness. We wish to serve notice right here and now, that there will be no cakewalk participated in by the best-colored people of Topeka. We are in favor of presenting an entertainment which will demonstrate the progress we have made in intellectual development, and recite the story of our commercial and material successes and triumphs, but we can find no time, and have no inclination to play the clown and furnish diversion of the minstrel sort for the delectation of an applauding and admiring public. We are aiming to reach the heights; we are shunning the depths. "Ad astra per aspera" is our motto.[8]

Source: *Topeka Plaindealer*, June 29. 1900, 2.

Other black newspapers condemned cakewalk events particularly because of their reinforcement of black subservience to whites. This essay from Cleveland is interesting because the event was not segregated, yet blacks were asked to stand aside and watch as the white attendees mocked them:

At a dance at Woodcliff Hall, where a cakewalk had been held, on Monday evening, some individual in charge of

---

[8]"Ad astra per aspera," "To the Stars through Difficulties," is the state motto of Kansas.

the alleged entertainment had the nerve and gall to ask our people in attendance to clear the floor so the white people present could have a dance—AND IT WAS DONE. Good Lord, deliver us! Are we in northern Ohio or southern Mississippi? Whoever heard of such damfool nonsense among our people here in Cleveland? Surely we are going backward if the occurrence referred to is any indication. Where did that fellow come from, anyhow?

Source: *Cleveland Gazette*, March 25, 1899, 3.

The final two examples illustrate the use of sarcasm in the black press to show disapproval of cakewalk dances. Although not stated specifically, the dim view of these affairs held by the Fair Play and the Freeman comes through:

... At North Alton, Ill. On Sunday, a rather unusual proceeding was enacted. It was the lockout of Rev Isaac Clark from the colored Methodist church. The scene on Sunday morning was a culmination of a series of differences between the church and the pastor. A new building was erected a short time since, and Rev Clark did some of the work. He obtained a mechanic's lien on the property and a wrangle followed over this. On Saturday night a cakewalk and barrel-rolling contest was given and the trustees claim that Rev Clark was the originator of that scheme to raise funds. They strongly disapproved of the performance and decided that Rev. Clark should not be their pastor any longer. Accordingly the church was locked on Sunday morning and the pastor was not allowed to enter ...

Source: *Fair Play* [Fort Scott, KS], May 26, 1899, 1.

A cake-walk in Stolle's Hall last Monday engrossed the exercises of two ambulances. Two of the steppers are in the city hospital and the others will appear in police court. The Quaker Club, which ranks second in society to the "400" arranged for the cakewalk and invited the Douglass Club and the "400" to compete for the prize, which was a step-ladder, copper-rivited, ironside, dyspepsia-breeding affair with a sign reading "cake" on the top.[9] It was in the middle of the hall, and the dancers walked about it. The deciding point in a cakewalk is the style and manner in which the corner is turned. Occasionally a couple would be declared out of the contest because of "coarseness." Soon the contest narrowed down to two couples— Dave Premer and Effie Smyth of the Quaker Club, and Alex Moore and Tootsie Ragdale of the "400." After an hour of walking up and down, the judges gave the cake to Dave and Effie, then hurriedly left the hall. The announcement caused consternation, and the members of the "400" revolted. In seconds, razors all over the hall glinted under the lamp lights and then the lights went out. When the police arrived those who had not been injured were gone, and the wounded were stretched out ready to be removed. The cake was scattered over the floor like a barrel of saw dust. The most seriously injured were John Watson and Alex Moore. They are at the hospital, and the others were locked up after their wounds had been dressed at the city dispensary.

Source: *Indianapolis Freeman*, January 23, 1897, 1.

The "Coon Song:" Reactions in the Midwest

HOW TO WRITE A COON SONG
First you take a Southern coon,
So he's black he'll do;
Then you find a yellow gal—
Name her Sal or Lou—
They must have a falling out,
Else be very thick;
She must follow with the "dough"
When he's living high on tick;
Don't forget his bill of fare,
Wine and chicken wing.
And when the song is finished through
Just add the rag-time swing.

---

[9]The "400" was a social club in Washington, New York, Chicago, and perhaps other cities. The name referred to the 400 most socially and economically elite members of African American society.

Now, you've done the best you can;
Choose a name for it—
Something silly, lacking sense—
And it will make a hit.

Source: *Topeka Plaindealer*, October 6, 1899, 1.

According to Dormon, the "coon song" phenomenon began in the early 1880s with the publication and subsequent popularity of several demeaning songs with the word "coon" in the title, and by the mid-1880s it was on its way to becoming a national fad.[10] However, the first appearance of the phrase "coon song" in the black press of the Midwest seems to be a notice in 1887 of a $10,000 lawsuit filed by an African American in Cincinnati, Arthur Rose, against a singer who, during a performance of "There's a New Coon in Town," pointed a finger at him while he was sitting in the front gallery section.[11] Although the result of his lawsuit for defamation is not known, the black press during the 1890s illustrates the conflicting views among African Americans in the Midwest regarding the songs. Some felt that the songs had artistic worth, or at least served as amusing entertainment, whether presented on the stage, or within their own community functions. Others, including most black newspaper editors, failed to see the humor and looked forward to a time when black people were represented in song and on stage with greater dignity.

An essay from Kansas City, Kansas provides an interesting contrast to William Marion Cook's belief that "coon songs" were offensive because they relied too much on the musical language of the Italian masters. This writer embeds his critique of a "coon song" composer within an overall statement regarding the need for determination to achieve racial progress:

> ... So I think we may feel encouraged when we see our strong men point the way, pushing into arenas where wealth and station array themselves and playing such conspicuous parts. The important feature is not the man's place at starting, but his aim, his direction, his ultimate objective. I heard some "coon songs" recently. The chorus was beautifully balanced and some of the songs, put to farcical words, were rich in harmony and so uplifting in the orchestration as to be worthy of grand opera. A colored man wrote that music and adopted a nom de plume

---

[10] James H. Dormon, "Shaping the Popular Image of Post-Reconstruction American Blacks: The 'Coon Song' Phenomenon of the Gilded Age," *American Quarterly* (December 1988): 452-453.

[11] *The Wichita Globe*, 29 April 1887, 1.

for the program. He has had no encouragement from the
colored people. But that makes no difference, because it
is in him to write strong music. He has had the best sys-
tematic training. If he will steadily keep in the middle of
the road and stick to his music he will have the world for
his audience and he will be grateful for present lack of appreciation.

Source: *Kansas City American Citizen*, August 26, 1898, 1.

As with cakewalks, the popularity of "coon songs" on stage led to their
use among amateur groups for community dances and charity events. In
Part Two of this charity event in Springfield, Illinois, there is a jarring
juxtaposition of "coon songs" with the opening piece "The Colored Four
Hundred." That exact song has been lost, but the phrase "colored four
hundred" at that time referred to the black elite:

Hit of the Season

The young people of the city participated in one of the
best entertainments that has ever been given in the city
of Springfield, on last Tuesday night at Hart's Hall, for the
benefit of Shiloh Court. There was a large and appreciative
audience and each number on the program was heartily
applauded. The concert was managed by the Missess Arminta and M. Retta Davis and Carrie Belle Lee, Mr. Will
Merrit deserves special comment as his specialties were
up-to-date and greatly admired by each and every one.
The can dancing by Messrs. Merrit and Reece was one of
the best numbers on the program. The songs and choruses
were comic and catchy. Each number on the program is
worthy of comment but lack of space will not permit us to
do so. The program was as follows:

PART ONE

1. Opening chorus: "Suwanee River"

2. "Henrietta"—Misses White

3. Guitar Duet—Messrs Beck and Singleton

4. "Arabella Jones"—Misses Susye E. Thompson and Gene
   Finley

5. "She's my Warm Baby"—Miss Mabel Donnegan

6. "Mississippi Rag" — Misses Arminta Davis

7. "Mamma's Pumpkin Colored Coon"—Miss Mamie Hicklin

8. "Twentieth Century Boys" —Mr. Oscar J. Buckner

9. "Armour Avenue March"—Miss Gene Finley

10. "Mr. Johnson Turn Me Loose" —Mr. Will Reece

11. Chorus—"On the Dummy"

PART TWO

1. "The Colored Four Hundred" —Misses R. Davis, S. Thompson, M. Hicklin and C. Lee

2. "Enjoy Yourselves"—Mr. Chas. Brown

3. "Brush By Nigger Brush By"—Mr. Will C. Merrit

4. "My Gal's a High Born Lady" —Mr. Bert Singleton

5. "All Coons Look Alike"—Miss Carrie B. Lee

6. "The Four Revelers"— Misses Lee and Davis, Messrs. Reece and Merrit

7. Guitar Duet—Messrs. Beck and Merrit

8. Specialties— Messrs. Reece and Merrit

9. "Black Ana Promenade"—Miss Gene Finley, promenade by Misses Davis and Lee and Messrs Reece and Merrit.

Source: *Illinois Record*, December 11, 1897, 4.

As the review states, the event was held by "the young [black] people of the city." Then, as now, young people drew the concern of their elders by adopting the latest fashions and singing the latest music, in this case, "coon songs" with the new ragtime accompaniment:

> One too prevalent error is that too many girls of the present are dazzled by the superficial attainments of the men they chance to meet, while those solid, sterling elements which alone make the man are overlooked and underestimated. The young man about town who pomades his hirsute adornment, wears the correct cut of clothes and the most recent

artistic triumph. In footwear, the man who can tread a measure in ragtime or sing the latest coon song is the most popular man in town, while the steady, industrious youth, the one who sees life as a reality and tries to live up to the highest ideals of manhood, is considered a boor and a ninny. And on the other hand our young men are too apt to fall into the habit of judging from the same false standards.

Source: *Topeka Plaindealer*, June 15, 1900, 2.

But not all young people were enamored by the "coon songs." In Kansas, a beauty queen from Wichita took a stand, and the black press took notice:

We do not want to be understood as believing for a moment that the queen of the Wichita festival is in any respect the equal in beauty and grace of the handsome, queenly colored girl to whom Topeka and all Kansas did honor last fall; but there is a vein of good, sound sense about the Wichita queen which makes us feel like rising up early in the morning, like the patriarchs of old, and girding up our loins and fleeing unto her. She denounces the modern craze—the coon song—and undoubtedly condemns ragtime music and the cakewalk—the twin relics of ignorant slavery. The time has come when our people should permit no opportunity to pass when we can condemn these degrading fads. We honor the queen of Wichita and would ask her to require her court musicians to refrain from the ragtime coon song.

Source: *Topeka Plaindealer*, October 20, 1899, 2.

Indeed, by the late 1890s, a backlash against the "coon song" phenomenon was rising among both the black press and their readership. One reader pointed specifically to the lyrics of the songs and disparaged their sentiment. For her, the model of African American portrayal in song was defined by Stephen Foster during the time of slavery:

WHY NOT

Ella Wheeler Wilcox, who has turned dramatic critic, has some well refined ideas on the sentiment of "coon songs," which are so rampart on the stage at present. She says:

"I wonder why the better order of freedmen do not rise in a body and protest against the indecent tone of most of the "coon songs." They are devoid of sense of morality, and make the colored men and women seem to be fools. The airs of the songs are often catchy and full of haunting bits of melody, even of harmony, and it is because of this, no doubt, that they are accepted and sung by people everywhere who do not stop to consider the sentiment.

It is a curious thing that during the time when the colored man was in slavery he inspired exquisite stanzas of verse in the brains of our poets and song makers. "Old Kentucky Home," "Suwanee River," "Massa's in the Cold, Cold Ground," and many others of the kind are full of pathos, refinement, and beauty. Now that the slave has become a freedman and is giving [sic] opportunity with his fellows, why should he inspire our song writers to only such vulgar and coarse doggerel as most of the "coon songs" of the time undeniably are?

Source: *Iowa State Bystander* [Des Moines], November 10, 1899, 1.

A Trip to Coontown: A Racially Conscious Minstrel Show

By the mid-1890s at least a few black theater producers were beginning to challenge the white exploitation that controled productions and box-office receipts and profited through the use of black stereotypes onstage. One of the first shows to defy the racial dynamic of minstrelsy was *Down on the Suwannee River*, featuring William "Billy" McClain. According to one reporter, "Mr. McClain is to the theatrical world what Fred Douglass and Booker T. Washington are to the education phase of the race today.[12] During the 1890s McClain appeared in several mixed-race theatrical extravaganzas, leading to his production in the summer of 1895

---

[12]Quoted in Bill Reed, *Hot From Harlem: Twelve African American Entertainers, 1890-1960* (Jefferson, NC: McFarland Press, 2009): 43.

of an exceptional show, *Black America,* which used an enormous cast of African Americans to present a sympathetic rendering of African American culture.[13]

Although the manuscript of the show *Down on the Suwannee River* has been lost, a careful reading of the following advertisement for its tour through the Midwest reveals a new attitude towards the portrayals of blacks on stage. The first Acts are typical minstrel fare; there is a depiction of "the Dark Continent," missionaries about to be boiled by an African king, enslavement and subsequent happier times on an orange plantation in Florida. Yet there was the use of "exact duplicate[s]" of African costumes, weapons, and musical instruments, and an emphasis on the extravagant production value, and a complete lack of "coon songs." And at the end of the second Act, the slaves are emancipated by Lincoln, and the scene switches to a concert hall in New York City, "and displays the life of the Negro as he is today," concluding with a massive cakewalk "more artistically presented than anything before seen:"

Source: *Leavenworth Herald,* September 14, 1895, 3.

---

[13]Reed,*Hot From Harlem,* pp. 43-44.

The achievements of Billy McClain led the way for other innovative productions. Despite its name, the show *A Trip to Coontown*, which debuted in New York in 1897, was seen both then and now as challenging the racial stereotypes that were a mainstay of 19th-century minstrelsy. Written and produced by black entertainers Bob Cole and Billy Johnson, the show did feature the fare expected by a minstrel audience: songs with the word "coon" in the title, and a main character who is drunk, lazy, and fascinated with chickens. But there was a twist: Bob Cole performed the main character in whiteface, leaving his exact race undetermined. His comedic talents were combined with fine musical performances, as, according to Riis,"Cole and Johnson apparently sought to demonstrate that black singers could work cooperatively to bring off nothing less than a complete and balanced musical banquet—a full evening's entertainment beholden to neither self-mocking minstrel show ditties, nor pious religious folk songs (so-called Negro spirituals)...."[14] In late winter and spring, 1899, the show came to Topeka, Cleveland, and Chicago, where it received glowing reviews in the black press:

"A Trip to Coontown"

Cole and Johnson's comedians and comediennes, who presented the *avoce* farce at the Crawford Theater Tuesday night, December 27, were certainly an agreeable surprise to the theater-going public of Topeka. A surprise because it had been thought all along that the Negro was not capable of producing any sort of entertainment successfully except that of minstrelsy in its crudest form. While there were several numbers of music on the ragtime order produced in *A Trip to Coontown*, there was also enough music suggestive of a very high class of opera. The voices were all good and strong and blended harmoniously. Particular mention is due Mr. Lloyd G. Gibbs, tenor, and Miss Juvia Roan, soprano, for their operatic selections, which gave flavor to the work of the other farceurs. Of course, Messrs. Cole and Johnson did excellent comedy work and performed in such a way as to suggest that they were a notch above their subordinates and supporters and deserving of the classification of "stars." Theirs was not horseplay but comedy pure and simple, and upon its merits

---

[14]Krystyn R. Moon, David Krasner, and Thomas L. Riis, "Forgotten Manuscripts: *A Trip to Coontown*." In *African American Review* (Spring/Summer, 2011): 7-24.

they relied wholly for the approval of disapproval of the theater-going public. Cole and Johnson forcibly remind one of Evans and Hoey and are to Negro comedy what Evans and "Old Hoss" Hoey were to white comedy.[15] Indeed, Cole's tramp make-up is as amusing as was that of Hoey, and his lines are spoken with a drollness that is irresistibly laughable. The specialty of the Freeman sisters— Pauline and Clara—should also be particularized; their contortion act is above the average and is the more appreciated because it comes on the line of a novelty, in that they are possibly the only colored women in the theatrical world appearing as contortionists. Tom Brown, character comedian, still retains his impersonations of the Chinaman and the Dago, and he also retains his hold upon the popular pulse of the people, judging from the applause with which he was frequently interrupted. About the best compliment that can be paid Brown is to say that he has a clever imitator in the person of Jay Harry Fidler, who is now with Richard's and Pringle's Minstrels. Both Brown and Fidler are Indianapolitans. There is a "plot" woven into *A Trip to Coontown*, but not enough to interest an audience as to what its final outcome will be. As a whole, the Coontown company is a good one. The girls are good-looking, but not pretty. But it is said that there is not much cleverness in beauty, which possibly accounts for their good acting.

Source: *Topeka Plaindealer*, January 6, 1899, 3.

A Trip to Coontown

Will give one week's entertainment at the Lyceum Theatre, commencing Monday evening. The Coontown Company, of such peculiar name, is the most talked of colored company in the country, for many reasons, particularly its clean performance. The only successful colored show

---

[15]Evans and Hoey were a white minstrel team famous for their show *A Parlor Match* that ran from 1884-1893. Frank Cullen, with Florence Hackman and Donald McNeilly, *Vaudeville Old & New: An Encyclopedia of Variety Peroformers in America.* Vol 1 (NY: Routledge Press, 2006): 364.

that does not do any cake walking or buck dancing. This show has made the biggest hit of any farce comedy company, bar none. The stars, Cole and Johnson, are quite well known here, as in all other places. Their music and songs are known throughout the United States, such songs as "The Wedding of the Chinese and the Coon," "I Hope These Few Lines Will Find You Well," "I Wonder What's That Coon's Game," and many others. Cole and Johnson are supported by such well known performances as Tom Brown, the great Chinese impersonator and change artist; Bob Kelly the "Real Old Man" (without a doubt the greatest in the business): Lloyd G. Gibbs, the greatest black tenor living; Jesse Shipp, the great pantomime policeman; Jim Wilson, the only man of color that is doing balancing and juggling; the marvelous Freeman sisters, contortionists and dancers, introducing Chicago's most noted church soprano, Miss Edna Alexander (positively her first public appearance); including a chorus of 25 people....

Source: *Cleveland Gazette*, February 4, 1899, 3.

The review of the Cleveland performance was just as glowing and also covered a labor dispute. The final outcome of the dispute and last sentence of this essay supports Kusmer's belief that Cleveland was one of the more racially progressive cities of the 19th century:[16]

There was some trouble with the orchestra, two of the members (the cornetist and bass player) refusing to play under the direction of Cole & Johnsons' Afro-American musical director Wm. Carle. In this reprehensible stand they were supported by the orchestra's leader, Faetkenhauer, and the theater's manager. The first three performances Carle was absent from the orchestra, as a result of the aforementioned prejudiced stand and Tom Brown and others sang without accompaniment, refusing to permit the orchestra to play for them unless Mr. Carle directed. Thursday morning the local musical association, which numbers among its member Messrs. Anderson H. Bowman,

---

[16]Kenneth Kusmer, *A Ghetto Takes Shape: Black Cleveland, 1870-1930* (Urbana: University of Illinois Press, 1978).

Charles McAfee and the members of the Lyceum Orchestra, took up the matter at the suggestion of Mr. Bowman,
and passed the following resolution: "That the association
(M.M.P.A. of Cleveland, O.) does not draw a color line, and
deplores and repudiates the actions of the Lyceum Theater
Orchestra against the 'Trip to Coontown Co.' now playing
in the city." This and the "roasting" and scoring given
the prejudiced fool members of the orchestra by Messrs.
Cole and Jonson, the members of their company and every other sensible person who learned the facts, had the
effect of forcing the orchestra to play with Mr. Carle, who
presided over it while at the piano the remaining performances of this week... It is indeed most unfortunate that
two or three "sap-headed" individuals with more prejudice than sense of education are thus able to bring unmer-
ited disgrace upon a community and city the size of this
and with its splendid reputation for fairness...

Source: *Cleveland Gazette*, February 11, 1899, 1.

The *Illinois Record* went a step further in their review, commenting not
only on the quality of the performance but also seeing the group as great
missionaries of the race who show new possibilities for the portrayal of
blacks on stage:

A TRIP TO COONTOWN

A Farce Comedy Composed Entirely of Colored People The Best

Entertainment Ever presented to the American Public by Negro Actors—Miss Edna Alexander a Decided Success as a Vocalist

Those who missed seeing *A Trip to Coontown,* played at the
Alhambra Theater last week, missed a pleasure passed,
though the writer hopes, not forever lost. For the first time
in the history of the race, a farce comedy composed entirely of colored people, has been organized and put on the
road, to excite the sensibilities of the theater going public.
And be it said to their credit, that through the sterling efforts of this aggregation of colored artists, the Negro as
a performer has for the first time been safely elevated to

his proper place in the theatrical profession, for this is the best Negro entertainment that has ever been presented to the American public. And it is no exaggeration to say of this band of merry makers, and others in the same line of work, that they are doing more to break down race prejudice in this country than the race gives them credit for, for as they pass from town to town, from city to city and state to state they not only hope to break through the bulwark of American prejudice, but it is also safe to say of them that they are the greatest missionaries of our race that we have before the public today. Their excellent achievement is a bright commentary on the possibilities of American cosmopolitan life. For just to think that our race, a little over a quarter of a century ago in bondage, are today challenging the admiration of the public, treading the stage as colored aristocrats, delighting the Colored 400 and the elite of white society, sitting side by side in one of the largest theaters in Chicago...

For a number of years the bright lights of this profession have held that in order to succeed a colored company would have to travel under white management. This fossilized theory has been exploded by Cole and Johnson, for they are under the management of Samuel Corker, Jr. a colored man, and as brainy a little fellow as you will meet in a day's travel. He has the distinguished honor of being the manager of the brightest, breeziest, and cleanest farce comedy on the American stage.

Those who went to the Alhambra with roseate anticipations of seeing the ladies of the company dressed in tights and other paraphernalia peculiar to farce comedy and burlesque were sorely disappointed, for instead of abbreviated costumes they witnessed a decently, thoroughly laughable farce, with a capable and judicious caste of players and singers that spoke their parts and sang their songs with a finish and mellow flavor that would please the most fastidious.

Trip to Coontown has great merit as a play and does not depend for success alone on race sympathy by delineating the obsequious and illiterate Negro of forty years ago. In it there are numerous bright lines and comic incidents furnished in abundance to give everybody present a chance to laugh, and not one was disappointed.

It is a pleasure to record the graduation of the Negro as a performer on the stage; He is no longer a burnt cork comedian with a big mouth and cooney witticisms, but an up to-date, well dressed performer. [Performers such as Kersands] were all clever, but products of their day and time; today they are considered luminous lights of by-gone days. Instead of the burnt cork minstrel of the past to delight us we have the up-to-date farce comedy of today, in the form of *A Trip to Coontown*.[17]

Source: *Illinois Record*, March 11, 1899, 1.

The Decline of the "Coon Song"

The staging of *A Trip to Coontown* and its positive reception among the black press and audience was one of many factors leading to the rapid decline of the genre at the turn of the century. To be sure, there were still a few more such shows that appeared after the tour of *Coontown*:

THE HOTTEST COON IN DIXIE

The Hottest Coon in Dixie, which will be seen for the first time in Topeka, at the new Crawford Thursday and Friday, October 5 and 6, with popular matinee Friday afternoon, is a pleasing combination of all the most popular features of farce comedy, vaudeville and comic opera. Thirty-six musical numbers are rendered including everything from "All I Want is my Chicken," to gorgeously costumed selection from grand opera. All the popular ragtime song "hits" of the day will be sung by these dusky children of the South, including "Miss Virginia," "An Oriental Coon,"

---

[17]Born in Indianapolis in 1866, William "Billy" McClain was an African American acrobat, comedian, and actor, as well as songwriter, producer, and boxing promoter.

"That's One Thing That Rag-Time Will Do," "I Long to Hear
That Old Song Once Again," "The Girl I love in Sunny Ten-
nessee," "I'm sorry, Mr. Jackson, but I've Got to Throw
You Down," "My Honolulu Queen," "Ma Honey Lu," "If I
Only Had a Job," "The Hottest Coon in Dixie," "My Gal
Done Wrong," "The Darktown Jubilee," "That's Where My
Heart is Tonight," "4-11-44," and a dozen others.[18] Many
of the selections are rendered with novel dances, marches,
and cakewalk accompaniments.

Source: *Topeka Plaindealer*, October 6, 1899, 3.

But by the turn of the century, such shows were wearing thin, at least
among an African American audience that wanted to challenge prevailing
white attitudes and stereotypes, both on and off the stage. This chapter
concludes with a reader's letter and an editorial from the progressive *Indianapolis Freeman* suggesting that, in the first days of the 20th century,
"minstrelsy, though it still drags its antiquated form down the corridors of
time, is in the rear of the procession."

NUTS TO CRACK

Dear Sir—As I go to the various shows that come to this
city I notice on the posters and programs the following
mentioned as a general thing: "Nothing said—or done to
offend the most fastidious." Now what I want to know
is, why is [sic] the colored classes excluded in the above
sentence, and why is every colored person in the audience,,,, insulted every time a comedy company or a minstrel troupe comes to the city? The popular ragtime songs
are always announced as "coon song," the women ... are
always referred to as wenches and whenever one of the
colored girls, or "gals" as the writers call them, speaks
to her lover he is a coon or Mr. Nigger. Now the white
troupes are not the only ones who do this but the colored
performers seem to take some kind of a peculiar delight in

---

[18]The phrase "4-11-44," was a common reference that signified a lottery number, and,
more specifically, the stereotypical idea of African Americans who were fascinated with the
lottery, but almost always lost.

berating their own for the white man's pleasure... I think it is about time that a colored man or woman can attend public performances without being made the butt end of every joke and held up as an object of ...ridicule, and more especially by members of his own race. When colored performers sing these songs, why can't they deliver them so that they will be agreeable to the colored man as well as to the white and not always be referring to his own as niggers, coons, and wenches.

Yours,

A Colored Citizen

Source: *Indianapolis Freeman*, November 3, 1900, 4.

Like everything else, "time's gradual touch" is making such changes and improvements in the theatrical profession, especially the colored part of it that unless our performers keep abreast of the times and keep their minds under the influence of good literature they will find themselves shelved to the ranks of the "has been." It isn't the big mouth, thick lipped performers whose salaries are in the three figure class nowadays, but it is those whose skills enclose an allotment of brains. The strides the colored branch of the theatrical profession has made in the last few years have been highly gratifying even to the most sanguine. Minstrelsy, though it still drags its antiquated form down the corridors of time, is in the rear of the procession. It is now recognized as the haven for the played-out performers, with, of course, a few notable exceptions. A minstrel show, compared with our modern, up-to-date shows, is like those big, clumsy machines of years ago compared with the beautiful, light running bicycle of to-day. It is strictly an institution of the past, and had fate dealt kindly with it, it should have been laid to rest in the theatrical graveyard long ere this. In spite of all the elements of modernity that can be infused in them they smack of "ye ancient times." The day of the ignorant performer is fast passing. Unless the profession, that is the colored part of it, familiarizes itself with the late happenings of the day, those things that stir the public pulse, it is doomed to an early demise. In these days of general prosperity and enlightenment, when pianos, books, magazines, newspapers, and the ordinary luxuries of life grace the average man's home, he demands a higher class of entertainment than his parents did. To meet this demand is what at present should be the concern of the colored profession. Possibly the greatest boon that could happen [to] the colored profession would be a first class, out and out playwright, one who is blessed with the powers of expression, humor, and who has a keen knowledge and insight of the habits, customs and nature of the race. There have been several meritorious plays produced for us by white men, but when one scrutinizes them rigidly there is a lack of something that is indescribable. At times they make the Negro an unnatural being, and this has been, I think, more than anything else, the reason why plays of this sort have not been genuine successes. The chief reason of the success of the minstrel show was that the Negro was true to life, he did not get out of his natural element, he did nothing more than bring his daily life on the stage, and from there, for the time being, portray it. The play of today must do the same thing, namely, portray the Negro as he is today, and to do that requires two things: First, brains to produce the play. Second, brains to interpret it. So, performers, my advice to you is while you are training your feet to execute the latest steps of ragtime, at the same time train the mind by familiarizing it with the latest thoughts of the day; then you need have no fear for the future.

Source: *Indianapolis Freeman*, October 6, 1900, 2.

Chapter 3:
Syncopation for a New Century, 1900-1910

The colored man writes the "coon" song, the colored singer sings the "coon" song, and the colored race is compelled to stand for the belittling and ignominy of the "coon" song, but the money from the "coon" song flows with ceaseless activity into the white man's pockets.

Source: *Chicago Broad Axe*, August 31, 1901, 1.

Pessimists tell us the world isn't growing better—even though the "coon song" craze has bumped the bumps.

Source: *Wichita Searchlight*, April 23, 1910, 7.

During the first decade of the 20th century, the *Cleveland Gazette* and the *Topeka Plaindealer* continued to provide extensive coverage of musical happenings in their respective cities. The *Indianapolis Freeman* maintained its national reporting of items pertaining to the theater. The *Chicago Defender* began in 1904, ultimately becoming the most widely-read and consequential black newspaper in the country. And three African American newspapers started up in Missouri, with the *Sedalia Times* providing interesting items regarding its native son, Scott Joplin. Also contributing items to our study of this decade were newspapers from Wichita and Kansas City.

Essays found in these newspapers reveal certain musical trends during the decade. Minstrel shows that were almost exclusively based on humor pertaining to racist stereotypes gradually declined, to be replaced in the next decade by more diverse vaudeville shows, featuring a wide range of singers, dancers, comedians, and musicians. The acts which made the biggest impact among blacks in the Midwest were led by comedian Burt Williams and singer Sissieretta Jones, the "Black Patti."While their shows did continue to employ some of the racist elements of 19th-century minstrelsy, the "coon song" phenomenon itself rapidly declined in popularity during the decade, especially among black audiences.

Also during the decade, newspapers discussed Ragtime the piano genre, as well as "ragtime" the generic phrase. As a piano genre, the black press celebrated piano Ragtime that was sanitized and commercialized for middle-class consumption. There was pride in the achievements of Scott Joplin and James P. Scott, and in their predecessor, now in the twilight of his career, "Blind" Boone. The press saw the popularity of Boone's concerts and Joplin and Scott's sheet music business as another step towards the advancement of the race. But, as the roots of Ragtime lay in the saloon and wine bar, the newspaper editors expressed at first an uneasy relationship with the new rhythms and dances the music inspired. In addition, the press editors and their readers often used the phrase "ragtime" as a term that connoted the syncopated rhythms that now accompanied music for the theater, including songs and productions that denigrated the race. Thus, the syncopations of Joplin were respectable music; the syncopations of a "coon song" accompaniment, although also called "ragtime," were not.

A discussion of this decade is also a good place to begin an examination of class structure in the newly emerging African American communities of the Midwest, and the impact of class tensions on music making. With any black migratory wave, whether the Exodusters of the 1870s or subsequent movements, new arrivals had to redefine their lives, and relationships needed to be established with those already living in the place of destination. Within growing communities, new class structures were defined, leading to new business and social relationships that played an important role in shaping a community's musical culture.

Syncopation, the Old Guard, and the New

Tom C. Cox's social study, *Blacks in Topeka, Kansas 1865-1915: A Social History*, reveals several aspects of the impact of immigration that can be extrapolated in our consideration of other Midwestern towns. As he writes, the black population of Topeka was 724 in 1875 but had risen to 4,807 in 1900. Such an increase led to the development of new churches and several black newspapers. Men who came with education or business experience created new businesses and an upper class; those who arrived with neither shaped a working class. In addition, there was a distinction between an "Old Guard," early arrivals to Topeka, who looked suspiciously on a "New Guard," or those who came later.

These boundaries and tensions were present in all of the black communities of the Midwest and perhaps account for the various and conflicting opinions regarding black popular music that can be seen in the press. Our first examples come from authors who strove to create a sense of propriety in middle and upper-class social clubs like the "True Eleven" of Atchison, Kansas. In these clubs, propriety meant European style music and dancing, without the seeming vulgarity of ragtime rhythms or "coon songs." This is especially evident in the final sentence of the first essay. And, as the title of the first essay implies, racial uplift was an important focus of these social organizations:

BUILDING UP THE RACE

The True Eleven of Atchison, KS sets a good example for people who will and want to do what's right …

Dancing Position

There should be at least two inches of space between the lady and gentleman. The gentleman first receives the lady by extending his left hand, palm upward, to receive the lady's right hand, palm downward: both lightly close their fingers on each other's hand. The hands should be carried without any swing, about the height of his shoulder, or a few inches below. The gentleman's right hand, fingers extended and together, should rest about the center of the lady's back, near the waist; a better place by which the lady can be gracefully glided. The left hand of the lady is then placed on the gentleman's right arm between the shoulder and elbow, fingers turned inward; this will enable her to keep comfortably the regulated distance. Both should slightly stoop forward. At no time should the lady's chin reach the gentleman's shoulder or should either take a leaning back position.

Professors of ragtime music are asked to stay away from the piano …

Source: *Topeka Plaindealer*, September 20, 1901, 1.

AN INTERESTING REVIEW OF THE WORK AMONG THE
CLUB WOMEN OF IOWA

The Committee on Social Purity, under the guidance of Mrs. Gertrude Culberson of Clinton [Iowa], has held its own [meeting]. The results of this committee should be more than thoughts and words, but deeds and actions should be its ultimate aim. Vulgarity of speech, disgrace of divorce, unlimited amount of gossip, intemperance both in drink and over-serving at the club, the begging for churches or charitable institutions by our girls, the playing of ragtime music and singing "coon songs," the attendance upon cheap colored minstrels which only shows the ridiculous side of the Negro's nature, these things and many more are discouraged by this committee. We would not presume to make entirely perfect the membership of this Federation, but we have attempted to build the moral walls so high and with a circumference so great that no one need escape its encircling influence ....

Program for January, 1906...Fourth meeting—Music day. Biographies of composers, instrumental and vocal selections. Discussion: Resolved that ragtime music should be eliminated...

Source: *Chicago Broad Axe*, December 30, 1905, 7.

NEW DANCES FOR WINTER

COME TO THE ELITE DANCING SCHOOL AND LEARN ALL
THE LATEST DANCES OUT

Rag Time Doomed—Dancing Masters Declare Dignity and
Grace Must be Restored

Five new dances will hold the attention of society. A striking and radical change will be instituted by dancing masters, and there will be another return to the slow, stately measures of the minuet. The Pembrook, the Debut, the Fantasia, the Brooklyn Schottishe, and the Dieux Temps quadrill complete the list of new conceptions in the art. Dignity and grace will characterize the ball room dances this winter. The undignified ragtime and cakewalk will be strictly eliminated from programs. The ban thus put upon onetime favorite dances for amusement is the outcome of the five days convention of the American Society of Professors of Dancing held in San Francisco. The dancing masters declare the ragtime type of dancing destroys all the grace and beauty which should represent terpsichorean arts, and they are loud in their denunciation of what they call a "deep rooted evil." With accord they proclaim its undesirability in the ball room and declared they would take measures to eradicate its influence from the realm of good society. Its departure from the ranks of popularity and respectability will be supplanted by a radical return to the slow and dignified minuet, the society two-step, the glide polka and the graceful glide two-step waltz.

Source: *Indianapolis Freeman*, January 26, 1901, 8.

The new rhythms may have presented a moral dilemma for some members of African American society, but their popularity, at least among the youth, could not be denied. The tension that was continuously present between an older black elite who wanted to adopt at least some European cultural tradition, and a younger generation excited by the new syncopated rhythms will be a continuous theme in this book:

Society Music

Mary will have to be asked to play when she goes out in society. A proud mamma will attend to that. And Mary will play, with faithful accuracy, something from Chopin or Beethoven or old Mendelssohn, and the young people will watch her chubby fingers thoughtfully and wonder when the selection will come to an end... they will applaud, too—when the end is reached—for that is good manners and everybody likes Mary anyhow. And then—well, Lucy Smith, who has never taken lessons, will rollick up to the piano and begin a "coon song," hands and feet will beat time all over the room, half the listeners will hum the refrain; everybody will see the difference between the piano as a penance and as a pleasure, and only Mary's mamma will make unpleasant side remarks about the degeneracy of popular taste in music.

Source: *Wichita Searchlight*, October 5, 1907, 3.

The newspaper editors also kept up their diatribes against the elements of the new music that they found demeaning. The attacks against "coon songs" and racist minstrel shows continued, and a new target, the cake-walk as an entertainment for whites, emerged:

Do you know why so many colored children use unpolished language and enjoy tough ways? You don't? Well, just wait until the next minstrel show comes along, and for months afterward you will hear the new slang, "See the new monkey act," etc. Keep your child away from this kind of a show! Stop them from playing a ragtime piece! Burn up the music, if you desire to make room for culture and refinement.

Source: *Topeka Plaindealer*, September 9, 1900, 4.

A cakewalk and entertainment was given one evening last week by Weddell House bellman at G.A.R. Hall for the edification of whites.[1] The early part of the program consisted of choruses and solos. Jackson and Turner, accompanied by banjo and guitar, told the audience that "Home Am Nothing Like This" and Mrs. Terrell sang "Hannah from Savannah." The event of the evening, of course, was the cakewalk. Six couples were in the contest, but the numbers were finally reduced to four.... It was some time before the judges... all white, were able to decide the winners. The question was put to a vote and by a large majority Mr. and Mrs. Terrell were awarded the prize. It is a matter of great regret and a detriment to the race, too— such pastimes as "cakewalks." If we desire to show to the world that "we are rising" we must stop such practices as cakewalks.

Source: *Cleveland Gazette*, May 9, 1903, 3.

---

[1]The Weddell House was Cleveland's most illustrious hotel at this time. G.A.R. [Grand Army of the Republic] Hall was a meeting place for Civil War veterans.

The Final Years of Minstrelsy

Despite the outcry from the African American public and press, minstrel shows and their racist "coon songs" continued to entertain through the first decade of the 20th century. Their largest market were whites on the east coast, but large all-black ensembles, called in the profession the "big shows," did on occasion play the cities and towns of the Midwest. Two of the most famous shows were led by Bert Williams and George Walker, and Sissieretta Jones, the "Black Patti."

Williams and Walker began organizing and touring shows in mid-1890s. They billed themselves as "The Two Real Coons," to counteract the many whites who were donning burnt cork to play the "coon" character onstage. This advertisement and subsequent review of their 1900 show *The Policy Players* is quite revealing. The large scope of the performance can be imagined, with several dozen actors, singers, and comedians, in addition to the two stars. And the review from the *Freeman* is glowing, even in spite of the presence of at least one "coon song": the comedians kept the audience in a "continuous uproar," the music, singing, and costumes demonstrated "beauty and refinement":[2]

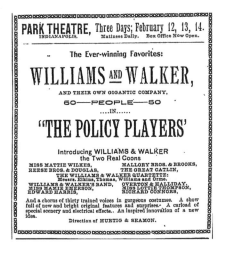

Source: *Indianapolis Freeman*, February 10, 1900, 5.

---

[2]For more on the career of Burt Williams, see Camille F. Forbes, *Introducing Bert Williams: Burnt Cork, Broadway, and the Story of America's First Black Star* (NY: Basic Civitas, 2008).

...Indianapolis theater goers have at last been able to see the well-known comedians, Williams & Walter at the head of their own big company of Negro celebrities. They began their engagement of three days at the Park Theatre...giving a matinee daily and judging from the thousands that witnessed these performances, they will undoubtedly keep Indianapolis on their route book in the future.... Williams & Walker are prime favorites in this city with the show-loving people and they were not slow in showing their appreciation by turning out in large numbers. They are presenting this season "The Policy Players," an original two act, musical farce comedy written by themselves. "The Policy Players," with of course Messrs. Williams and Walker in the chief roles as "Dusty Cheapman" and "Happy Hotstuff," respectfully, tells the tale of the doing of a policy fiend, who has won a large sum of money on policy and wishes, afterward, to enter and mingle with the Colored 400, and the many difficulties that he encounters in so doing never fails to keep the audience in a continuous uproar. Some of our critics spoke of the similarity of the play with one given by another colored company at the same theatre several weeks ago, unaware of the fact, as we have often heard before their appearance here, that the other, in its unabridged form, was nothing more or less than a steal from this, the original which was given in its entirety. The majority of the audience looked upon this as a fact and showed their approval. Messrs. Williams and Walker are ably assisted by some of the leading stars in the profession, among them being George Catlin, who is undoubtedly the greatest of all Chinese impersonators. His makeup, considering the fact that he is of a very dark complexion, with a very heavy mustache, is something wonderful; while his "pigeon-English" is remarkable.

Miss Mattie Wilkes the star soprano, was received with rounds of applause. Miss Wilkes has a beautiful voice and good judgement has been used in the selection of her songs which were rendered in an artistic manner. Messrs. Mallory Bros and Miss Mazie Brooks opened the second act in about the most refined musical act heard in this city; the instruments and stage setting making a beautiful picture. Their playing showed the effect of artistic training and they were heartily encored. Misses Overton and Halliday, as the "Honolulu Belles," do a very clever singing and dancing turn. Another act which deserves special mention is the Reese Bros. and Douglass in a gun and baton spinning act that challenges the world. The Reese Bros. are also acrobats of no mean ability. Mr. Walker in the second act with the assistance of Miss Ada Overton, in his latest creation: "The Broadway Coon," was the recipient of repeated encores. The Williams & Walker Quartette, composed of Messrs. Williams, Elkins, Orme, and Thomas sing in a manner and tone not heard here before and they were compelled to answer several encores. They are ably assisted by Miss Ann Cook, an accomplished soprano. The costumes were beautiful and the chorus singing grand. Several new songs written by Messrs. Williams & Walker are presented during the two acts, prominently among them being "The Medicine Man," "The Man in the Moon Might Tell," "Honolulu Bells." The show as a whole fully came up to the expectations of those that attended and their return next season will be awaited with much interest.

Source: *Indianapolis Freeman*, February 17, 1900, 5.

Williams and Walker continued with several shows throughout the decade, including *Abyssinia* and *Bandanaland*. Walker became ill with syphilis in 1909, and Williams took a new show, *Mr. Lode of Koal*, as far west as Chicago. The following review refers to Williams as "The Funny One" of the duo, and remarks that the show was clean and free of smut, and alludes to Mr. Williams' famous comedic persona, that of a "sorrowfully sedate" victim of life's misfortunes. Noticeably absent is any mention of "coon songs":

"The Big Fellow"—The Funny One, of Williams and Walker, in *Mr. Lode of Koal,* now playing to crowded houses at the Great Northern Theater

BERT WILLIAMS MAKES GOOD AT THE GREAT NORTHERN THEATER

Any number of musical comedies might with advantage emulate the offering which is being presented at the Great

Northern Theater by that most unique and drollest of Negro fun makers, Bert Williams, in *Mr. Lode of Koal*. It is a carnival of clean, hearty romping mirth. In the whole performance there is not an off colored joke or suggestion of smut.

The production goes with a dash and exuberance of gaiety. The humor is of the rampant, irresponsible sort, as though everybody, upon the stage, chorus and all, were thoroughly enjoying the fun.

But, no, that statement cannot be allowed to stand unqualified, for it is part of the comicality of Mr. Williams to appear sorrowfully sedate. Drearily sober in his method of producing gales of laughter, he seems never to have learned how to smile or enjoy himself. Perhaps it is this assumed lack of a sense of humor which makes him so uproariously funny. As Mr. Lode he is seen to better advantage than in any of his previous offerings. His eccentric singing, his loose-jointed eccentric dancing, his slow, ambling drollery and in fact, his whole range of fun-making talents are much funnier this time than they ever were before.

Of course, he is not the whole show. He is surrounded with an organization of spirited singers and dancers who make the three acts of the musical comedy welcomely [sic] alive to the very end of the performance.

As for the piece itself, it is precisely the vehicle it should be to deliver such car loads of laughable whimsies. The music itself is a sort of ragtime jubilee, which goes with a bewildering abandon, giving an effect of almost primitive wildness.

So enthusiastic are the audiences at the Great Northern Theater that the outlook should be very favorable for excellent patronage during the balance of Mr. Williams' engagement.

Source: *Chicago Broad Axe*, October 9, 1909, 1.

The Black Patti Troubadours were one of the biggest of the "big shows" working in the first decade of the 20th century. They were headlined by singer Sissieretta Jones, designated by the press as the "Black Patti," in comparison to the famous European prima donna Adelina Patti (1843-1919). Sissieretta was classically trained and had been performing since the mid-1880s. In 1896 when her managers Rudolph Voelckel and John J. Nolan formed the Troubadours, she was already one of the most famous African American singers in the country. In fact, the black press felt that she was every bit the equal of Adelina Patti:[3]

SINGERS AND SINGING

... The Topeka theater-going public has been fooled so frequently by over-estimated singers that we are loath to say anything complimentary of any [of them]. There is only one thing which prevents Sissieretta Jones from being classed as the greatest singer in the world, and that is her persistence in being styled the "Black Patti." In this wise Sissieretta Jones, while making herself great, makes another woman greater. And we do not think [Adelina] Patti is a greater singer than Sissieretta Jones. We have heard both. Though [Adelina] Patti's notes are a trifle higher in quality, and a great deal higher in price, her singing does not surpass that of Jones. If anything, Sissieretta Jones has a softer and a more melodious voice. Even critics who have heard both will concede this much. Therefore, it is not the part of wisdom that Madam Jones should give another a greater advertisement that she herself might gain thereby. The name "Jones" can be made as highly revered in the household as that of "Patti." "Jones" is much in common parlance; it can be made more in song. Madam Jones has the voice, and she is not compelled to wait for the opportunity; it is here. She should take advantage of it.

We regret that there are not so many more singers in the race like Madam Jones—those who take of themselves, their voices and their several talents—but we also dislike the advertisement which the greatest singer in one race is giving the greatest singer in another.

---

[3]For a detailed biography of her life, see Maureen D. Lee, *Sissieretta Jones: The Greatest Singer of her Race 1868-1933* (Charleston: University of South Carolina Press, 2013).

A few years ago when we first heard Sissieretta Jones sing
in the rooms of the Young Men's Christian Association, at
Kansas City, Mo. we were surprised that a woman with
so intelligent a countenance was advertising the accom-
plishments of another not any greater. Sissieretta Jones
is a truly great singer. This may be unpopular to several
who lay claim to greatness, but truth is always unpopular. However, Sissieretta Jones does not need any illustrious nicknames to accentuate her greatness. She is a host
within herself, and a marvel even as plain "Mrs. Jones."

Source: *Topeka Plaindealer*, February 2, 1900, 2.

...The main hall of the Exposition building was uncomfort-
ably crowded last night to hear Miss Sissieretta Jones, the
Black Patti, sing. The young colored woman sings like
[Adelina] Patti, without the slightest visible effort; her
voice is well cultivated, her high notes enable her to ef-
fectually render the most difficult compositions, and her
low tone is peculiarly deep, intense, and masculine. This
sable diva is highly cultivated, of profound insight into
the spirit of her art. Yet she sings intelligently, wholly
without affectation and with sound musical feeling. Her
voice coming from a skin as white as her teeth would be
counted the wonder of all lands—it is a strong and beautiful voice that sounds with the steadiness of a trumpet.
Though it does not ring with passion, it shakes the heart,
not your ears, with the pathetic warmth that marks all Negro singing. Her skin has a soft lack-luster tint as of pale
plush in shadow. Her eyes are expressive and intuitively
play sympathetically a colloquial part. Her teeth would
be the envy of her fair sisters and the despair of dentistry.
Her rather thin lips are fond of exposing their even rows,
snowy white, whether in song or conversation. She entirely captivated her magnificent audience last night, and
her every performance this week will likely attract just
such a crowd as she entertained last night....

Source: *Cleveland Gazette*, October 1, 1892, 1.

Although the Black Patti Troubadours toured mostly the east coast and
the South, they did make trips west and played smaller towns as well as

large cities. Each year's tour featured new additions to the cast of several dozens and new acts. These two reviews, from Topeka in 1900 and Wichita in 1904, illustrate the diversity of the program and the large scale of the troupe:

Black Patti Troubadours

This world-famous organization will be the attraction at the Crawford Grand tomorrow afternoon and evening. This will be joyous news to the lovers of rag-time, sweet Southern melody, buck dances, "coon" fun, cakewalks and operatic ensemble singing. These merry, musical Troubadours are preeminent in this style of entertainment. During the past four years they fairly carried the country by storm through their rag-time melodies, merry jests, characteristic dances, gyrating cakewalks and superb operatic ensemble singing. Every section of the Union and all of the Canadas are toured annually by this remarkable aggregation of Afro-American singers, dancers, and comedians, and no traveling company of players attract the crowds or give so much universal delight and satisfaction as do these talented and versatile Troubadours.

The personnel of the company, which numbers two score or more, includes the most talented stage artists known to the Negro race. "Black Patti (Mme. Sissieretta Jones), whom nature has endowed with a marvelously sweet voice, is the stellar attraction, and prominent among the other principals are Al and Cecil Watts, "coon eccentrics;" Mattie Phillips, the greatest living interpreter of rag-time, and the champion colored lady cakewalker of the world; Ida Forcen, the "Senegambian Sylph;" Bland and Bailey, "The Charleston Gal and the Elongated Coon;" Judson Hicks, "The Warmest Coon in Town;" W.C. Stewart, "The Essence of 'Old Virginny';" Anthony Byrd, "The Black Edouarde de Reszke:"[4] Lesilie Triplett, "King Koon Kop;" May Lange, "The Louisiana Levee Lassie;" James Lightfoot, "The Afro-American Meister-singer;" James H. Gray, the wonderful baritone; and James H. Gaston, the accomplished lyric tenor.

---

[4]Èdouard de Reszke was a Polish bass singer and international opera star during the late 19th century.

In addition, there are the Troubadours, buck dancing and cakewalk contingent, and the superb ragtime and ensemble chorus. The stage scheme is entirely new this season, and as attractive and fascinating as any of the Troubadours previous offerings. "A Ragtime Frolic at Rasbury Park" is the title of a new opening skit. This is said to be the very incarnation of coon fun, melody and dance, and serves to introduce the entire company with the exception of Black Patti. Here are where hilarity, ragtime, buck dancing, and cakewalk reign supreme, and when these happy sons and daughters of Ham are seen in their merriest mood, a very strong olio follows, including sterling specialties by the Watts, Mattie Phillips, May Lange, The Troubadours' Sextette in their new grouping, entitled "Happy Ante-Bellum," a selection of classical ballads and sweet melodies of the Sunny South. The new operatic kaleidoscope arranged for the final half hour of the stage performance, is prepared with dignified, musical taste, and is of the same high standard as formerly, excepting that the selections are almost entirely new. In this portion of the program the talented Troubadours demonstrate their exceptional gifts of voice and rare musical training. Their exquisite rendition of solos, duets, quartettes and ensemble masterpieces of the great operatic composers is unequaled and incomparable, and won for them the fame and exalted position they now maintain in the stage world. While the ragtime melodies, the buck dancing, the cakewalk and the coon fun which precede the operatic kaleidoscope are inimitable and immensely enjoyable, it is universally acknowledged that the inspiring melodic masterpieces, and the manner in which they are rendered are what give authority and supremacy to the Black Patti Troubadours and their stage performance. Another pleasing feature is the taste shown in costumes and stage appointments this year. The management have indulged almost to the point of elegant extravagance in their aim to make the Troubadours and their stage surroundings pleasing to the eye....

Source: *Topeka Plaindealer*, February 2, 1900, 3.

BLACK PATTI

Songs of the southland by the sweetest singers from Dixie, fascinating fun by furious funsters swell specialties by the smartest vaudevillianists under the sun, and the most graceful dancers and cakewalkers that ever appeared before the footlights will be in evidence when the Black Pattie Troubadours appear at the Crawford Opera House, Tuesday, Jan. 26.

This season's company excels all former ones. New features and new people are the rule. Bob Kelly, "The Real Coon;" Abie Gidam, "The Shinin' Light;" the Troubadour Comedy Four; Ward and Dobbs, "Champion Specialty Artists;" Mack Allen, "The Equipoise Marvel;" Emma Ohacus, "The Black Lily;" Ida Forcen, "The Honolulu Dancing Wonder;" Sisters Turner, "The Tennessee Tornadoes;" Ada E. Robinson, "The Louisiana Lassie;" Ed Green, "The Chesterfield Comique;" Nettie Lewis "The Unbleached Soubrette;" Sarah Green, "The Indiana Nightingale;" Leslie Triplett, "The Funny Policeman;" William Nichols. "The Elongated Comedian;" Will Cook, "The Comic Monk;" Anthony Byr, "The Black Eduard de Reseke;" James P. Reed, the "Unrivalled Bass;" Black Pattie (Mm. Sissieretta Jones), "the Greatest Singer of her Race;" and two score other highly accomplished singers, dancers, vaudevillians and funsters making this season's troubadours absolutely unrivaled by any varied stage organization irrespective of race, creed, or former conditions.

The big new acts include a hilarious, stunning, and laugh-provoking Weber and Field skit called "Darktown's Circus Day..." The "Troubadour Comedy Four," an act that made the smart set in New York, Newport, Saratoga, and all points en route rave with enthusiasm and laughter; Bob Kelly "The Real Coon," in songs and monologues, William Nichols, a mimic second to none; Ward and Dobbs in the singing and dancing specialty "Soldiers and Camp Girls," a happy revival of the sweetest melodies of the camp, battlefield, and plantations. Ten new specialty acts. A festival of operatic melody with Black Patti and the entire company. A splendid rendition of excerpts selected from the standard grand and comic operas.

Source: *Wichita Searchlight*, January 23, 1904, 3.

As appreciated as they were by the black press and audience, the Troubadours were still managed by whites, and a large percentage of their revenue came from white audiences, who expected "coon songs" and other racist imagery, as well as segregated seating accommodations:

> **With the exception of about three "acts," Black Patti's Troubadours this season give a performance that ought to be suppressed. The "show" is neither pleasing nor instructive, but is positively insulting and a bore at times. Our people should not patronize the present combination known as "Black Patti Troubadours." About the only redeeming features are the "star's" singing....**

Source: *Cleveland Gazette*, April 6, 1901, 2.

> **...Black Patti, with her famous reputation, and her company, will appear at the Grand February 8, beginning Sunday at a matinee at 2:30. The company has a complete and up-to-date show. The accommodations for the Colored people are guaranteed by the tour. They will have access to the first and second balcony. We shall expect you to appreciate the opportunity....**

Source: *Kansas City Rising Sun*, February 6, 1903, 4.

New Composers and Compositions

While "coon songs" and racial discrimination continued on the stage, a few African American songwriters were finding success without employing racist imagery. The song "Under the Bamboo Tree," by Bob Cole and J. Rosamond Johnson, was published in 1902 and became a big hit, appearing in musicals in 1902 and 1903, and was reprised by Judy Garland in the film *Meet Me in St. Louis* in 1944. Like Will Marion Cook, the brothers James Weldon and J. Rosamond Johnson were classically trained (Rosamond studied at the New England Conservatory of Music). As a performer, composer, and educator, Rosamond dedicated his career to advancing the dignity of African American artists: As his song swept the country, the *Cleveland Gazette* reprinted an autobiography that had appeared in the January 25, 1903, edition of the white but progressive *New York Sun*:[5]

[5]Sandra Jean Graham "J. Rosamond Johnson," *Grove Music Online*, accessed September 28, 2015.

BAMBOO TREE

Noteworthy Success Being Achieved by Many of Our
Songwriters

How Rosamond Johnson got his Inspiration from
Paderewski—Opera by Bob Cole and Johnson
Brothers—Rosamond's Career—Encouraging

The success of the song "Under the Bamboo Tree" is noteworthy because it is the work of three Negroes, J. W.
Johnson, Bob Cole, and Rosamond Johnson....In recent
years the Negro song writer has usually depended on a
white man for collaboration. Most of the "coon songs"
were written by white men, who revived old plantation
melodies. Up to a few years ago... there were few Negro
composers. Rosamond Johnson was born at Jacksonville,
Fla. He comes of a musical family. He is inclined to at-
tribute his musical career to the stimulus given to his ambition by a meeting with Paderewski. In 1880, when he
was 16, he came north and got a job as bell boy in the Hotel Brunswick in Boston. He received $189 a month and
spent his spare money and time in studying music. [As he
recalled] "One day... Paderewski came to the hotel. He
used to practice daily and I found infinite delight in paus-
ing on the stairs to hear him play. One particular piece
impressed me a good deal. It was his minuet.

"One of my teachers taught me how to play it, and I wanted
to find out how Paderewski rendered it himself. I used to
make excuses to go to his room to listen to him. I would
bring up some ice water or ask him if he wanted anything
done. On one occasion I went to his room while he was
away and began playing the minuet on the piano after the
way I had heard him play it. I was just in the middle of the
number when Paderewski and his manager entered. The
manager flared at me and began to jabber something in
either French or Polish. He waved his hands and ordered
me from the room. Paderewski smiled and I tried to plead
with him to let me remain and play it out. But he could not
comprehend me and I went down stairs. To my surprise,
the clerk ordered me to the desk a little later and I was

politely told that I was discharged. The manager had made a complaint, it appeared."

In spite of this misadventure, Paderewski had inspired Johnson with a desire to follow a musical career. He got a job at another hotel and became acquainted with Charles Dennee, composer of the "Defender," and William Dunham, who were connected with the New England Conservatory of Music, and helped him in his studies....

[He recalled] "I returned home in 1883," Mr. Johnson says, "and father and mother were agreeably surprised at the progress I had made in my studies. Mother did not have much time to instruct me and I was sent to a white lady who had just me with reverses and was in need of money. I tell you every time I went to her house to study I thought my life was in danger, because of the race prejudice. She begged me not to tell anyone that she was giving me lessons, because had the secret been divulged I'm sure she would have been ordered out of town. I came north again in 1898 and met Bob Cole. We formed a partnership and have been together ever since."

Source: *Cleveland Gazette*, May 9, 1903, 1.

Although he never traveled to the American Midwest, the African British composer Samuel Coleridge-Taylor was widely admired by African Americans throughout the country, including the Midwest press. His trio of choral pieces based on Longfellow's *Hiawatha* caused a sensation among American blacks, especially on the east coast, where an S. Coleridge-Taylor Choral Society was formed. Coleridge-Taylor represented the aspirations of all those involved in the movement for racial uplift. He created an art music, suitable for the concert hall and upper society, which incorporated African American themes and musical inspiration. He was also familiar with the work of Will Marion Cook, the Johnson brothers, and Bob Cole, and had seen the London performance of *In Dahomey*. In the fall of 1904, he traveled to Washington D.C. for a festival dedicated to his music. Upon his arrival, he was asked for his opinion of the American "coon song," and African American theater. His response, against the "coon song" and in support of more progressive music and composers, was conveyed by the *Cleveland Gazette* to their readers:[6]

---

[6]For more on the American reception of Coleridge-Taylor and his trip to the U.S., see

TAYLOR TALKS

And gives "The Popular American Music" A "Lusty Kick."

What he says, worthy of careful consideration and Thought—"Cook, Cole, and Johnson Furnish Some Exceptions to the Rule."

I firmly believe that ["coon songs"] have done much to detract from the dignity of the colored people. This is especially the case in England, where all serious musicians hold the "coon songs" in great contempt, and as their information regarding the birth of this class of music is somewhat hazy they are inclined to ridicule the colored people of the United States with the songs. Many think the colored man can only speak in the absurd dialect of the "coon song" and many think he aspires no higher than the sentiments expressed in this music.

Apart from these points, I cannot see much to admire in the majority of "coon songs." Some of course are infinitely superior to others but they are so much alike and the harmonies so common and vulgar that from a musical point of view, they are altogether hopeless.

On the other hand, those I heard at "In Dahomey" were mostly distinct and expressed sentiment in both words and music.

There are exceptions to every rule and the examples by Will Marion Cook and Cole & Johnson are of immensely superior type. They are dainty, fresh, and musical, which is not the case with most of the others.

Believe me, yours truly,

S. Coleridge-Taylor.

Source: *Cleveland Gazette*, December 24, 1904, 1.

Ragtime Doin's

The term "ragtime" or "rag-time" begins to emerge in the Midwest black press in the late 1890s. The term did not just signify a specific genre

Doris Evans McGinty "'That You Came so Far to See Us:'" Coleridge-Taylor in America," *Black Music Research Journal* (Autumn, 2001): 197-234.

of piano music; rather, it was often used in reference to a new kind of syncopated rhythm that could be for solo piano, piano accompaniment, or orchestral dance music, or even band music. Music described as ragtime could be featured at a ladies auxiliary meeting:

RAG-TIME DOIN'S

"Rag-time Jimmie gave a rag-time ball, you had to be rag-gedly dressed or you couldn't enter the hall." Such a lot of raggedy folks you never saw as were those who attended the "tacky party" given by Misses Bertha Harlan, Hattie Harper, and Bessie Hawkins at the residence of Miss Harlan Friday night. Some of the young ladies were a great likeness to a "Zulu Babe," some resembled "Aunt Jemima," others the "Gold Dust Twins." The young men in coming and going home were compelled to keep to the dark side of the street and out of the policeman's sight with a fear of being "vagged."[7] Everything was rag-time, except the lunch, which consisted of cornbread, beans, and milk that is the daily ration of many a poor child who would of [sic] felt more at "home" than at a "tacky party." Each guest was presented with a souvenir, a little black doll, with a red ribbon around its neck. At a seasonable hour all departed expressing their pleasure along the streets.

Source: *Topeka Plaindealer*, March 7, 1902, 3.

Or a "ragtime carnival" could be combined with a "Monster Cakewalk:"

MONSTER CAKEWALK

Big Ragtime Carnival at Tomlinson Hall January 8

The ragtime Carnival and Monster Cakewalk at Tomlinson Hall (Indianapolis) on Tuesday, January 8 ...will be one of the most stupendous affairs of the kind ever presented in this country. It will be unique in that it will combine all the elements of melody, motion, beauty, grace, and picturesqueness in one grand panorama of color, action, and harmony.

---

[7]To arrest someone for vagrancy.

When the thousands of spectators have taken their seats, the first scene presented to their view will be of a cotton field, with scores of colored men, women, and children busily engaged in filling gunny sacks with fleecy balls. As the pickers proceed naturally with their task they will sing, "Way Down upon the Old Plantation." There will be many present, no doubt, in whom the opening scene will revive tender memories of long ago.

The cakewalk itself will be the most notable on record. It will be for the Championship of the State of Indiana and the prize will be a solid gold medal....

One of the most interesting features of the night will be a unique contest for pickaninnies. Ten of the colored cupids, with eyes blind-folded and hands tied behind their backs, will be stationed in front of an equal number of pans of flour. Someone will toss a gold coin into one of the pans of flour and the cupids will dive for it. One, and only one, will get it in his teeth, but all will undergo a ludicrous transformation in that all will be as white as they were black previously. It will be a big night for those who attend to see the fun and enjoy the music and dancing, all of which will be of high quality....

Source: *Indianapolis Freeman*, January 5, 1901, 4.

This announcement and advertisement, suggests the interplay of white audience expectations and an African American determination to turn these expectations on their head. Both pieces ran in the *Indianapolis Freeman*, one of the most progressive black newspapers in the country, with their motto "We lead—others attempt to follow" in their banner. The advertisement mentions specifically the "Colored 400," a phrase that designated the black elite. Yet it took place in a segregated theater, opening with a scene of singing slaves picking cotton, for the revival of "tender memories of long ago." But the show will progress to exhibit "Negro life from plantation to palace." It will feature a "thrilling athlete" doing a high-dive, and music and dancing "of high quality" to ragtime and minstrel melodies.

Ragtime the rhythm and ragtime the song accompaniment became in the hands of Scott Joplin a respectable vehicle for solo piano. His compositional abilities and his achievements in the publishing industry began to find praise in the black press around 1902. Although he wasn't "raised in Sedalia," but in Texarkana, Sedalia was his base of operation from 1894 until his move to St. Louis in 1901. With pride, the *Sedalia Times* reported Joplin's achievements in St. Louis to a readership who must have remembered him from his days at the Maple Leaf Club:

Our Trip to the World's Fair City

The editor and publisher for the [Sedalia] *Times* spent Monday and Tuesday in St. Louis, and while there called on many Sedalia boys, who appear to be doing well. Our first visit was to Mr. Scott Joplin, who is gaining a world's reputation as the Rag Time King. Mr. Joplin is only writing, composing, and collecting his money from the different music houses in St. Louis, Chicago, New York, and a number of other cities. Among his numbers that are largely in demand in the above cities are the "Maple Leaf [Rag] Club," "Easy Winner [The Easy Winners]," "Rag Time Dances [The Ragtime Dance]," and "Peacherine [Rag]," all of which are used by the leading piano players and orchestras....

Source: *Sedalia Times*, April 26, 1902, 1.

SCOTT JOPLIN A KING
His Long Suit is Catchy Rag Time Music
WAS RAISED IN SEDALIA

He is Now Claimed by St. Louis and There He Is Making
Fame and Fortune

The following, published in Sunday's Globe Democrat will
be read with interest here for the reason that it refers to a
composer hailing from Sedalia, whose publisher is also a
Sedalian.

St. Louis boasts of a composer of music who, despite the
ebony hue of his features and a retired disposition, has
written possibly more instrumental successes in the line of
popular music than any other local composer. His name
is Scott Joplin, and he is better known as "The King of
Ragtime Writers," because of the many famous works in
syncopated melodies which he has written. He has, however, also penned other classes of music and various vocal
numbers of note.

Scott Joplin was reared and educated in St. Louis. His
first notable success in instrumental music was "The Maple
Leaf Rag," of which thousands and thousands of copies
have been sold. A year or two ago Mr. John Stark, a
publisher of this city and father of Miss Eleanor Stark, the
well-known piano virtuoso, bought the manuscript of "The
Maple Leaf" from Joplin for a nominal sum. Almost within
a month from the date of its issue this quaint creation became a byword with musicians, and within another half
a twelve month circulated itself throughout the union in
vast numbers. This composition was speedily followed by
others of a like character until now the Stark list embraces
nearly a score of the Joplin effusions. Following is a list of
some the more pronounced pieces by this writer, embody-
ing these oddly titled works:

"Elite Syncopations"

"The Strenuous Life"

"The Rag Time Dance" (song)

"Sunflower Slow Drag"

"Swipsey Cake Walk"

"Peachrine Rag"

"Maple Leaf Rag"

Probably the best and most euphonious of his latter day
compositions is "The Entertainer." It is a jingling work

of a very original character, embracing various strains of a retentive character, which set the foot in spontaneous action and leave an indelible imprint upon the tympanum.

Joplin's ambition is to shine in other spheres. He affirms that it is only a pastime for him to compose syncopated music and he longs for more arduous work. To this end he is assiduously toiling upon an opera, nearly a score of the numbers of which he has already composed and which he hopes to give an early production in this city.

The Times was the first Sedalia paper to begin giving Mr. Joplin a public boon as a Negro music writer and composer of the catchy music known as "Rag Time." Among the first was that of the "Maple Leaf Rag," which was named after a social club in our city known as the Maple Leaf. The next was the "Sunflower Slow Drag," which was and is now a great favorite among Sedalians.

Source: *Sedalia Times*, June 13, 1903, 1.

By 1903 Joplin was gaining a national reputation, not only for his piano music but also for his larger theatrical aspirations. However, little is known about his 1903 ragtime opera *A Guest of Honor*. The tour which inspired this review met with disaster when its receipts were stolen, and the score was never published:[8]

BEST ON THE AMERICAN STAGE

World's Fair Band Give Third Grand Ball—Against "Jim Crowism."

St. Louis, MO, Special. Hogan's *Smart Set* opened at the Imperial on the 2nd [of February] to a crowded house, and was considered by all to be one of the best on the American stage .... The World's Fair Band will give their third grand ball at Stolne's Hall on the 19th. All the churches and societies met at their respective meeting places and elected delegates to go to Jefferson City [MO] to protest against the "Jim Crow" bill, which is now pending before the legislature. The leading musicians of the city have declared that the ragtime opera [*A Guest of Honor*] which is now being written by Scott Joplin, will be the finest thing of the

---

[8]Edward A. Berlin. "Scott Joplin," *Grove Music Online*, accessed September 28, 2015.

kind ever produced. Louis Copperidge's World's Fair band and orchestra is the real thing in this city.

Source: *Indianapolis Freeman*, February 14, 1903, 2.

Scott Joplin, who is termed "the king of ragtime writers" has written a ragtime opera, entitled *A Guest of Honor*, which is a most complete and unique collection of words and music produced by any Negro writer. The opera is in two acts, something on the order of grand opera, with not a piece of music in the whole opera other than that from the pen of Scott Joplin, in which he introduces a lot of big numbers, some of which are "The Dude's Parade," "Patriotic Patrol," and many others which go to make it grand.

Source: *Indianapolis Freeman*, September 12, 1903, 6.

The success of Scott Joplin opened the door for other composers of ragtime piano music. James Scott was born in 1885 in Neosho, southwest Missouri. His family moved to Carthage where a teenage Scott took a job at the music store of Charles Dumars, who recognized Scott's talent as a pianist and composer. This essay describes Dumars' efforts towards the teenage Scott's first publication, "A Summer Breeze—March and Two Step." Although Dumars did not sell enough of Scott's works to stay in business, Scott ultimately moved to St. Louis and established himself as one of the top ragtime composers, working with Joplin's publisher John Stark in St. Louis. He moved to Kansas City in 1914, becoming a music teacher and bandleader, and silent film organist:[9]

A NEW COLORED COMPOSER

Jimmy Scott, a bootblack in one of the Carthage, Mo. barber shops, has composed a two-step which promises to be one of the season's best hits. So says C. R. Dumars, leader and director of the Carthage Light Guard Band, and so implicit is Director Dumars' faith in the future of the selection that he is having it published, paying the colored lad a royalty, and states that already a big Philadelphia house

---

[9]For more on the life and career of James P. Scott see William H. Kenney, "James Scott and the Culture of Classic Ragtime," *American Music* (Summer, 1991): 149-182.

has made an advance order for 100 copies of the piece. "A Summer Zephyr" is the name of the new two-step, and contrary to what might be expected of a Negro boy, it is described as no ragtime air, but of high-class merit.

Scott is somewhat of a phenomenon as a musician, and is ranked by many who have heard him, with Blind Tom.[10] His musical education consisted of a dozen piano lessons, given by a man he once worked for as a coachman. He can now read music at sight. Scott is now working on other compositions.

Source: *Wichita Colored Citizen*, March 14, 1903, 2.

Although for most of his career the repertoire of pianist John William "Blind" Boone consisted of classical works and spirituals, by the early 1900s he was beginning to compose and incorporate ragtime-based pieces into his shows. Boone concertized from the 1880s to 1927, and his reputation, especially among African Americans in the Midwest, was stellar. These are two of the hundreds of announcements and reviews concerning Blind Boone to be found in the Midwest black press over the course of almost 40 years:

For more than a quarter of a century the Blind Boone Concert Co. has been before the public. They have played before audiences in every city of any size in American and in the principal cities of the East [coast]. That this is a grand organization goes without question. The writer can remember when he was a wee small boy of once hearing this company. The recital impressed him and since that time he has never lost an opportunity to hear Blind Boone and his company. On a trip a few years ago to Columbia, MO, which is the home of Blind Boone, the writer visited the large, fertile, and well stocked farm of this wonderful player, and at a glance one would become interested in its grandeur. We hope that the colored people will give Mr. Boone and his company a royal reception on the 30th when they play at Garfield Hall.

Source: *Wichita Searchlight*, April 19, 1902, 2.

---

[10]Tom Wiggins (1849-1908), an African American pianist and musical prodigy from Georgia, who concertized from the late 1850s to 1904.

The Boone Concert Company gave two concerts in Topeka this week. One at the Parkdale M.E. Church, and the other at the St. John A.M.E. Church on Tuesday night. A crowded house greeted Blind Boone on Tuesday night, made up of all classes, who thoroughly enjoyed the unique performance of this prodigy. Boone played with marked ability some of the most difficult compositions, mixing just enough ragtime to keep the spirit of the audience on the tiptoe of expectancy. Boone played with vigor responding to the requests of the audience. Among the pieces played was a very creditable composition by Mrs. Geo W. Hamilton, of Topeka...one of our ladies of whom we are proud. The singing of Miss Maria Wingo was pleasing to the audience. She received many encores. Her singing of the "Honey-suckle and the Bee" brought out the full strength of her fine contralto voice. The concert was a financial success bringing good returns to the Sheldon league and the church.

Source: *Topeka Plaindealer*, October 4, 1901, 2.

A Reflection on "Progress"

This chapter concludes with a letter to the editor of the *Chicago Broad Axe*. In her essay singer and choir director Martha Broadus-Anderson places the music composed and performed by African Americans since Emancipation alongside other achievements that have contributed to racial progress. She feels certain that, given enough time, blacks will make musical contributions equal to their European counterparts. She also attests that the black audience is discriminating, and demands the best from its performers. This essay thus looks forward to a future filled with more African American musical achievements:

Evidences of Musical Progress among Colored People
By Martha Broadus-Anderson[11]

[11] Ms. Broadus-Anderson is described in the article as a "Graduate of the Chicago Musical College, leader of the choir of Quinn Chapel, and a member of the Choral Study club, who has become a prominent and successful figure in the musical world."

Much has been said concerning the Negro in America and
his progress. The race question has been discussed pro
and con till at times it has taken on a ridiculous aspect.
We have been told by various writers and lecturers of the
amount of property accumulated by him how many doc-
tors, lawyers, milliners, dressmakers, mechanics, ect. he
has produced in a little more than forty years of freedom,
but it seems that very little or nothing has been said as to
his musical progress. It is because he has not made any?
Absolutely no! Along with the steady progress in other
lines he has not failed to advance just as steadily musically. Quite true that as a race, they have not reached the
fullest development, but today they are far in advance of
the place from whence they started. It has been proven
that whatever has happened in this country that was of
interest to the nation, the Negro has had a hand in it. It
is none the less true in the musical field. American is fast
becoming a power among the nations musically and just
as the country grows so will the Negro grow. If it took two
hundred years for Germany to produce a Johann Sebas-
tian Bach, we are not surprised that the progress among
the Colored people in America has not been greater. Who
knows that a few generations from now the colored people
may not produce composers and musicians equal to those
produced by any other race?

Already they have given the world some musicians whose
work compares favorably with the best. Have they not had
a Flora Batson-Bergen, a Selika, a Black Patti, and others
whose voices have thrilled thousands? Have they not a
Joseph Douglass and a Clarence White among the violin-
ists?[12] These are young men who still have a great deal
to which to look forward. Have they not pianists and or-
ganists without number who need only to be heard to be
admired? The Colored young men and women are not all
idling their time away. They are to be seen here and there

---

[12]Here the author references five important concert performers. Marie Selika Williams
(c. 1849-1937) was a soprano, and in 1878 became the first black artist to perform at the
White House. Flora Batson-Bergen (1864-1906) was a mezzo soprano, known as the "double-
voiced queen of song." Clarence Cameron White (1880-1960) was considered the finest
black concert violinist of his generation, a student of both William Marion Cook and Samuel
Coleridge-Taylor. Joseph Douglass was the grandson of Fredrick Douglass, and the first
African American concert violinist.

wherever good music is heard. Some of them are striving up the ladder of art slowly, but steadily.... It is said by some that the Negro has a greater sense of rhythm than any other of the races [and] that he loves song. If that be true, great things are expected for him. In the years to come, I have the confidence to believe, he will not disappoint as the doors of opportunity are opened to him. Here and there he will make the opportunity for himself and will be so persistent that the world will be forced, as it were, to sit up and take notice....

And what of the Colored audience? Do they appreciate the real worth of the Colored musician? We feel safe in saying "yes." Our audiences are becoming educated musically. We are to the place where we can no longer throw just anything before them and call it music. If we play we must do more than play the notes like a machine; if we sing, we must do more than be the possessor of our excellent voice and the ability to carry a tune; we must in every instance be able to express to our audiences what the composer meant as nearly as possible, or, in other words, we must be able to interpret. If we have not succeeded in telling something to an audience, we have fallen short of our one aim and at some time or other we will be made to feel only too keenly our deficiency. Sometimes one is inclined to feel that a Colored audience is even more discriminating than the average white audience.

The word to the student then is to press onward and upward. Aim high, and if we do not reach the goal, we will at least be higher than if we had not made the effort. It is for posterity to bring to perfection that which is begun by the parents.

Source: *Chicago Broad Axe*, January 2, 1909, 2.

Chapter 4:
Ragtime, Blues, Jazz, and a World War, 1910-1920

A Harvard professor rises to remark that "syncopation in harmonization has no immoral connotation," which, being roughly translated into idiomatic English, means "Ragtime is de pure goods."

Source: *Chicago Broad Axe*, November 18, 1911, 7.

"Jack" Johnson, Negro prize fighter, married at Chicago Lucile Cameron, the white girl who escaped the custody of her mother. Ragtime music and scenes of revelry followed the exchange of vows and then the wedding "feast" given by Johnson to his friends, which ended in an orgy.

Source: *Cleveland Gazette*, December 7, 1912, 4.

A Night of the Blues for the Blues

Mrs. McCullough cordially invites patrons to attend the Blue Monday party and March Soiree given by the Autumn Leaf Dancing Club, Monday evenings March 6th and March 20th at Lane's Hall ... Come and hear your favorite "Blues" sung while you dance.

Source: *St. Paul Appeal*, February 26, 1916, 4.

By the early 1910s, "coon" songs and minstrelsy were clearly in decline throughout the country, including the Midwest. New types of songs,
dances, and other musical entertainment were now to be found in traveling
vaudeville shows that presented a variety of acts, not all of which featured
racist imagery. Vaudeville, together with sheet music and the recording
industry sustained the popularity of ragtime for a few years, and also introduced the "blues" and, by the late 1910s, music that began to be called
"jass" or "jazz."

The term "blues" as a musical genre begins to appear in the Midwest
black press around 1914, disseminated in the publications of W.C. Handy,
and a few lesser-known composers and entertainers. "Blues" songs quickly
became part of the vaudeville repertoire, as well as sheet music for purchase. The term "jazz" emerged in the newspapers in 1916, again in advertisements for vaudeville shows, but also as a descriptor of local bands
who played in nightclubs, or, in St. Paul, on riverboats. While we can get
an indication as to the nature of the "blues" songs from the sheet music
of Handy, it is more difficult to surmise from the press what qualified a
band as a "jazz" band, as distinct from a ragtime band, or the exact musical definition of that term. But it is clear that the word "jazz" was used
by bandleaders, composers, and arrangers to describe music that was new,
exciting, and innovative.

In the second decade of the 20th century, The *Indianapolis Freeman* continued to provide its readers with national coverage of theater happenings
until its publication ceased in 1916. The *Chicago Broad Axe* and *Chicago
Defender* also maintained an important national presence and the editors
of the *Cleveland Gazette* and the *Topeka Plaindealer* still strove to connect
African American music with racial uplift. Each of the Kansas Cities had
their own black newspaper, the *Kansas City Sun* in Missouri and the *Kansas
City Advocate* in Kansas. And the *Appeal* of St. Paul, Minnesota reveals that
jazz was popular in the upper Midwest as early as 1917.

Two other important topics will be covered in this chapter: the arrival
of New Orleans jazz at Chicago's Pekin Inn, and the role that jazz played
in World War I. The transformation of the Pekin into a jazz cabaret established Chicago's South Side as one of the premier centers for the new
music in the country. And, as we will see, ragtime entered Europe at the
dawn of the War, and the band attached to the African American Battalion
356, led by James Reese Europe, caused a sensation towards the end of the
hostilities. Mr. Europe's musical and military career was a source of pride
and hope for African Americans, and his tragic death was deeply felt.

Theater Music and Ragtime: New Horizons

In 1913 black theater was at low ebb; Bob Cole, Ernest Hogan, and George Walker, of Williams & Walker, had all died by 1911, and the Black Patti Troubadours were drawing smaller crowds. Black vaudeville acts struggled to find an audience and the T.O.B.A. circuit had yet to be formed, but popular taste runs in cycles, and new and exciting opportunities were just around the corner, as foretold in this essay:

By Lester A. Walton in the A.M.E. Quarterly Review

The Negro on the American Stage

Not for a decade has the dramatic field been so barren and so unproductive to the colored performer. However, as our advancement is oftimes [sic] measured by individual success, it can be said that the race is slowly but surely assuming a higher and more prominent status in theatrical realm....

The first of the year will mark the departure to Europe of a number of colored acts of high standing, which have found it difficult to get booking in the best vaudeville houses this season. In London just now they are ragtime crazy, and the situation is being greeted with pleasure by colored vaudevillians of ability.

As has been the case with all races and classes of people, the Negro performer's lot has not been strewn with roses. He has and is experiencing ups and downs, trials and tribulations that are inevitable in order to reach the goal spelled success. The career of the Negro on the American stage has been interesting, but the part he is bound to play as an actor, singer and dancer will be more so. Nature has fitted him to be an entertainer of the first order, and as soon as he learns that with an educated throat and feet he must combine educated brains, there is no telling how brightly he will shine as a disciple of Thespis.

Source: *Topeka Plaindealer*, February 14, 1913, 6.

This period of transition from minstrelsy to ragtime and vaudeville allowed black composers and musicians to examine the past, realize the worth of African American musical creativity, and imagine a future offering expanded horizons. Indeed, they were witnessing the continued popularity of ragtime and the rapid rise of African American syncopated dance music. Juli Jones Jr. was the stage/pen name for William D. Foster (1884—?), an African American film producer, actor, and writer. With an extensive experience in vaudeville, he offered his version of the evolution of ragtime:

Great Colored Song Writers and Their Songs

How they have helped the American to be recognized in the Musical World

...Ragtime really came from the Mobile buck, combined with the banjo. The tap of the feet and the stop time on the banjo formed some kind of a combination that sounded like a thousand different taps were going on that the same time. The biggest asset was they kept good time. The success of the Mobile buck found its way to the river cities on the Ohio and Mississippi rivers, when steamboats held sway in this country and hauled all the freight and passengers that traveled north and south. Sometime along in the early eighties a triple combination of song, walk, and dance by the name of "Coon Jine Baby, Coon Jine," sprang up amongst the roustabouts on the many boats and spread like wildfire. The song and dance found its way into the levee resorts, where all prosperous houses had old hand-me-down square pianos with a half dozen broken keys: yet these instruments were considered the jewels in those days, as it only required a few keys to play the "Coon Jine." This is where the original ragtime started from—the quick action of the right-hand fingers playing the "Coon Jine." Some claimed St. Louis as the father town for ragtime; some claimed Louisville, Ky. Anyway, St. Louis turned out the first and best players. Following the "coon Jine Baby" was "Ta-a-ra ta Boom de ya." This song was put on the stage by May Irwin and Lottie Collins.

In supporting "Coon Jine Baby, Coon Jine," and "Ta-a ra ta Boom de ya," the writer is not overlooking "Mary's Run off with a Coon," and "Sleeping on a Corncob Bed." They were coon songs, but not ragtime coon songs, and were not filled with the ginger of ragtime. Coon songs have always been popular, as all of Stephen Foster's songs were coon songs, but did not carry the triple syncopated time that has upset the musical world.

The credit for the popularity of the ragtime has been given to first one then another. To be plain and to the point, Edward Harrigan, of Harrigan and Hart, was the first to present Broadway, New York in the middle eighties, with a good, live ragtime coon song, a song by the name of "Crow, Crow," in his play Pete. "Crow, Crow" did not have the sting that many songs have had since, but it was a good example. Dave Braham, the leader of the Grand Opera Orchestra, New York, set the music to "Crow, Crow." There was a very little improvement on Mr. Braham's style of music for a long time, as the cultured musician could not read ragtime or play it. This was a big holdback to ragtime. Some leaders refused to allow their men even to try to play ragtime. At last the real ragtime song came to the front in "Mr. Johnson, Turn Me Loose" by Ben Harney, a white boy, who lived among Negroes in St. Louis, MO. It was arranged by Carl Hoffmann, a white man, the leader of the Olympia Theater Orchestra, Chicago. Mr. Hoffman's arrangement was the key to arrange ragtime so any orchestra could play it. Ben Harney, the writer...was readily hustled out of the Negro concert hall where he was playing and learned the Negro's secret of how to play ragtime: put it on the vaudeville stage, headlining all bills as the only white man that could play ragtime on a piano. Mr. Harney was a tremendous hit everywhere he appeared. From good authority we are told there were fifty colored piano players in St. Louis that were better players than Ben Harney. At that time the vaudeville door was not open to the colored man. With May Irwin singing "Mr. Johnson, Turn Me Loose," and Ben Harney playing ragtime on the stage, the country went ragtime wild.

Our great band master, John Phil Sousa, when leading the Marine Band in Washington, D.C. added a lot of fame to ragtime when he wrote the "High School Cadets" march. This march was well filled with ragtime. Up to this time only a few songs could be arranged in ragtime. One Wm. Tyers, a colored arranger, perhaps the first colored arranger of ragtime, came on the scene who could arrange or take down any song in ragtime. For a time he had every publishing house in New York at his mercy, as he was the only arranger in the city who could put out ragtime that any orchestra or band could handle. His arrangement of "Georgia Camp Meeting" stormed the country. The band leaders of this country denounced ragtime for a while. The audience wanted it so bad that plenty of times they would raise up in their seats and openly demand it to be played. The leaders would put on a selection from Wagner instead.

Mr. John Philip Sousa broke the chains on his first tour of the country. He always put on a rag number as his third selection. The air of it would set the crowd wild. Ragtime music had its final and first test in the early '90s. Some of the great music critics in New York were very outspoken about the craze and put it at the doors of the common people, that the high cultured, refined people detested such trash. Contrary to this there was a big demand for ragtime music from the patrons of the Metropolitan Opera House at Sunday night concerts which were given weekly for the benefit of the orchestra and a few solo singers who belonged to the grand opera company, as their salaries were not up to the standard....

The critics who have been so harsh on the Negro about his lack of help supply the world with something besides trouble would do well to look up the music end of literature. They will find that the Negro has cultivated the only thing that America can boast of being better than the old world has ever been able to produce.... There are hundreds of writers the world will never hear of because they have no way of producing their music. The colored song writers of this country have been robbed out of enough melody inside of the last 25 years that, if one should put a commercial value on it, would amount to millions of dollars....

Source: *Indianapolis Freeman*, December 23, 1911, 6.

In 1915 the *Cleveland Gazette* ran an article written by James Reese Europe (1881-1919) that had previously appeared in the progressive *New York Sun*. Europe led the innovative Clef Club Orchestra whose syncopated rhythms, accompanying the new dances by Vernon and Irene Castle, were just then revolutionizing dance music. In this essay, Europe attributes the popularity of African American music to the combination of "natural" gifts and new forms of training:

Afro-American Cullings

"Why does society prefer the Negro musician?" The question was recently asked by one of your correspondents. If the Negro musician enjoys any preference at all, he does not enjoy it solely because of his color. His color is a handicap; and wherever he achieves success he does so in the face of doubly severe competition. In certain branches of his occupation the Negro musician has been successful: In furnishing entertainment at dinner parties, receptions and other social functions similar in character and in furnishing dance music. For work of the former kind his services have always been in demand, because of his unfailing good nature, his genial, kindly humor, and his versatility. Until recently, those who were engaged in this work were for the most part untrained musicians who relied on their natural talents.

In the last few years, however a new type of Negro musician has appeared in response to the demand for dance music of which the distinguishing characteristic is an eccentric tempo. Such music usually takes the form of a highly syncopated melody, which in the early period of its development was known as "ragtime" music. Since the dance is born of music, it is quite apparent that the modern dance is a creature of the syncopated melody. Thus a new field has been opened to Negro musicians. The Negro's success is due to the following facts: He is a natural musician and throws himself into the spirit of his work with spontaneous enthusiasm; so that the music rendered by a Negro orchestra rarely has the mechanical quality which is fatal to dancing. He has a superior sense of rhythm, peculiarly adapting him for dance music. The art of playing the modern syncopated music is to him a natural gift.

He excels in the use of the guitar, banjo, and mandolin, instruments which are now being generally adopted by orchestras playing dance music to obtain the "thrum-thrum" effect and the eccentric accentuated beat so desirable in dance music; and he was the first to discover the availability of these instruments for such purpose.

In addition to his natural talent in the above respects the modern Negro musician is well trained in his art. He reads readily, memorizes marvelously well, interprets naturally, and not only understands the principles of technique in the use of his instruments, but is remarkably skillful in execution, as is to be expected when one considers that the Negro possesses a rare facility for arts requiring physical skill.

Perhaps it is fair to say that the Negro has contributed to American music whatever distinctive quality it possesses. Certainly he is the originator of the highly syncopated melody so much in favor today. Some years ago in Cole & Johnson's show, of which I was musical director, there was a number containing a peculiarly syncopated passage which not a single white orchestra ever succeeded in playing correctly, while colored orchestras played it without effort, unconscious of its intricacies.

Such preference as the Negro musician enjoys is therefore due to efficiency which is the result of a natural inheritance and to his application to the serious study of his music....

Source: *Cleveland Gazette*, November 6, 1915, 4.

James Weldon Johnson was one of the leading civil rights activists of his generation, ultimately becoming the leader of the NAACP. He was also a poet and a novelist, and a collector of spirituals. In this essay, Johnson, like Europe, discusses the musical gifts of African Americans, and shows that the new black dance music and ragtime had, and will continue to have, a great impact upon the world:

The Negro in American Art

The influence which the Negro has exercised on the art of dancing in this country has been almost absolute. For generations, the clog and the jib, which are strictly Negro dances, have been familiar to the American theater audience. Several years ago the public discovered the turkey-trot, the eagle rock, and several other varieties that started the modern dance craze. Half the floor-space in the country was then turned over to dancing, and highly paid exponents sprang up everywhere. The most noted, Vernon Castle...never danced except to the music of a colored orchestra, and he never failed to state to his audiences that most of his dances had long been done by your colored people, as he put it.

Anyone who witnesses a musical production in which there is dancing cannot fail to notice the Negro stamp upon all the movements, a stamp that even the great vogue of Russian dances could not affect. That peculiar swaying of the shoulders which you see done everywhere by the blond girls of the chorus is nothing more than a movement from the Negro dance referred to above, the eagle rock.

...Ragtime is the one artistic production by which America is known the world over. It has been all-conquering, and is everywhere hailed as "American music."

Of course there are those who will deny that it is an artistic production. American musicians, especially, instead of investigating ragtime, dismiss it with a contemptuous word. But it has always been the course of scholasticism in every branch of art. Whatever new thing the people like is pooh-poohed: whatever is popular is spoken of as not worthwhile. The fact is, nothing great or enduring, especially in music, has ever sprung full-fledged and unprecedented from the brain of any master; the best that he gives to the world he gathers from the hearts of the people, and runs it through the alembic of his genius....

We are all familiar with the great influence that ragtime has had on music in America. Most people will recognize that influence on the musical comedy stage, but not many know that ragtime has even influenced our religious music. I do not know how many of us here are familiar with Gospel hymns, but if you are you can at once see the great difference between the songs of thirty years ago, such as "In the Sweet By and By," "The Ninety and Nine," ect., and the up-to-date syncopated tunes that are sung in Sunday schools and like meetings today....

I believe the Negro possesses a valuable and much needed gift that he will contribute to the future of American democracy. I have tried to point out that the Negro is here not merely to be a beneficiary of American democracy, not merely to receive. He is here to give something to American democracy. Out of his wealth of artistic and emotional endowment he is going to give something that is wanted, something that is needed, something that no other element in all the nation has to give.

In spite of the bans which musicians and teacher have placed upon it, the people still demand and enjoy ragtime. One thing cannot be denied; it is music which possesses at least one strong element of greatness; it appeals universally to not only the American, but the English, the French, and even the German people who find delight in it.

In fact, there is not a corner of the civilized world in which it is not known, and this proves its originality, for if it were an imitation, the people of Europe at least would not have a found it a novelty. And it is proof of a more important thing; it is proof that ragtime possesses the vital spark, without which any artistic production, no matter how approved its form may be, is dead.

Source: *Topeka Plaindealer*, November 30, 1917, 1.

Numerous articles of the time support Johnson's statement that European nations were encountering and enjoying African American music. An essay in the *Cleveland Gazette* reveals that, on the eve of World War I, ragtime was finding popularity in Germany. This article appeared two days after Austria-Hungary had declared war on Serbia:

Germany Takes to Ragtime

Notwithstanding the prevalence of folk songs among the peasantry, the deeply-rooted love for classical music that pervades all Italy retards the introduction of American "ragtime" music which is making its way but slowly in that kingdom. In Germany, on the other hand, American music, especially ragtime, is very popular and has a good and ready sale, says a United States consular report.

A German music publishing firm in Berlin is said to copy the popular and "catchy" instrumental music and sell it in all parts of Germany; songs are also translated and published by this firm, and some of these American songs are quite popular. Music dealers in Strasbourg say the German firm referred to can sell the copied music more cheaply than the original can be imported from America.

Source: *Cleveland Gazette*, August 1, 1914, 3.

The terms "ragtime" and "minstrel" continued to be found in the black press during this decade, but the new terms, "vaudeville," "blues," and "jazz," emerge and grow. By 1920 those words dominate the discussion of popular music in the press, indicating a shift towards new, exciting forms of entertainment and dance. Vaudeville presented its audience with a wide assortment of acts. There was less burnt cork and racist, anti-Bellum imagery, and a greater emphasis on modern music and dancing. Although most of the venue owners were white, Chicago's Pekin Theater was an exception. It was founded and owned by black entrepreneur Robert T. Motts, whose goal was to create "a playhouse worthy of the name and a credit to the Negro race," and who only hired African Americans.[1] All of these features are revealed in this announcement:

An All Star Colored Vaudeville Bill at the Pekin Theater

Beginning on Monday, May 29th another unique feature bill will be offered at the Pekin. The management has secured an all Star Colored vaudeville bill for the week's program. This should prove most interesting and is the only program of its kind that has been arranged for a vaudeville performance for a regular bill since the Colored artists have become foremost in the vaudeville field. The acts have been selected because of the difference of one from the other and a most pleasing entertainment should result.

The famous Byron Musical family in an entirely new set of selections will head the bill, with Perrin & Crosby in their charming singing and dancing number, an act new to Chicago will be shown, the Owsley Brothers, who have an offering presenting the old fashioned Colored men. Clayborn Jones, the Zulu King, with his well-known specialty. Beside, five other well-known and pleasing acts will complete this unique bill for the coming week which should prove very interesting and pleasing to the patrons of the Pekin. At this season the house is most attractive owing to its fine system of cooling, and its open sides make an evening at the show most comfortable notwithstanding the heat of the evening. No doubt a strong attendance will turn out to see the All Star Bill of Colored artists.

---

[1] Robert T. Motts, quoted in Thomas Bauman, *The Pekin: The Rise and Fall of Chicago's First Black-Owned Theater.* (Urbana: University of Illinois Press, 2014): xv.

Source: *Chicago Broad Axe*, May 27, 1911, 2.

In the early 1910s, most of the vaudeville producers and theater owners were white. However, the black vaudeville performer Sherman H. Dudley purchased a collection of theaters, and working as treasurer of the Colored Actors Union created the "Dudley circuit," which booked only black artists. As we shall see, the Dudley circuit built upon its success, becoming the Theater Owners Booking Association in the 1920s. Like the Pekin, the Alpha Theater in Cleveland catered specifically to a black audience, and strove for entertainment appealing to all:

THE ALPHA THEATRE

3206 Central Ave.

The Most Complete Colored Theatre in America

Showing only

The Best and Highest Priced Colored Vaudeville Traveling

Our acts are booked direct from New York, Chicago, and Philadelphia, through the

Dudley, Owsley and Kline Circuit

Showing also

The Best in Motion Pictures

A Place for Ladies, Children and Gentlemen

Gilbert B. Johnson.   Florence Ferguson,   Jas. A. Hicks,
Stage Mgr.   Musical Director.   Gen. Mgr.

Source: *Cleveland Gazette*, November 8, 1913, 2.

The "Blues" and New Dances

In 1912 W. C. Handy published his "Memphis Blues," establishing in the popular lexicon a new 12 bar, three- chord song form and a rhythm for dancing. During this decade Handy's blues appeared on the vaudeville stage and the dance hall, reshaping both American song and dance. In this essay, written at the time that Handy published his seminal "St. Louis Blues," vaudeville performer Salem Tutt Whitney places Handy among the top African American composers in the country:[2]

Seen and Heard while Passing
By Salem Tutt Whitney with the Smart Set Co.

---

[2]For more on W. C. Handy, see Eileen Southern, *The Music of Black Americans: A History* (NY: W.W. Norton, 1997): 338-40.

W.C. Handy, Composer of the Memphis blues, the Man
Who is Making Memphis Famous.

Not many persons outside of Memphis and vicinity may
have a personal acquaintance with Mr. Handy, but who
has not been moved and thrilled by the peculiar rhythm
and minor strains and cadences of the "Memphis Blues?"
Mr. Handy wrote the "Memphis Blues" just to please the
people of Memphis. He sold it. Since then it has brought
thousands of dollars to its purchaser. An enviable reputation to Mr. Handy and added publicity to the city of Memphis.

Mr. Handy is just at the meridian of life, pleasant and
unassuming in manner, and an interesting conversational-
ist with that lack of self-assertiveness that is peculiar to the
true genius. He has been a close student of music for more
than 30 years, was vocal director, arranger, and bandmas-
ter with Mahara's Minstrels, managing 60 men 17 years
ago. He was also teacher of vocal and instrumental music
at the A & M College, Normal, Ala. Mr. Handy has received
complimentary press notices for his work as a director of
music from the American, Cuban, Mexican, and Canadian
press. He has one of the most complete musical libraries
owned by a Negro anywhere.

Mr. Handy's band is always in great demand, and he makes
a specialty of featuring compositions by Negro composers.

When Mr. Handy wrote the "Memphis Blues," he builded
[sic] better than he knew. He was censured by many for
writing what they claimed was an inferior piece of music and greatly below his standard as a composer. It is a
unique composition, having twelve measures to a strain
instead of sixteen. Its rapid increase in popularity everywhere makes it a psychological study and it is bound to
become a classic of its kind just as the real Negro compositions of Will Marion Cook, Scott Joplin, and other Negro
composers are now considered to be the only real expression of the Negro in music and the only genuine American
music....

Source: *Indianapolis Freeman*, September 26, 1914, 6.

The next three essays describe the spread of Handy's blues from the east coast to the Midwest. The popular dances of New York City's Vernon and Irene Castle, accompanied by the syncopated rhythms of James Reese Europe's Society Orchestra, soon spread to the Midwest. By the middle of the decade dancing to music now being called "blues" and "jazz" was a popular new pastime, especially for the upper classes. Dancing schools and clubs inspired by the Castles sprang up, where patrons could learn the newest steps, the Tango and the Foxtrot:[3]

African American Cullings

By James Reese Europe

There is much interest in the growth of the modern dances in the fact that they were all danced and played by us Negroes long before the whites took them up.... The fox trot was created by a young Negro of Memphis, Tenn. Mr. W. W. Handy, who five years ago wrote "The Memphis Blues." This dance was often played by me last season during the tour of the Castles but never in public. Mr. Castle became interested in it, but did not believe it suitable for dancing. He thought the time too slow, the world of today demanding staccato music. Yet after a while he began to dance it at private entertainments in New York, and, to his astonishment, discovered that it was immediately taken up. It was not until then that Mr. and Mrs. Castle began to dance it in public, with the result that it is now danced as much as all the other dances put together. Mr. Castle has generously given me the credit for the fox trot, yet the credit, as I have said, really belongs to Mr. Handy...The one-step is the national Dance of the Negro, the Negro always walking in his dances. I myself have written probably more of these new dances than any other composer, and one of my compositions, "The Castle Lame Duck Waltz," is, perhaps, the most widely known of any dance now before the public.

Source: *Cleveland Gazette*, February 6, 1915, 4.

...Mr. Barksdale is conducting a dancing school in his new place, at 10550 Euclid Ave. [Cleveland, OH], every Thursday evening. The high moral tone of this school merits the

---

[3]For more on the impact of the Castles on black dance music, see Eve Golden, *Vernon and Irene Castle's Ragtime Revolution* (Lexington: University of Kentucky Press, 2007).

patronage of our race who enjoy clean dancing and good association. Mr. Barksdale teaches one of the new dances every Thursday evening and also demonstrates new positions and styles of dancing. The ballroom may be rented for private parties and private lessons may be arranged for by special appointment. Remember that on New Year's night the "Jazz" will be taught.

Source: *Cleveland Gazette*, December 22, 1917, 3.

Cosmos Club [Kansas City, MO]

The M & O Hall has been newly papered and painted for the Fall Opening of the Cosmos Club, Friday, September 7th. All members are expected to be present without fail. Invite your friends to come also and let's make this the grandest affair in the history of this the most famous dancing club of Greater Kansas City. Prof. Frank Buckner will lend the magic of his presence to the floor and the Cosmo Club orchestra will furnish both jazz and jizz for the occasion.

Source: *Kansas City Advocate*, August 31, 1917, 1.

Jazz Arrives in the Midwest

The origins of the term "jazz" or "jass" are of course not precisely known. But in the black Midwest press, the word starts to appear in 1916. In 1916 the *Indianapolis Freeman* had a brief announcement of a "singing Jazz band" that was touring Indiana and Iowa in December of that year.[4] More substantially, an African American pianist/composer named W. Benton Overstreet was writing new material for vaudeville singer Estelle Harris, and calling her backup band "Jass Entertainers," whose popularity at Chicago's Grand Theater was such that a strike by the theater's union carpenters could not stop the show:

Estelle Harris a Big Hit at the Grand Theater in Chicago

Despite the little bunch, in other words, gang, that loitered around the Grand Theater nightly with their little hammers discussing why, how, and what should be done the

---

[4]*Indianapolis Freeman*, December 2, 1916, 8.

week of October 2nd, Estelle Harris and her Jass Entertainers turned people away and stopped the show throughout
the week. The house was sold out Sunday night before
the orchestra went into the pit. Some of the carpenters'
union said that the act went over owing to the fact that
they carried their own crowd with them, which was absurd. The act played the old Apollo Theater at 47th street
and went over nicely. Life is too short to worry over somebody else's act when you need one yourself. The music for
the act was composed and arranged solely by W. Benton
Overstreet, with the exception of two numbers, "The Shi-
mashwabble," and "Don't Leave Me, Daddy." Miss Harris'
introductory number, "That Alabama Tango Band," was
written overnight by Mr. Overstreet, who is writing a new
number to replace the "Happy Shout," which has been
turned over to one of the leading publishing companies.
William Busch, banjo-mandolin player, has been added to
the orchestra.[5]

Source: *Indianapolis Freeman*, October 21, 1916, 9.

By 1918 venues were springing up on the South Side of Chicago that
featured dancing to the new jazz music. The famous Pekin Inn had undergone a difficult period after the death of owner Robert Motts in 1911,
but the new owners were trying to revive the old theater, saving it from a
criminal element, as the final sentence of this notice indicates:

THE OLD PEKIN THEATER HAS COME TO LIFE AGAIN AS AN ATTRACTIVE DANCE HALL

The old Pekin Theater, 27th and State streets, is now running at full blast again as a dance hall, under the management of Wallace K. Tyler. Each evening the original New
Orleans Jazz Band discourses music for the merry dancers
and the others who enjoy themselves sitting at the tables
on the main floor and upper balcony while sipping soft
drinks of various kinds. No liquor is sold on the premises.

Everything seems to indicate that it will continue to be
conducted in a more law-abiding manner or method than
what it was in the past.

---

[5] Eileen Southern cites Overstreet as one of the first to use the word "jass," in 1916. For
more on this topic, and Estelle Harris, see *Southern, The Music of Black Americans*, p 366.

Source: *Chicago Broad Axe*, March 9, 1918, 3.

But now the Pekin had competition. With the population boom of the Great Migration, several cabarets opened up, making Chicago's South Side the center of a musical movement that had come north from New Orleans:

THE DREAMLAND CAFÉ, WILLIAM BOTTOMS, PROPRIETOR

Less than two years ago the Dreamland Café at 3520 South State Street threw its door open to the public and from that time to the present it has been one of the most pleasant places of amusement on the South Side. At the present time, it has the best ragtime band in Chicago, accompanied by Bertha Hall, Albert Hunter and Mr. Tom Mills, the most popular entertainers. The New Orleans Jazz Band hits the rail all the time at a high rate of speed, and it really makes one feel that they are in Dreamland while listening to the sweet strains of the music and the almost crazy antics of its performers. My Host, William Bottoms, really and truly understands how to provide first-class and "catchy" amusement for his many patrons.

Source: *Chicago Broad Axe*, September 7, 1918, 12.

The South Side of Chicago became a haven for new arrivals during the Great Migration, who formed a fresh audience for African American music in the Midwest's largest city. But Chicago was not the only place where the new dances and music were to be heard. Bands long lost to history were playing jazz for dancers in places like Fort Scott, Kansas:

The Airdome is the one place in Fort Scott where colored people can go and get an evening's entertainment and be treated right. They are carrying a Jazz band now and the music is charming; the manager has used every effort to make this a place of amusement and recreation and it is up to you to make the best of the opportunities extended you for your own pleasure and entertainment. Why suffer with the heat after a hard day's labor, when you can comfortably sit down and rest in the coolest place in Fort Scott and enjoy yourself? When they named it "The Airdome" nothing more appropriate could have been selected in the way of a name, because you certainly get the cool breeze at night in this place.[6]

Source: *Fort Scott Messenger*, August 23, 1918, 1.

And Topeka:

Goodly number of friends and neighbors enjoyed an old fashioned barbecue at the home of Mr. and Mrs. Richard Slaughter in Pierce [Pierce City, MO, in the southwest corner of the state, near the Kansas border] Saturday night of last week. The meats, fish, etc., were delicious and with good, cold, "almost" beer fresh from the keg, the meats were devoured without mercy, and those who desired pop, ginger ale, etc., did not have to go wanting for it too was in abundance. It reminded us of the good old days when stuff drawn from a keg had the "authority." The feature of the evening however was the music by Hamilton's Jazz band: Joe Tolbert, violin; Andrew Harris, clarinet; "Doc" Gilbert," cornet; Clinton Duke, piano, and Preston Smith, traps. Each man knows his "stuff" and plays every note on the score from beginning to end. Clear and sweet as a bell the notes of the inspiring jazz thrilled those who heard them, and when they struck up "Home Sweet Home," the crowd clamored for just one more. It can be truthfully said that this organization is the equal of any in Topeka and the best of their race the city has ever boasted.

Source: *Topeka Plaindealer*, July 23, 1919, 3.

---

[6]An ad in the *Messenger* two weeks later provided the name of the band: Paul Reno and His Dixie Players (*Fort Scott Messenger*, 6 September, 1918, p. 1.

And Indianapolis:

Source: *Chicago Broad Axe*, December 7, 1918, 7.

But by far the black newspaper with the most elaborate advertisements for jazz events in the late 1910s, even more so than the Chicago newspapers, was the *St. Paul Appeal*. Below are just a few chosen selections:

Source: *St. Paul Appeal*, July 28, 1917, 4.

Source: *St. Paul Appeal*, January 28, 1918, 3.

Source: *St. Paul Appeal*, February 9, 1918, 3.

Jazz And a World War

By the beginning of World War I American syncopated music was cir-
culating in some parts of Europe, in the form of sheet music. The War
enabled a closer contact between Europeans and Africa American culture,
as many black men were willing to serve in the hope of gaining greater
respect at home. And the all-white draft boards were happy to ship black
men out of the country so that fewer whites would have to serve. Ultimately there were four all-black regiments: the 9th and 10th Cavalry and
the 24th and 25th Infantry. While African Americans made up about 10%
of the American population in 1917, they represented 13% of the American fighting forces.

The best known African American unit, both for its military accom-
plishments and for its band, was the 369th Infantry of the 93rd Division,
the "Harlem Hellfighters." The director of the regiment's band was James
Reese Europe, who had previously worked with the Castles to popularize
new, syncopated dance music. He and his regiment saw fighting on the
front lines through most of the spring and summer of 1918, fighting with
French units near Aisne-Marne in a successful counter-offensive.[7]

This essay is one of the few in this book by a white author, a correspondent for the *Saturday Evening Post*. It was subsequently reprinted in
the black *Kansas City Advocate*. The amount of racial bigotry that black
fighters had to endure, from inadequate food and clothing to being directly
and purposely placed in harm's way, is well-documented. It is not often
that one finds a white person writing with respect about African Americans at this time, but seeing the formerly besieged French people so moved
by the music of Reese's band seems to have made a deep impression on
the writer:

**Correspondent Irvin S. Cobb, observing 369th
(Hellfighters) regiment for the Saturday Evening Post:**

**...As for the dwellers of the French towns in which this
regiment has from time to time been quartered, they, I
am told, fairly go mad when some alluring, compelling,
ragtime tune is played with that richness of syncopated
melody in it which only the black man can achieve; and
as the regiment has moved on, more than once it has been**

---

[7]Information on the African American contribution to World War I taken from
Jami Bryan "Fighting for Respect: African-American Soldiers in WWI" http://-
www.militaryhistoryonline.com/wwi/articles/fightingforrespect.aspx, accessed October 6,
2015.

hard to keep the unattached inhabitants of the village that the band was quitting from moving on with it.

If I live to be a hundred and one I shall never forget the second night, which was a night of a splendid flawless full moon. We stood with the regimental staff on the terrace lawn of the chief house in a half-deserted town five miles back from the trenches, and down below us in the main street the band played plantation airs and hundreds of Negro soldiers joined in and sang the words. Behind the masses of upturned dark faces was a ring of white ones where the remaining natives of the place clustered, with their heads wagging in time to the tunes.

And when the band got to "Way Down Upon the Suwanee River," I wanted to cry, and when the drum major, who likewise had a splendid baritone voice, sang, as an interpolated number, "Joan of Arc," first in English and then in excellent French, the villagers openly cried; and an elderly peasant, heavily bewhiskered, with the tears of a joyous and thankful enthusiasm running down his bearded cheeks, was with difficulty restrained from throwing his arms about the soloist and kissing him.

Source: *Kansas City [Kansas] Advocate*, August 30, 1918, 1.

James Reese Europe's band was not the only ensemble which brought jazz to France during the war. Probably every African American unit that could get access to instruments, a score, or a phonograph played or sang something from their community, and the French were appreciative. This essay was written one month after the Armistice. The regiment and location are unknown, but we are told about the popularity of jazz among the French, and the determination and industriousness used to acquire songs and instruments in war-time conditions:

ANOTHER "MOST POPULAR" BAND

Our Soldier Boys Overseas Will Have Their Music—The French "Go Wild" Over it.

Somewhere in France—American music greatly interests the French population, and every night there is a concert by one of the army bands, the natives turn out en masse. They listen with undisguised approbation to the latest "hits" from the States and stay until the final notes of the "Star Spangled Banner" close the program.

The French fairly go wild over the American "jazz" tunes. They call that sort "chic." And when the band plays one of those rollicking one-steps they keep time with the music and vociferously applaud for more.

In one of the larger American base cities these military concerts are given about three times a week. The plaza, nearly a quarter of a mile long, is always crowded with the inhabitants as well as American soldiers. The bands alternate from the various surrounding army camps.

One of the most popular and best known American bands in the "service of supplies" in France is composed of the Afro-American stevedores. The men are in a draft outfit and come principally from western Pennsylvania and Tennessee. They are all natural musicians, and when they are not trucking guns, food, and other supplies from American ships and loading them on waiting freight cars they are practicing for their next concert.

They scraped up their instruments wherever they could. Some brought their horns and flutes along with them from the states. By saving their payday francs etc., they managed to get enough ahead to furnish their complement of instruments from the French shops.

But then they lacked music. So their leader turned on the phonograph in the Y.M.C.A. hut and jotted down the music for each of his men. They play for retreat each night, take part in the infrequent parades and celebrations in their district and each Sunday entertain huge crowds of visitors to their camp.

Source: *Cleveland Gazette*, December 28, 1918, 1.

Upon returning home African American soldiers were welcomed as heroes in their communities. One such event took place in St. Paul in December 1918, organized by the Minnesota Home Guard (M.H.G. in the announcement). The Minnesota Home Guard was organized by the Governor of the state to replace the newly federalized Minnesota National Guard. A group of African Americans petitioned the Governor for their own battalion in the M.H.G. and the 16th was formed. Their duties included homeland security, drilling, band concerts, and escorting new black Army recruits to the train station. And when they returned, the celebrations included music by Steven's Sharp Jazz Band:

Source: *St. Paul Appeal*, December 14, 1918, 3.

The celebrations of victory in the African American communities were soon tarnished by the murder of one of their war heroes, James Reese Europe. His sudden death was felt by blacks throughout the country. Every black newspaper carried notices of his passing, but this one, from the *Topeka Plaindealer*, is particularly detailed:

EUROPE, JAZZ KING. SLAIN BY DRUMMER

Herbert Wright, Member of His Band, is Charged with Stabbing Leader in Neck at Boston Concert.

Boston, May 9—Lieut. James Reese (Jim) Europe died at a hospital here at 11 o'clock tonight as a result of a wound in the neck, said to have been inflicted by Herbert Wright,

drummer in the band of the "Hell Fighters" (369th Infantry), of which Europe was the leader. The two engaged in an altercation at Mechanic's Hall, where the band has been giving a series of concerts.

Europe, who was standing in the wings while the band was playing, called out to Wright to "put more pep in the sticks." Wright left his drum and walked hastily over to Europe, who retreated to his dressing room.

Wright followed him, and after some words the police allege he drew a knife and slashed Europe in the neck. Wright was arrested. Both men came from New York.

Born in the South

Lieut. Europe was born about 37 years ago in Mobile, Ala., his father being at the time in the Government service. Europe early in life showed the Negro's aptitude for music and studied in Washington. He came to New York about fifteen years ago and immediately became prominent in the musical activities of his own people. He founded the Clef Club, which comprises some 200 musicians and which has at times been heard in public as a symphony orchestra and in other capacities.

A Composer of Note

Europe acquired much fame by providing musicians and composing a large part of the music used by Mr. and Mrs. Vernon Castle when the dance craze was at its height. "The Castle Lame Duck" waltz was his best known composition of this nature.

When the call of war came, Europe answered and went to France as a machine gunner. He was soon asked to organize a band from the colored fighters who were abroad, and Europe gathered a band made up of colored men from all parts of the United States. When this band gave its first concert in Paris, the so-called jazz features made a great sensation, and Europe had to play in Paris for weeks.

When the Fifteenth returned to America in February, Europe's band got much recognition and a fine welcome. After the Fifteenth was mustered out, Europe and his band gave two performances at the Manhattan Opera House, to the delight of crowded houses. They then started on a transcontinental tour of the country.

Members of the Clef Club last night, when told of the death of their popular founder, said it would be a distinct loss to the club and to the Negro colony here. It was said at the club that Europe leaves a widow ... a brother in New York, and a mother and three sisters in Washington.

Source: *Topeka Plaindealer*, May 16, 1919, 1.

As life returned to a new kind of normal after the war, jazz in the Midwest became infused with a new energy. Some returning soldiers began their own bands:

Source: *St Paul Appeal*, July 12, 1919, p. 4.

And dancing to jazz was done not only in cabarets and taverns but at public parks and picnics:

Moseley's
Dixie Land Park and Stadium
33rd Street and Wabash Avenue
NOW OPEN
7 TO 11:45 P. M. DAILY

Sundays and Holidays 2 to 12 P. M. Band Concerts;
Dancing to the best Jazz music. Shows and all kinds of
concessions.

Show your Race pride and spend your money with
your own and are welcome. Furnish employment as well
as amusement for your own.

Source: *Chicago Broad Axe*, July 12, 1919, 9.

And jazz was heard not just in the big cities of the Midwest, but in the small towns as well:

Town Gossip

Mr. Marion Martin, Prop. of the pool hall located at 504 S. Main, has installed a new electric piano, also a new and large tobacco case and a new cigar show case. These are valuable additions to the pool hall and add greatly to its appearance. The electric piano has several real snappy jazz pieces and adds new life to the spectators and patrons. A noticeable effect has already been recognized in the increased parsonage. Mr. Martin conducts his pool hall along strictly up-to-date lines, and lays special stress on maintaining order. There is also an up-to-date barber shop in connection, conducted by Mr. Joe Bell and Mr. Harrison Wickliffe.

Source: *Hutchinson [Kansas] Blade*, April 10, 1920, 4.

Town Gossip

The boys are glad that there is a piano in the pool hall, as the Jazz pieces delight their hearts.

Source: *Hutchinson Blade*, April 24, 1920, 4.

Jazz came not just to the underworld, but it also came to polite society as well. The following two advertisements are from African American versions of the men's fraternal Elk's Club (Improved Benevolent Protective Order of Elks of the World, or IBPOEW) and the Knights of Pythias. We will examine in greater detail the role of jazz in men's and women's social organizations in the next chapter:

Source: *St. Paul Appeal*, June 19, 1920, 3.

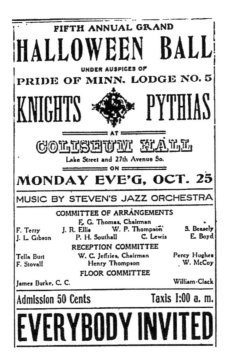

Source: *St. Paul Appeal*, October 16, 1920, 3.

Thus, as the country entered the post-war, optimistic, and for many, more prosperous 1920s, the energy of jazz captured the mood like no other music could:

My Jazz Soul!

I am no better than the musical atmosphere under which I breathe. For what inspires like music? It is elixir to my soul, wine to a heart that yearns, fire to a sense of motion such as the mad dance, the dance of dances.

Oh yes. I know something of the pure cold tones of the so-called classic. It satisfies an ideal, but like all else that's human—comes with a mood. Likewise the sacred psalms enrapt with glow so elevating that wings of heaven seem to hover near, and that I, poor soul! am about to know translation from this lowly state forever and forever.

But what is this that makes me feel so humanly human, delightful, glorious, abandoning all cares that worry and turn human experience gray when we are yet young and should see through the youthful lens of green? IT MUST BE MY JAZZ SOUL! Ah! to drink this in. The sweet spell, the charm of swinging around on time with the music, stepping to the exact beat of the drum, the plan of the piano, the moan of saxophone, and, most lately, the exhorting appeal of the singer—all mixed in the frenzy of the exhilarating noise. Again it must be my Jazz Soul!

Source: *Kansas City Sun*, September 25, 1920, 8.

Chapter 5:
Dancing in Kansas City, 1920-1929

By the early 1920s, Kansas City and Chicago were major Midwestern cities with growing African American communities and subsequently vibrant musical cultures. Both cities received thousands of African American migrants during this decade, expanding preexisting black communities, their social institutions, and economic systems. As a result, each city also had a strong black newspaper, which covered musical happenings in great detail. These next chapters will focus on the reflections of music, musicians and the black culture that supported them in the *Kansas City Call* and the *Chicago Defender*, two of the most widely disseminated black newspapers of the period. Moving from a survey of several newspapers to a focus on just one per chapter will reveal the richness of the material to be found in each and will enable detailed insight into the hopes and aspirations of their editors, the writers, and the readership.

Kansas City jazz of the 1920s and '30s is commonly perceived as deeply connected to the city's notorious vice and corruption of that era. This image has been perpetuated in books such as Ross Russell's *Jazz Style in Kansas City and the Southwest*, Nathan Pearson's *Goin' to Kansas City* and Robert Altman's movie *Kansas City*.[1] There was indeed a symbiotic relationship between jazz and vice in Kansas City, but that relationship is only part of a much larger picture. The music was also integral to the middle and upper class African American community, most of whom did not patronize the gambling dens and taverns where illicit activities took

---

[1]Ross Russell, *Jazz Style in Kansas City and the Southwest* (NY: Da Capo Press, 1973); Nathan Pearson, *Goin' to Kansas City* (Urbana: University of Illinois Press.1994); Robert Altman, *Kansas City* (Fineline Features, 1996).

place. They in fact endured such establishments, as they had to endure the segregation and racism that led them to create their own social structures isolated from the larger, white Kansas City community. For middle and upper-class blacks, jazz- influenced dance music was featured in charity events, political meetings, outings at the park, and many other activities that had little or no connection with vice. And this community celebrated the professional successes and achievements of the musicians who lived and worked among them. This is the story of jazz as told in the pages of the *Kansas City Call*.

This chapter focuses on the 1920s in Kansas City, when two band leaders, George E. Lee and Bennie Moten, rose to prominence. There were others as well, including Paul Banks, Chauncey Downs, and Jesse Stone to name just a few. The intention of this chapter, and this anthology, is not to focus on detailed biographies and performance timelines of the musicians, for that has been done elsewhere, most notably in Driggs' and Haddix's illuminating work *Kansas City Jazz: From Ragtime to Bebop—A History*.[2] Rather, my purpose is to provide a collection of essays and advertisements from the *Call*, allowing its writers and readers to speak once again, in a kind of detail that is not possible in a historical narrative written in the third person.

The *Kansas City Call* was founded in 1919 by Chester A. Franklin. It eventually became the sixth largest African American weekly in the country. It featured strong editorials, including a column about black life written by future NAACP leader Roy Wilkins, and another column that covered musical events written by his brother Earl Wilkins. It is an indispensable source for anyone researching not only the music, but also the political, economic, athletic, and social history of African Americans in the Midwest. Migration and Segregation

Migration and Segregation

Kansas City was the destination for many participants in the Great Migration of African Americans from the rural South to the urban North during the late 1910s until the 1930s. Whereas many migrants to Chicago were from Alabama and Mississippi, Kansas City was a closer destination for those from Texas and Arkansas. According to the U.S. Census reports there were 23,704 blacks in Kansas City in 1910, 30,893 in 1920, and 42,005 in 1930, by then making up more than 10% of the city's total pop-

---

[2](NY: Oxford University Press, 2005).

ulation.[3] The new immigrants merged with a pre-existing black community that, through racism and violence, were confined to specific neighborhoods. The main black commercial district was the 18th and Vine area,
where African American leaders established businesses, churches, and a
school, in defining space for their community. Our first two examples are
editorials that aimed to ease the tensions as new arrivals from the south
entered this established society:

The Search for an Ideal Home is the Cause for the Negro Migration

High wages in the northern industrial centers has been the
occasion of tremendous migration from the South, but not
the reason for it. Migration has given Negroes peaceful
firesides, but safety was not the reason. It will be fatal to
those who are considering measures for the good of southern industries, if they do not understand that the impelling
force which has emptied field and hamlet and city, is [the]
Negro's desire to give their children a better chance in life
than they themselves have had. For this they have left the
South and dared the unknown North.

Courage is a relative term. For a Negro who has gained
what he knows of the North from the lips of whites who
have profited by his ignorance, to go where snow is measured in feet, and leave the certainties of his existence,
however meager, is an adventure not to be undertaken
simply for higher wages. In the case of the highly paid pro-
fessionals, whose incomes are as great as any made in the
North, they too are leaving, and it is not money that lures
them. When Negroes thought schooling the open door to
opportunity, they stayed and old and young crowded into
the schools.

When they thought money meant a chance in life, they
saved even though paid one-half and one-third what other
men get. But when their hopes have been disappointed,
they have risen like the Pilgrims of old and fared forth, let
come what may. Having given up Dixieland for an ideal,
we will not be led back by anything short of a recognition
that we too are men. Color which has been the distinguishing mark of the worker, and leisure, which has been the ev-

---

[3] *Statistical Abstracts of the United States 1930* (Washington, D.C: United States Census Bu-
reau, 1930): 22-23.

idence of good breeding must join with the other dead and gone memories of the "chivalrous" south. In their place, must rise what will be the realization of Henry W. Grady's New South. "Labor conquers all … ."[4]

When we can look up at Old Glory, and call it our flag, with every star shining with promise for him who serves and endures to the end, we may go back. But until that day, though golden apples could grow on the trees, and though every southern breeze is keen with the fragrance of flowering nature, we will be men of the bleak shores of northern lakes, rather than be "good" Negroes in a land of plenty.

Source: *Kansas City Call*, August 24, 1923, 9.

Get Acquainted with your New Neighbor

Take a walk around your block and get acquainted with your neighbors. There are some mighty fine people whom you do not know. Suppose you had gone a thousand miles to see a new home, where your children could be educated and your wife could be safe, and then you found no welcome, would you like it? Would you give of your best to the new community? Would you be able to do your best for yourself?

Take a walk around your block, and meet all the new people, and shake hands with all the old ones. Tell them that twice a year the government whose benefits they wish to share, sends its representative out to assess property, and they should bear their share of the cost. Tell them Negroes vote in Missouri. Tell them they can vote for any man or any party they choose. Explain the registration, explain the voting.

Take a walk around the block and see if there is not an adherent of your church who needs your hand shake and your guidance to services. Shouting on Sunday is a lesser Christian service than neighborly kindness on Monday.

---

[4]Henry W. Grady was the managing editor of the white newspaper the *Atlanta Constitution* in the 1880s. Nicknamed the "Spokesman of the New South," his newspaper in the post-Reconstruction era called for northern investiment, diversified farming, and white supremacy.

Singing and praying are necessary and comforting, but they are the shadow of which helpfulness is the substance.

Take a walk around your block and see if anybody is keeping the children home from school. Maybe a little ignorance of conditions, possibly a little false pride about clothes, possibly sickness keeps the child at home, but whatever it is, Kansas City is a good place to live in and we all can help it do its best by everyone within our gates.

Source: *Kansas City Call*, September 28, 1923, 9.

While there were certain cultural tensions between the native Kansas Citians and the new arrivals from the South, all of the city's African Americans shared the experience of racism and segregation that denied them equal housing, education, and a political voice. The coverage of each of these topics in the *Call* could be the subject of more chapters or even a book. An incident regarding the week-long stay of a black jazz orchestra from Denver will provide a glimpse of life in this segregated society. The boycott was organized by women, who communicated through the network of ladies auxiliaries that were a vital part of the community's social life, as we shall see:

Boycott Jim Crow Show as Protest

Community Makes Common Decision Against Attending

"Special" Performance

The appearance of a colored entertainment organization is a very common place event at the local theaters down town. At some, no opportunity is given to hear them, [the theater] Pantages, for instance. In others segregated seats are sold, the range of seats being from the worst in the house to those slightly better. It remained for the Empress Theatre to make a new step in caring for colored patrons, by giving a special performance of the Morrison Orchestra from Colorado, with the time set at 10:30 p.m. on last Thursday night. At the announcement, at first came astonishment—the idea was so novel—then quickly followed indignation that accommodations could not be made in regular hours.

As a result, a body of women from the Federation of Clubs, a representative of Community Service, and a number of the local musicians, picketed the theater. Negroes bound thither were accosted, reasoned with, and turned back. The result was not over 70 persons attended the performance, and they were largely visitors to the city. Of the performance itself, people judged by their appearance at the social events which took place Tuesday and Friday nights. Thus ended one of the most unexpected assertions of the race spirit that Kansas City has ever known. The streets resounded with just one sentiment—that no person ought to go under such conditions. Without organization, simply on the initiative of individuals, the boycott was organized and it was put into effect with telling effect.

Since the performance, and the boycott, owners of this theater have stated to a [*Kansas City*] *Call* representative that the whole matter of colored persons was new to them, since they had just come into possession of the theater, that they were new owners with no experience with this particular custom there, and that only after this event, when it was too late, did they know that they had done so much violence to the feelings of colored people. They assured him that this would not happen again.

Some years or so ago an attempt was made to organize a boycott of a grocery man whose signature was among those signed to a petition against Negroes being left in peaceful possession of homes out south. It failed. The housewives who started it were unable to get all the women to leave off purchasing from this particular grocery man. The shifting population has left this particular store now surrounded by colored people and its trade is largely Negro ... the change in a few years' time is most significant, and shows the growth of race solidarity.

The consensus of opinion is that the whole incident of the orchestra has given a decided impetus to the disposition of Kansas City Negroes to spend their money where they are made welcome. The stores down town with toilet rooms barred to the race's women, the department stores where they may not be fitted, and all the places where prejudice rather than courtesy rules, are about to realize that it is a new Negro that has come upon the scene since the Great War.

Source: *Kansas City Call*, February 11, 1922, 1.

Vaudeville and the Female Blues Singers

Kansas City was an essential stop in the tour cycle of vaudeville productions that traveled throughout the country. It is a geographic point where the South, the Midwest, and the West meet, and thus served as a beginning and/or ending point for countless acts. The shows that were most often advertised in the *Call* were those on the black-owned T.O.B.A. (Theater Owner's Booking Association) circuit. This is just one of the many T.O.B.A. advertisements that appear in the *Call* during the 1920s:[5]

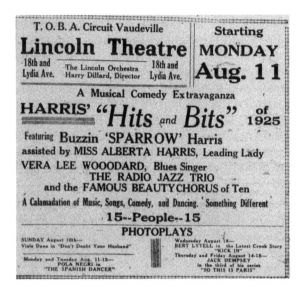

Source: *Kansas City Call*, August 8, 1924, 7.

As the T.O.B.A. vaudeville shows found success, so did the first commercially produced blues records. Mamie Smith's recordings of 1920 initiated the "race record" phenomenon when record companies awoke to the economic buying power and musical taste of African Americans in the wake of the Great Migration. Mamie Smith and Bessie Smith were among the many female blues divas who came to Kansas City in the 1920s. Their

---

[5]For more on the T.O.B.A., or this show, in particular, see Bernard L. Peterson, *A Century of Musicals in Black and White* (Westport, CT: Greenwood Press, 1993).

appearances were announced in the *Call* by elaborate advertisements, announcements, and sometimes reviews.[6]

Winston Holmes was the African American owner of a Kansas City music store who also worked in the recording industry. He served as manager for a time of the Bennie Moten Orchestra, and he created his own recording company, Meritt Records. He frequently purchased advertising space in the *Call* to announce the arrival of the latest blues records:

Blues Singer at Gillis Theatre

Mamie Smith, the famous colored phonograph star and her big company of entertainers have been booked for ten appearances at the New Gillis Theatre on April 3rd. Ever since Mamie Smith made her first appearance on the phonograph records, she has been a tremendous favorite both in New York and throughout the entire country. NO colored singer has ever attained the degree of popularity in so short a time as has come to Mamie. She carries a full company of well-known colored players with her, including her own jazz band, known as the "Mamie Smith Jazz Hounds." This season her company has been augmented and entirely new scenery, costumes, and lighting effects of a gorgeous nature have been provided. The show is said to be one of the cleanest and cleverest colored attractions ever seen on tour.

Mamie Smith's present revue scored a record breaking success through the East and South. The Gillis Theatre has been thoroughly renovated; the house has also been recently redecorated.

Source: *Kansas City Call*, April 1, 1922. 7.

---

[6]For more on the female blues singers of the 1920s, see Daphne Harrison, *Black Pearls: Blues Queens of the 1920s* (New Brunswick, NJ: Rutgers University Press, 1988).

Source: *Kansas City Call*, March 11, 1922, 3.

Source: *Kansas City Call*, May 9, 1924, 7.

A staple of the blues repertoire is sexual innuendo and double enten-
dre. While the *Call's* editor Chester Franklin accepted advertising money

for blues records and performances, he must have found the most explicit blues records objectionable, and not just for moral reasons. In this editorial, Franklin sees the "filth" of blues sexuality as another degradation forced upon them by whites. A boycott of the records in his view would thus be a step in resistance to white authority:

Boycott the Vile Records

Negroes must stop the deluge of filth which makers of records are marketing among them. The music of the "Blues" is one thing, but whether good or bad, it is indefensible to put to it all the stench which ingenuity can drag out of the underworld, and camouflage with words of double meaning. The same companies which appeal for white patronage with the best artists, disregard common decency when they sell to Negroes. One record, the vilest of the many gutter scrapings, actually reached a sale of 800,000 copies. And we pay good money to have our reputation for indecency thus established!

At the same time that commercialism is demoralizing our race, distributing perversion and sensuality in our homes, culture is denying us a share in uplift. The Negro who seeks after art, is just as unwelcome as when he wants work, or food, or shelter. Filth and filth alone is his with ease, and so much his that makers actually have the nerve to call their foul product "race records." There is even a difference in our degree of welcome, accordingly as the art gets worse. For instance, the Shubert Theatre held open many seats for Negroes to see "The Bird of Paradise" but none for Sothern when he appeared in Shakespearian plays.[7] In the former was told the story of the fall of a white man who loved a Hawaiian woman and of the regeneration of another white man, already fallen, who had casual contacts with a white woman, a very vivid comparison of the opposite effects on white men by women, the one dark and the other white. To cheap sophistry we are welcome, but no seats for Shakespeare.

It may be just coincidence that our moral atmosphere is polluted and our cultural opportunity cut off. But cold calculation could do no worse. That selling sewage makes

---

[7] E. H. Sothern (1859-1933) was one of the most famous American Shakespearean actors of the day.

money is no excuse, because selling art is also profitable. Concerts, such as occur in Convention Hall and Ivanhoe Temple, would not be lowered in tone because blacks as well as whites heard them.

Filth and prejudice are a fearsome combination for us to overcome. Either is opposition enough. But with the necessity of fleeing one and breaking thru [sic] the other, we are lost unless we exert ourselves mightily. We may not be able to compel white people to open up their heart to us, prejudice may continue to make race count more than merit or humanity. But we certainly can control our own money.

We ourselves have the solution of the filthy records. Don't buy them! Don't go to people's houses who do buy them. Don't permit your race newspaper to hear that name and at the same time advertise flagrant immorality set to music. Do anything, do everything, filthy records must go!

Source: *Kansas City Call*, March 12, 1926, 4b.

Bennie Moten and the Paseo Dance Hall

Much has been written about the connection between vice and jazz in Kansas City. The *Call* often condemned places of vice like the notorious Yellow Front, especially when they had a negative impact on schools and residential neighborhoods. However, jazz and jazz- inspired dance music were also heard in the city's more refined dance halls and ballrooms. Several of these venues were established for and patronized by the black middle and upper classes, and these events the *Call* covered in vivid detail. Indeed the newspaper offers some of the most important material for tracing the evolution of Kansas City jazz, especially the rise of the famous dance orchestras such as those led by Count Basie and Andy Kirk.

Pianist Bennie Moten (1894-1935) began as the leader of a trio in 1919, and through his entrepreneurship and his support from the African American men's fraternal lodges and women's auxiliaries, grew his band into a five- piece by 1923. Here is an early advertisement for an appearance at a cabaret, a venue that served dinner with dancing. Notice the emphasis on "clean entertainment:"

Source: *Kansas City Call*, May 18, 1923, 7.

In 1924 Bennie Moten leased a dance hall at the corner of 15th and Paseo, formerly known as Dahomey's. Now called the Paseo Dancing Academy, it served for several years as the band's home turf. Weekly dances were held there, many sponsored by the black elite. The announcements of the Grand Opening (with capitalization in the original) read:

First Time Colored People Use this Fine Hall

Society is demanding higher standards in all of its social phases. BENNIE MOTEN and his MUSICAL COHORTS have raised the standard of Dance Pleasure and announced the lease of the BIG HALL located at FIFTEENTH AND PASEO for the indulgence of COLORED DEVOTEES OF TERPSICHOREAN DELIGHT. This is indeed the Hall of Halls—with every up-to-the-moment CONVIENIENCE for PATRONS. Mid these luxurious surroundings you will want to attend every EVENT pulled off in this REAL EMPORIUM OF PLEASURE. With the best possible dance floor, the best installed

acoustics for carrying the best Music—a good time is assured at all times....

Source: *Kansas City Call*, March 14, 1924, 2.

Bennie Moten Secures New Dance Palace

For the first time in its history the dancing palace at 15th and Paseo will be leased to colored patrons. This has been brought about through the efforts of Bennie Moten and his orchestra who have been playing there for a number of years. The hall is one of the most spacious in Kansas City and will rent for the reasonable sum of fifty dollars. The opening dance will be held Sunday night March 23.

Source: *Kansas City Call*, March 14, 1924, 8.

In this segregated society, a venue that attracted a large African American audience struck fear among certain members of the white community. The white newspaper *Kansas City Star* reported that a group of white citizens protested the presence of black dances before the Board of Public Welfare, with no opportunity to respond. The *Call* investigated, and the chair of the Board admitted to C.F. Franklin, owner/editor of the *Call*, that such dances were out of the Board's jurisdiction:

Dance Hall Not Closed to Negroes

Following an investigation made by *The Call* of the report that Negroes were to be refused the use of the dance hall at 15th and the Paseo, Matt Foster, chairman of the Board of Public Welfare, said that no such action has been taken, but that a hearing of those for and against the licensing of the hall to Negroes would be held soon.

The daily press [the *White Star*] of last Saturday reported a decision of the Board of Public Welfare, made the day before at the request of a delegation of white citizens, concerning dancing in the hall at 15th and Paseo. The press said that the board would refuse Negroes permits to dance in this hall in the future. This is the hall known formerly as Dehoney's, and was opened only recently to the use of colored dancers. To this some neighbors objected, and several made up the delegation that visited the welfare board.

So far as the newspaper report said, no opportunity was given for the Negroes to say why they should be free to use the hall, the appearance of the whites only being recorded. Another bit of silence, failure to say there were charges of badly conducted Negro dances, led to the conclusion that all had been disorderly.

Thereupon *The Call* made an investigation. In an interview with Col. Matt Foster, who is president of the welfare board, he said there were no charges made by the Whites against the Negro dances alleging rowdyism, or any other impropriety. Their sole argument was that it was not best to allow Negroes to dance in the hall. The board decided, says Mr. Foster, to have a hearing with opportunity for complaint and defense; when next a permit was asked by Negroes for the use of the hall. His letter in reply to *The Call*'s inquiries is as follows:

"Dear Mr. Franklin;

At the regular Board meeting on last Friday afternoon, there appeared before us a delegation of white property owners who live in the neighborhood of 15th and The Paseo, protesting against the issue on dance hall permits to Negroes in this hall. The Recreation Department had been issuing blanket permits for this purpose without consulting the Board, a permit being issued for a dance on Sunday night last. We took the position inasmuch as the dance probably had been advertised we would permit it being held, but in the future when permits are requested it will be necessary for the persons promoting the dances to appear before the Board to offset the protest made by the white business interests...."

Since the Board of Public Welfare has no jurisdiction over private businesses, its power being restricted to public dances, the presumption is that the hall will continue in use for them, several of which are scheduled here.

Source: *Kansas City Call*, May 16, 1924, 4.

For the next several years the Bennie Moten Orchestra continued to lease and to be featured at one of most elaborate dance halls in the Midwest. Announcements such as this one are common in the *Call* from 1924 to the Great Depression:

Source: *Kansas City Call*, February 5, 1927, 8.

And holiday dances received special treatment:

Source: *Kansas City Call*, April 2, 1925, 7.

Source: *Kansas City Call*, December 24, 1926, 4.

To create a sense of autonomy from the larger, oppressive white community, and to serve their own institutions, blacks in Kansas City formed dozens of social and benevolent organizations. Among the men's groups, there were the Knights of Pythias, the Masonic Lodge, the Breau Brummels, the Cheerio Boys, and the I.B.P.O.E.W., the African American version of the Elks Lodge. For women, there were the 12 Charity Girls, the Kewpie Club, and, for students and alumni of Lincoln University, the Delta Sigma Theta sorority. In these groups black Kansas Citians focused much of their efforts on charity work to benefit their own churches, schools, and hospitals. And one of the best ways to raise money was to hold a dance featuring one or more of the city's jazz orchestras.

Charity work was a necessity because all of the black health and educational institutions were underfunded by the city and the state. Favorite causes were the Wheatley Provident Hospital and the Niles Orphan Home. There was one black school, named Lincoln, and one black college in Jefferson City, Lincoln University. For these causes and many others, the men's fraternal lodges and women's auxiliary groups organized dances, sometimes with themes, and charged either 25 or 50 cents.

These events did not resemble the image of Kansas City jazz and vice commonly portrayed in books and movies. In 1996 I interviewed a frequent attendee of the dances, Fred Hicks. According to him, "you couldn't go in there dressed any old way. You had to have your best on." And the Paseo Hall, the scene of many of the charity dances, "was a palace.

There was a crystal ball on the ceiling, and velvet covered chairs against the wall." And the dancing and music were dynamic: "those dancers could cut any rug you wanted cut. One-step, two-step, foxtrot, the waltz, and the Hesitation."[8]

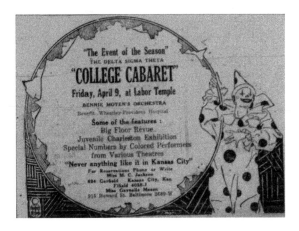

Source: *Kansas City Call*, March 19, 1925, 5.

Source: *Kansas City Call*, March 16, 1923, 7.

---

[8]Fred Hicks, personal interview, 16 May 1996. Mr. Hicks lived in the 18th and Vine neighborhood for the entirety of his 90-plus years. He worked as a hod-carrier and was also the custodian of the building that housed the Musician's Local 627, now the Mutual Musician's Foundation at the corner of 19th and Highland in Kansas City.

Source: *Kansas City Call*, November 16, 1923, 5.

Source: *Kansas City Call*, May 21, 1926, 7.

Source: *Kansas City Call*, December 3, 1926, 7.

Source: *Kansas City Call*, April 6, 1928, 2.

Sometimes the dances would accompany other, non-musical activities. Fashion shows and costume displays were common, as were athletic events:

Source: *Kansas City Call*, December 6, 1923, 7.

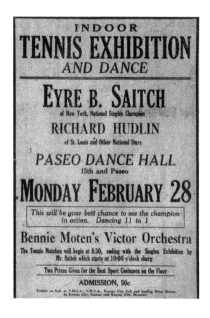

Source: *Kansas City Call*, February 18, 1927, 7.

When summer came and it was too hot for dancing indoors, the jazz orchestras played at the pavilion of Liberty Park, the city's only park open to blacks:

Source: *Kansas City Call*, June 17, 1922, 7.

Ultimately the Bennie Moten Orchestra began to emerge in the mid-1920s as the city's most commercially successful band. Moten had a strong relationship with the city's social organizations. He began in 1919 with a trio performing at the Labor Temple, a building used by both white and black unions, and available to blacks for special events. He became a favorite of the Elk's Lodge, and his status and ensemble grew quickly. In 1923 his band could be heard on the local radio, WHB, and with the help of Winston Holmes, the Moten band was chosen by Ralph S. Peer the director of operations for the Okeh label, to make six recordings with a sextet and two singers in 1923. In 1924 Moten began to lease the Paseo Hall for his dances, furthering his control over the orchestra jobs in the black community.[9]

After two more recording sessions, the Moten Orchestra was dropped by Okeh. Ralph Peer, who had moved to Victor Records, brought them into the Victor studio in December 1926. By now the band was much improved, and these recordings, combined with Victor's wide distribution and publicity, enabled the band to gain a reputation outside of the Kansas City area. The Orchestra lasted until 1932, and from this point on they toured the east coast frequently.

Ever the astute publicist, Moten sent to the *Call* a letter that he received from Peer regarding the band's first recording session for Victor.

---

[9]For a far more detailed account of the early years of the Moten Orchestra, see Driggs and Haddix, *Kansas City Jazz: From Ragtime to Bebop*, pp. 40-50.

The newspaper published the letter in its entirety, praising the band for its efforts. Peer's letter is revealing, as he compares the Moten recordings with white records, and states that they will be able to be marketed in the same way. Peer also mentions one of the band's signature features, the sound made by clarinetist Woody Walder, who created "novelty" effects by playing his mouthpiece into a water glass:

Moten Orchestra Commended by Victor Musical Director

Bennie Moten is in receipt of a letter from R. S. Peer, musical director for the Victor Record Company, formerly with Okeh, commenting Bennie and his organization very highly on the showing they made at the Victor recording laboratory recently. The Orchestra was requested to come there for a tryout and made such a hit that a group of records were made immediately, for future release. The letter follows:

"Dear Bennie; Your records have just come through and I am mighty glad to tell you that they are the best you have ever made. I have interested one of our Musical Directors and, after listening very carefully to the records, he agrees with me that your work is good enough to justify listing in the white list along with Olsen, Whiteman, Coon Sanders, ect.

In Chicago I told you of this possibility but really felt that you did not stand a very good chance. Your constant rehearsals and hard work during the past years have given the band an unusual style and, for the first time, I hear a colored band which is always in tune.

To put the proposition over with the record committee, I must be able to guarantee Victor exclusive rights to use your name. This seems fair enough as they will spend many thousands of dollars in publicity.

All the boys did splendid work. All solo work is good, including the glass trick, piano, and tuba solo. Every man in the band distinguishes himself in one or more of the selections.

The Record committee meets in Camden [N.J.] next Monday and Tuesday and in order to get action, I will have to know that you have signed the contract. I presume that everything will be satisfactory but request that you wire me

to that effect. These chances only come once and I want to be certain that I am free to go ahead.

Yours very truly,

R. S. Peer"

Bennie has reached the position in the musical world desired by every orchestra director—that of being recognized by the big record companies. The surest road to national recognition now is via the graphophone and the radio and Bennie has been the entire distance. He first recorded for [radio station] WHB a local broadcasting station, then made records for the Okeh and is now in the catalog of the biggest of them all—-Victor.

Source: *Kansas City Call*, January 28, 1927, 2

For the next nine months, until the beginning of a long tour in September, the Bennie Moten Orchestra held court at Paseo Hall. There was a dance every Sunday night, and often special events during the week. In February 1927 the Fletcher Henderson Orchestra visited, and Moten assisted "by special request" of the bandleader. The event called for a full-page advertisement in the *Call*, the first for a dance at the Paseo. The ad requested by the Henderson organization proclaims the Orchestra's popularity and its history of sellouts throughout the Southwest. The telegram communication between the Henderson Orchestra and the *Call* on the left, and between Henderson and Moten on the right are used in the ad. Henderson writes "Have heard a great deal of your Victor Recording Orchestra. Will you favor us with several numbers at my Kansas City appearance and oblige." On the bottom left side of the ad are reviews from other newspapers:

Source: *Kansas City Call*, February 11, 1927, 7.

On the bottom right side are accolades from black Kansas City busi-
nessmen: Carl Beckwith was the sports editor for the *Call*, Homer Roberts
owned a large car dealership, Felix Payne was a club owner, and Q.J.
Gilmore was the business manager of the Monarchs baseball team:

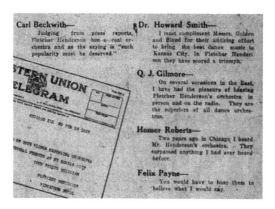

Source: *Kansas City Call*, February 11, 1927, 7.

In March cameramen from the Pathé movie company were hired to
record "A Super Movie Picture of the Negroes of Kansas City." The movie's
directors and sponsors remain a mystery, but clearly, the intent was to
portray black Kansas City at its best, with the event called a "progressive
movement." Dancing to the Moten Orchestra at the Paseo was filmed,
prizes were awarded, and all of the city's clubs were urged to participate:

Source: *Kansas City Call*, February 11, 1927, 7.

Source: *Kansas City Call*, March 18, 1927, 7.

Source: *Kansas City Call*, March 18, 1927, 7.

By late 1927 the Moten Orchestra was making frequent and lengthy tours to the east. When the band was away, the *Call* reported their successes, and when they returned, celebratory dances were held at the Paseo:

Bennie Moten Home in September

Bennie Moten and his Victor Recording Orchestra will be home in September, after triumphs in Buffalo, where they played at the Statler Hotel and 20th Century Night Club and broadcasted nightly over [radio] station WGR.

Bennie and his aggregation have already started home and are now playing at the leading amusement park of Jamestown, Ohio, where he is making his usual hit.

The local paper there is speaking about Bennie and his boys said:

"The Pier Ballroom is proving immensely popular these warm evenings, not only because of the appearance here of Bennie Moten's Victor Recording Orchestra, the best colored dance band in the country, but also because the big pavilion is cool and comfortable even for dancing."

Moten's organization itself is capable of drawing a crowd wherever it plays. In a recent cup competition at Chicago this orchestra was awarded first prize. Not only do they furnish music as only colored artists can, but they present several of their own compositions that have made enormous record sales.

Source:*Kansas City Call*, July 20, 1928, 7.

Moten's Band Draws Crowd at Paseo Hall

That Kansas City's music and dance lovers are glad Bennie Moten and his orchestra are back was vividly illustrated Wednesday night when 1,700 people crowded into Paseo Hall to hear and see what the boys had brought back in the way of syncopation, after their nine months absence. Apparently, from the reception given the orchestra, the boys brought back plenty.

The same 10 men who left with Bennie last year showed their pleasure in being back again by rendering the latest music with such an improvement in style that encore after encore was necessary to satisfy the huge crowd.

James "Tiny" Taylor was more than well received in the song numbers, and his unique style of orchestral direction excited much comment. And when Thaymon [sic] Hayes sang "Ramona" to the muted accompaniment of soft brasses and whispering reed instruments, a distinct ripple of approbation stirred the crowd to heavy applause. A new way of playing the popular "Coquette" song also pleased the crowd, and when "Tiny" Taylor, Woody Walder, and Leroy "Buck" Berry featured "Mississippi Mud" it became plain why Moten's orchestra played in some of the best places in the east while they were away.

The boys all expressed themselves as being glad to get home, and Bennie told The Call representative that he had turned down a year's contract in New York in order to return.

William Little, who promoted the dance, was all smiles in spite of the fact that the dance inspector enforced the 12 o'clock closing law.

Source: *Kansas City Call*, September 21, 1928, 2.

George E. Lee and Chauncey Downs

Although Moten's Orchestra was the only Kansas City band with a recording contract and extended tours, there were several other bands in the city, notably the ones led by George E. Lee and Chauncey Downs, to entertain the dancing public:

Orchestras to Hold Contest

Downs and Lee in Heavyweight Music Go, with the Public the Referee

Listening to the sizzling, snapping, swinging, crooning, soothing sax! Catch step with the drum! It is joy night at Paseo Hall Wednesday, July 25, with two great orchestras, Chauncey Down's Rinky Dinks and George E. Lee's Novelty Singing Orchestra playing their hearts out to see who is the best.

It is going to be a gala night at 15th and Paseo, with everybody coming out as they always do, to see the musicians strut their stuff. Lee says he wins, because winning is his habit. He won when he was here and he won down in Oklahoma. But Downs says youth must be served. His orchestra has been at work as never before. The folks who dance will get no rest on this night, because the lilting tunes will tease them on.

Source: *Kansas City Call*, July 20, 1928, 7.

In the months leading up to the market crash of October 1929, the *Call* provided coverage of a vibrant dance and social scene. There were frequent "Dance Wars" at the Paseo, in which two bands were engaged in a friendly contest of non-stop musical action. There was also a sharing of music between the races. By 1927 the Moten and Lee orchestras were playing at white venues, events which the *Call* never covered. But in late 1928 two white bands from California "challenged" George E. Lee's group at Paseo Hall. The final example for this chapter illustrates the *Call's* rhetorical touch of pitting one band against the other, and printing quotes from both leaders to generate excitement among its readers. It is a poignant read when we remember the coming economic disaster of the Great Depression that would befall them all in just a few months time:

Music War Next Thursday George E. Lee to Contest for Supremacy with Pacific Coast Orchestra

Are Negro orchestras superior to white orchestras? This long debated question will have a show-down next Thursday night at Paseo Hall when George E. Lee and his Novelty Singing Orchestra meets Jack Owen and his Atcan Aces in an orchestra contest. The Atcan Aces is one of the famous white orchestras of the Pacific coast. They have scored triumph after triumph over the radio, on the stage, as Victor and Brunswick recorders, and in the exclusive dance palaces of the west. They are enroute home from fresh recordings in New York and Mr. Lee, who is personally acquainted with Jack Owen, issued a challenge to the Aces to meet him and his orchestra at Paseo Hall.

First time in Kansas City

This is the first time in Kansas City that the colored audience have had the opportunity to dance to a white orchestra or that a white orchestra has appeared in a contest with a Negro orchestra. It is quite common in the eastern cities, however.

Both Leaders Confident

Both leaders are confident of victory. Jack Owen of the Atcan Aces in a wire the the Call says in part "You may say for me that I have no fear of the outcome of this contest between George E. Lee and myself. All I ask is a square deal from the audience. I am confident of receiving that. We welcome this opportunity to play before a Negro audience and they may be assured that we will do our best."

George E. Lee said last night that he didn't want any favoritism shown him because he was playing a contest with a white orchestra. "I will beat them on my merits. There never was a white orchestra born that can stomp it out like we do."

A record attendance is looked for with a grand and glorious time for all.

Source: *Kansas City Call*, March 8, 1929, 8.

Chapter 6:
Kansas City Jazz and the Great Depression, 1929-1935

As the spring of 1929 turned into fall, there was no mention in the *Call* of the financial chaos occurring on Wall Street. Indeed, the newspaper never covered the stock market or the white institutions that it impacted, before, during, or after the crash in late October. On the front page of the Friday, November 1st edition of the *Call*, the first edition to come out after Black Tuesday, the main stories were the success of a local charity drive, the deaths of Moorfield Storey, the President of the NAACP and Nick Chiles, the editor of the *Topeka Plain Dealer*, a murder in St. Louis, and the political campaign of Harlem's Hubert T. Delany to join Oscar DePriest as the only two blacks in Congress.[1] But certainly, the stock market crash and ensuing Depression were to impact the lives of all in Kansas City, with African Americans hit first and hardest. The economic collapse would also dramatically change the nature of jazz and dancing in the black community.

This chapter begins in the spring of 1929 when dancing to Kansas City jazz in both white and black dance halls reached an exciting peak. There were four large orchestras competing for both the black and white venues; the bands led by Bennie Moten and George E. Lee were at the height of their popularity, and Andy Kirk's Twelve Clouds of Joy and Paul Banks Rhythm Kings had recently formed. In the black community, bands played

---

[1]In 1929 Delany won the Republican nomination to represent New York's 13th district, which included Harlem, but he ultimately lost to his Democrat opponent Joseph A. Gavagan. He later became a judge and an advocate for the National Urban League and the NAACP.

the Paseo Hall and the Labor Temple; whites heard them at the Pla Mor and the El Torreon. And during the summer the black orchestras entertained at the black Liberty Park and the white Fairyland Park. Bennie Moten, in particular, had aspirations of acquiring national recognition, as his band continued to record for Columbia, and took several tours east during the early 1930s.

But, for a variety of reasons, this chapter ends with the sudden death of Moten, in April 1935. First, from the early 1920s to his death, Moten was the largest presence in Kansas City jazz. He was not the best pianist, and sometimes his bands lost battles to other bands. But he was the best organizer and promoter, his orchestra recorded far more than any other Kansas City band at the time, and it was covered more extensively in the *Call* than any other band.

Second, although the immediate effects of the Depression were delayed in Kansas City, the black community and its entertainment industry were ultimately hit first and hardest by the economic decline. The city's politicians, most prominently political boss Tom Pendergast, were able to stall the financial impact of the economic collapse in the short term. Political corruption meant that the city's vice and entertainment industries were booming.

The Pendergast machine also built its economy by issuing city bonds, which were used for massive construction projects, and which employed companies and cronies controlled by Pendergast. The construction projects did keep the economy moving, but with Pendergast's decline in 1936 and subsequent arraignment for tax evasion in 1939, the house of cards that was Kansas City's 1930s economy came crashing down.[2]

In addition, by 1935 the city's black dance venues had changed substantially, and with these changes came a declining coverage of their activities in the *Call*. Large dance halls such as the Paseo Hall and the Labor Temple gave way to smaller nightclubs, which, like Harlem's Cotton Club, featuring stage shows. In 1933 the Cherry Blossom nightclub opened, and the Paseo Hall was turned into the Harlem Night Club and closed to blacks. The Cherry Blossom and other nightclubs did not feature the extensive promotion in the *Call* as the dance halls had but simply used smaller ads to announce its performers. And as the Depression tightened its grip, less and less can be found in the *Call* about the city's jazz bands after 1935.

---

[2]For more on the Pendergast machine, especially Pendergast's economic policies, see William M. Reddig, *Tom's Town: Kansas City and the Pendergast Legend* (Columbia: University of Missouri Press, 1986).

Band Battles and Break O' Day Dances

In 1929 and 1930 George E. Lee's Novelty Singing Orchestra and Bennie Moten's Victor Recording Orchestra were the two most popular bands in Kansas City. They were playing in both white and black venues, and the scene at Paseo Hall had never been more exhilarating. There were fashion shows, band battles, and Moten had begun a new tradition, the "Break O' Day" dances that started Saturday nights at midnight and went until dawn. Below are just a few of the many advertisements and announcements regarding their activities as the Great Depression approached:

George Lee to Give Fashion Ball April 11

Prizes will be given to Best Dressed Lady and Gentleman There's going to be a homecoming and a general rollicking and gamboling around on Thursday, April 11, when George Lee and his Novelty Singing Orchestra, idols of all lovers of the dance, will play for the big Fashion Revue Ball at Paseo Hall. Those "hot to death" Easter outfits, which were not able to be worn Sunday because of the rainy weather, should be dragged out of the attic and donned for this party because prizes will be given for the best dressed lady and gentleman. This dance will be George's first appearance since he took a close decision over the far-famed Atcan Aces in a band contest at Paseo recently.[3] Since then he has been playing at the Pla-Mor Ballroom to large crowds of rabidly enthusiastic white dance-lovers and has been broadcasting over the radio. He comes back to this first re-appearance at his own stomping grounds ready to greet his friends with a lot of new tricks.

"White people like good music," Mr. Lee said, "but, try as they will, they can't get perfectly attuned to the playing of an orchestra as the average colored audience does. Between a colored orchestra and its colored dancers, there is a very noticeable bond of feeling which causes the orchestra to play its best and the dancers to get the most out of the music. We've got a lot of new songs and features that we are anxious to put over for our regular patrons and we're rarin' to go for this Fashion Revue Ball."

Source: *Kansas City Call*, April 5, 1929, 10.

---

[3]The Atcan Aces were white band from California.

Paseo Hall to be Scene of Music War

Hurley Kaylor and his Radio-Ballroom Orchestra to
Avenge the Defeat of the Atcan Aces

George E. Lee is going to lead his Novelty Singing Orchestra into action again. He will meet the "enemy" Monday night, April 15, at Paseo Hall. And what a "battle" is in prospect. Hurley Kayler and His Ten Piece Radio-Ballroom Orchestra (white) are out to avenge the defeat of the Atcan Aces. A crowd of more than 2000 witnessed George and his boys down these white lads from California last month. George's fondest admirers, and they are many, said they never heard him play as he did that night in March. George won't admit it but the truth is he has a hard contest on his hands. The rumor was being circulated yesterday that Kaylor called George at the Pla-Mor Wednesday night where George was broadcasting on the "Nighthawk Frolic" and told him if that was the best he could do he would need a lot of practice before Monday ... It is not known what George said in reply to Kaylor.

Both Leaders Confident

Both leaders are confident of victory. "I welcome this opportunity," said Kaylor, "to appear before a colored audience. I know that you will give us a square deal because you treated the Atcan Aces more than well. We have a better and larger orchestra than those boys and we are going to prove it Monday. I have heard George Lee at both the Pla-Mor and on the air. I am confident that we can beat him. Win or lose, we will give you our best."

"We have known," said George Lee, "ever since our first victory over the white orchestra in March that Kaylor and his ten piece orchestra were after our scalps. But we have been getting ready and when the smoke of battle is over our scalps will still be where they belong. I am not underestimating our opponents, they have a "hot" orchestra but you all know competition helps me and my boys."

Kaylor has a Real Outfit

These white boys have a real outfit. They have played opposite Gene Goldkette at the [white] Pla-More, they have
worked in the finest ballrooms of the southwest, and recently closed an engagement at the [white] Uptown Theater. They have also been heard repeatedly over the radio. Their accordion player, John Kaido, is a regular daily
feature over WDAF. There are two other outstanding musicians in their orchestra, Walter Headlin, sensational drummer, and William Marshall, celebrated saxophone player.
The other seven boys are said to be mighty "hot."

Source: *Kansas City Call*, April 12, 1929, 12.

Cleopatra to Reign Tonight At Paseo Hall

Mrs. Addie Porter Williams Chosen for Title Role: Doors Open at 8

A committee for five discriminating people last Friday selected Mrs. Addie Porter Williams to portray Cleopatra at
Cleopatra's Court tonight at Paseo Hall.

And what a court it is going to be! From the time the doors
open at 8 p.m. until the last witching strains of orchestra
music die away at 1 a.m., there is going to be something
doing. Fittingly, the evening opens with dancing from 8
until 9 with special music.

Promptly at 9, a presentation of a ten dollar gold piece
will be made to Mrs. Will Shaw Monroe, who submitted
the winning name for the dance, and awards will be made
to each of the seven unsuccessful candidates for the title
of Cleopatra. Tap dance specialties will be offered at this
time by Lenny and Van, boy dance wizards. This portion
of the program is scheduled to take not more than twenty
minutes. Following it there will be uninterrupted dancing
with George Lee and his singing boys, presiding until 11
p.m.

Then, with a grand blare of trumpets, a flashing of lights
on jewels, and a winding train of brilliantly dressed court-
iers, comes the Grand Court scene from the life of Cleopatra. J. Oliver Morrison is directing the scene and the incidental dancing is under the supervision and direction of
Miss Zelma Taylor.

Cleopatra will be attended by Virginia Bryant and Rosa Lee Jamison. Marcus Antonius (Oliver Bell) will have Edward Harris and Junior Johnson as guards. A chorus of dancing girls will feature the scene with historic Egyptian dance numbers ... the scene will be laid against a background of a massive oriental throne with soft lights, drapes, and incense playing a heavy part in carrying out the authenticity of the court display.

After the court scene dancing will be resumed until one o'clock, and George Lee has promised some new stunts in the way of Egyptian jazz. Cleopatra's Court is an annual frolic of the Beau Brummel club whose proceeds go entirely to charity. According to Burt Mayberry in charge of arrangements, the box seats are nearly all sold out but a few are still available ... Members of the club will be distinguished by an arm band which they will wear.

Source: *Kansas City Call*, April 19, 1929, 10.

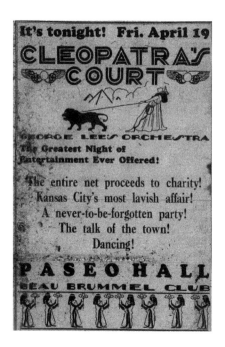

Source: *Kansas City Call*, April 19, 1929, 5.

Source: *Kansas City Call*, December 6, 1929, 10.

The Writings of e.w.w.

From 1929 to 1933 Earl Wilkins, the brother of *Call* columnist and future NAACP President Roy Wilkins wrote a column for the newspaper called "Dance Gossip."[4] Signing his columns simply "e.w.w.," Wilkins' writings are a valuable source. As with this following example, Wilkins reviewed new bands, here the first performance of Andy Kirk's ensemble at the Paseo. He reported on the established bands, and how new additions to the ensembles were working out. Wilkins also describes for the reader the energy of a dance, the characters, and activities as the bands played into the night:

---

[4]Roy had left for Harlem in 1928 to begin his work with the NAACP but continued to write columns for the *Call*, mainly regarding life in Harlem and national concerns of African Americans. Earl's son, Roger Wilkins, became a Civil Rights leader and received a Pulitzer Prize for reporting on the Watergate scandal.

Kirk and 12 Clouds of Joy at Paseo Hall Aug 29

Everybody who went to hear Andrew Kirk and his Twelve Clouds of Joy perform at their initial appearance before a colored Kansas City audience last Monday night will be back with all their friends to hear these joy dispensers Thursday night, August 29. For the boys are GOOD with plenty of capitals!

It is part of my job to check new orchestras, and I went to Paseo last Monday night with my usual cynical smile and a store of hollow guffaws to release when the blues music got sour and "blue." I sat in my usual place in the balcony where I could watch the antics of the performers, smoke my pipe, and chuckle my he-hahs to myself.

But I didn't' have the opportunity. When I got there the orchestra was finishing a slow number which fairly made my feet itch (and I have heard some good bands), and then swung into the asinine but compelling rhythm of "Tight Like That." Everybody in the hall was infected with the punch of that music and the dancers were captivated by it. Toward the end of it a tall windy clarinet player held a long note for about 3 minutes while the rest of the orchestra did a nasty patter. Then they revised the arrangement and gave the lead to a man doubling on the steel guitar who plucked some mean notes from the shiny instrument.

There were more clever tricks uncorked than I have seen in a long time, but for me the crowning feature was the number—I don't know the name of it—in which the orchestra impersonated a railroad train with startling reality. Every member donned an engineer's cap and bright colored kerchiefs to which the leader added a pair of heavy white fireman's gloves. To start the number, he reached up with a pulling motion and the hoarse train whistle startled the crowd. Then came clearly the sound of the wheels slipping before they started to grip, the blowing of the steam exhaust, and then the rhythmic clicking of the wheels as they band broke into a captivating dance number.

I've said plenty, but I haven't said enough. As George Lee opined, this band is going to make all the local orchestras look up and get up. They're good with a band, and that's honest to Gosh! e.w.w.

Source: *Kansas City Call*, August 23, 1929, 2.

Dance Gossip

There is something infectious about a lively dancing crowd .... Take Bennie Moten's dance at Paseo Hall a week ago .... It was chilly outside and I was feeling low in spirit until I walked in the door, where the lights, the music, the chatter, and the gaiety enveloped me and made me part of it all. The music, of course, was the keynote of the festivity–and what music! This orchestra has increased in size and improved in both arrangements and technical execution .... It is impossible to detail the work of each artist, but they are so good and the ensemble is, if you will allow the vernacular, "really correct." The audience must have felt as I did for it turned out to jam the hall and applauded long and vociferously. There were several interesting side happenings including two incipient fights which the smooth-faced majesty of the law quickly quelled. And one tall young man who had drunk a bit too much decided to entertain the whole balcony with an eccentric (and shaky) tap dance .... The gay attitude of the dancers was well reflected in a portion of conversation I happened to overhear: "What in the world are you doing wearing a pink shirt?" a good looking woman asked a man who approached her. "See all those women down on the floor?" he countered. "All of them having a good time, and a lot of them wearing red and green dresses, why can't I have a good time and wear a pink shirt?"– and forsooth, why not? e.w.w.

Source: *Kansas City Call*, March 14, 1930, 7.

This next example is brief but important. Here Wilkins reports on a special "Break O' Day" dance that foreshadows the changes coming to the Paseo Hall and dancing in Kansas City in general. As mentioned previously, by 1933 the big dance halls were replaced or converted into nightclubs and cabarets with shows, in imitation of the black and tans of Harlem. That this early cabaret dance was a "literal knockout" illustrates the ever-changing tastes of the dancing public:

Dance Gossip

Every once in a while someone decides to promote a "cabaret" dance, but they usually fall flat for want of the proper atmosphere. It remained for Bennie Moten and his Orchestra last Saturday night to provide a cabaret Break O' Day dance that was a literal knockout.

Tables were placed all along the north side of the hall next to the dance floor, and white jacketed waiters were kept busy between dances providing cool things to drink. With the tom-tom music, the dancers crowding back and forth from the tables to the dancing floor, and with the trick lighting effects and decorations, old Paseo had lapsed for the time from grace and sank rather gracefully into the role of a metropolitan night club.

Entertainers there were too. Henrine Shaw, a dancer, took the cleared space in the middle of the floor and executed a number of steps that kept people pushing forward and standing on chairs, the better to see them. And LeRoy Reed and Van Osborne, a local tap dancing team, found the usual amount of favor with their excellent dancing. It was a cabaret dance plus! Here's to more of them! e.w.w.

Source: *Kansas City Call*, July 18, 1930, 9.

In January 1931, Wilkins snuck into a white-only dance and reported this forbidden experience to his readers. Here we have another account of the energy brought by the Moten bands and the singers and dancers who performed with them, and we see black Kansas Citians looking at whites who were looking at, and dancing to, members of their own community:

Dance Gossip

Bein' as how the Mainstreet theater doesn't cater to colored people, and bein' as how Bennie Moten and his orchestra, who have thousands of dusky followers in the city, played there for a week ending last night, and bein' as how I managed to creep in the stage door for a peep at the band's number, it looks as though this account of what went on is going to serve as a free pass to the readers of this column, entitling them to one long view of how Herr Moten and his cohorts looked when they were doing their stuff for the palefaces.

... The boys are all there: Jack Washington, Ed Lewis, Thamon Hayes, Bill [Count] Basie, and the rest. They are all dressed up and look good enough to take a spot on anybody's program.

Then we get a call and we all march up on the stage, behind the umpteen curtains they used to divide off the various sets. The boys take their places behind the instruments, stage managers and "prop" men run everywhere, actors in other numbers stand around peeping at the act in front of the curtain, and everything looks like one big jumble ... .

The act ahead finishes, the rear curtain goes up, the lights blare on the boys in the orchestra, and they cut loose with a hot number which is guaranteed to take the roof off.

And it darned near does! The audience claps and roars as the band swing into its second number. Bus Moten is out front, dapper as always, cutting with that baton, pressing the band to better and better efforts.

They swing into "Travelin'," and [Jimmy] Rushing steps out from the wings to do the vocalization. He is dressed in blue overalls, an old gray hat, and wears a red bandanna about his neck; over his shoulder, he sports a stick with a bundle tied in an old handkerchief. Slowly he sidles across the stage as he sings the number. As he finishes, he skips off the stage and the house comes down with applause.

Then Grayson and Ellis strut out for their fast tap-dancing number. They get a big hand from the audience in their two appearances. And so, the ever-hotter music goes on for the thirty minutes that the band plays. The white actors who are standing around in the wings watching the act with me comment to each other on the excellence of the music. "Good," they said, and good it was. e.w.w.[5]

Source: *Kansas City Call*, January 16, 1931, 8.

Our sample of Wilkins' writings concludes with his coverage of one of the most significant dances of this period. The Moten Orchestra played an

---

[5]The musicians were of course well-known to the Kansas City dancing public. Washington was Moten's baritone saxophonist, Lewis his trupmpet player, and Hayes his trombonist. Bus Moten was Bennie's nephew, and played accordion. Count Basie joined the band in 1929, as did singer Jimmy Rushing. As Haddix and Driggs write, Moten was preparing for a tour east and had engaged Broadway producer Aaron Gates to hire dancers Roy Ellis and Billy Grayson (Driggs and Haddix, *Kansas City Jazz: From Ragtime to Bebop*, p. 100).

east coast tour from October 1931 to January 1932. While in NYC, Moten heard the Henderson and Ellington bands, and in fact, purchased arrangements from Henderson. In addition, his pianist Count Basie and alto saxophonist Eddie Durham were working on arranging techniques that they had developed during their time with the Oklahoma City Blue Devils. Seeing the future of dance music, Moten fired half of his band upon returning to Kansas City and hired musicians such as bassist Walter Page who could play the new, faster music required for dances like the Lindy Hop. The fired musicians reformed with a vengeance, under the leadership of Thamon Hayes, and the new band made their debut at this dance, playing opposite the new Moten Orchestra. According to interviews with musicians on both sides, Wilkin's review goes easy on the Moten band. Their annihilation by the Hayes ensemble was complete, and ended Moten's reign as the city's top bandleader:

Dance Gossip

In the face of a bitter cold night, some 1,500 people braved the worst weather Kansas City has had this winter and trooped in a body to Paseo Hall last Monday night to hear a parade of the best dance music this section of the country could muster.

The little bands and the big bands were all there, and all of them were eager to show what they could do. And what they did do!

Judged solely by popular acclaim, the feature of the evening was the first appearance of Thamon Hayes and his band. Going on late at something after midnight, the Hayes band received from the crowd such an ovation as has rarely been tendered any orchestra ever to play the hall.

When Maceo Birch, master of ceremonies, announced that the next band to play would be Thamon Hayes and his band, the crowd went wild. There were hoarse cries, shrill whistles, staccato hand clapping, and thuddings of feet on the floor.

Nattily attired in new uniforms of rich tan with shirts and ties to match, this new band made a pleasing appearance. Before they started their stint, the crowd insisted that Thamon Hayes, the organizer, take a bow. And then the Hayes group swung into its numbers.

The dancers were interested. They stopped dancing and

milled about the platform to watch. They crowded the balcony rail, straining to see the men in action. The first number rocked them, and they went into frenzies before the Hayes band had finished. There were cries of "Play it, boy!" "Listen to those fellows go!" "They've really got a band, haven't they!"

The Hayes organization has a pleasing combination of the kind of rhythm which has made Bennie Moten's orchestra famous, and the trick style which has stood George Lee in such good stead. Their one novelty number, an imitation of an old-fashioned Holy Roller meeting, with the lead trumpet "preaching," and the lead trombone "praying," turned the dancers into admiring watchers.

"We were all naturally pleased," Hayes said afterward, "to get such a good reception from the crowd. The fellows have all worked hard in the past and will continue to do so to give the public the very best we've got. Much of the credit for the band's achievement so far must go to Jesse Stone, the director, who is handling our arrangements for us."

Bennie Moten's band wound up the evening. Bennie himself was on the platform, busy. He also received generous applause from the audience. The Moten organization has recently undergone some changes. e.w.w.

Source: *Kansas City Call*, March 11, 1932, 7.

The Musician's Union 627 Ball

In 1917 Kansas City's black musicians established an African American chapter of the American Federation of Musicians, Local 627. By the mid-1920s Local 627 was serving the professional needs of bandleaders and musicians, with George E. Lee, Bennie Moten, and Paul Banks on its Board of Directors. The Union established salaries for musicians and helped them to organize jobs in the city's dance halls and theaters. By the late 1920s membership was over 80, and in 1929 Local 627 held the first of its annual spring balls. These events could feature six bands or more, with attendance approaching 2,000. Also in 1929, the union purchased a house at the corner of 19th and Highland for its headquarters. When the white and black unions merged in 1970, the building became the Mutual Musicians Foundation, a social club for musicians recognized as a national historic landmark. Today it is a place where musicians rehearse, teach classes for younger musicians and hold jam sessions. It is located two blocks from the American Jazz Museum.[6]

Six Bands to Stage the Year's Biggest Battle Next Monday Night

Six Bands to Stage the Year's Biggest Battle Next Monday Night The greatest concerted effort on the part of local musicians in the history of the city will greet dance fans next Monday night, Dec. 2, at Paseo Hall, with a giant battle of bands featuring six well-known local orchestras. The event is being sponsored by the Musicians Union Local 627.

Bennie Moten, George Lee, Andrew Kirk, Paul Banks, Walter Page, and George Wilkerson are the band leaders who will lead their bands onto pitched combat at the Monday night event. Every type of jazz music will be presented at this biggest of big dances. Dancing will be continuous from 9 on, with the doors opening at 8.

Nothing like this dance has ever been held here before. In point of musical magnificence, dancing revelry, and general fun, it must be classed alone. Indications are that the largest crowd ever to attend a dance in Kansas City will be at Paseo Hall to hear the respective merits of these six great musical organizations. Proceeds will go to the completion of the Musicians home recently purchased...

Source: *Kansas City Call*, November 29, 1929, 10.

Musicians Open House

National Music Week opened auspiciously for the musicians connected with Local 627, A.F. of M., with a huge parade and open house which lasted all afternoon Sunday, May 1. With the American Legion drum corps in the

---

[6]For more on Musicians Local 627 see http://library.umkc.edu/spec-col/local627/index.htm and the Mutual Musicians Foundation at http://www.mutualmusiciansfoundation.org/.

lead, more than 200 musicians took part in the winding parade which took its way all through the business section. Following the parade, the whole gathering together with friends of the musician's organization went to Musician's Headquarters at 1823 Highland, where lunch was served. The last visitors drifted away at about 5 p.m.

The most eventful Musician's Ball in the history of these colorful events was given last Monday night at Labor Temple. According to officials of Local 627, A.F. of M. approximately 1,400 people enjoyed the affair and at least 200 more were turned away because of lack of checking facilities.

In the eyes of the spectators, however, there were several happenings ranking on a par with the large attendance and the truly excellent music. Among these extra-curricular divertissements were two fist fights, the turning off of the lights for about five minutes at 1 a.m., the fainting of a woman in the balcony, and the appearance of the winner of a bathing beauty contest. Oh, yes, it was a great night, and the people who went to that hall got their money's worth and more.

The bands themselves got underway with Bill Little and his Little Bills doing a stellar piece of curtain raising. This is perhaps the hardest spot of any dance bill, but Little and his chaps swung into the spirit of the whole evening with some syncopation that got things moving rapidly. A. C. Hayden and his Nighthawks followed. This band is small, but in many respects it is a slick band. The dancers seemed to like it and I must say that I did too. It has improved tremendously since the first time I heard it.

Paul Banks and his Rhythm Aces followed. Paul's boys are no longer apprentices, knocking at the gate. They have arrived as a big time band. From natty new uniforms to hotcha performance, they were good. If I heard one person in the balcony comment on the good work of this band, I heard a dozen.

With the evening growing late, Thaymon Hayes and his orchestra took the stand and received an ovation from the crowd. Their zippy novelty style, up to the second melodies, and unusual arrangements drew a great hand from the crowd. It was during the work of this band that the lights went off. There were oh's and ah's from the women in the crowd and the big brave men began striking matches to offer some feeble illumination.

Displaying fine headwork, the band continued to play and the crowd quieted down. Shuffling feet indicated that in spite of the pitch blackness, the dancers were continuing to enjoy themselves. Below me, I heard one boy as he oozed by on the floor murmur, "What a break for me, baby!"

Finally the lights went on again and after a time Bennie Moten and his band took the stand for the final burst of music and fun. Bennie warmed up after his first few numbers and had the crowd howling for more. As I listened to the band work, I realized again that Joe Smith is one of the sweetest trumpet men I know. e.w.w.

Source: *Kansas City Call*, May 6, 1932, 7.

Record Crowd Celebrates at Musicians Annual Ball

Anyone who happened to be in the vicinity of Fifteenth Street and the Paseo Monday night knew that something unusual was going on. There was. Dance lovers were celebrating their homecoming at Paseo Hall as guests of the Musicians Protective Union at their annual ball.

More than 1,800 attended the festivities and made merry until the wee, small hours. This was one of the largest crowds in the history of these annual affairs.

The Paseo Hall until a few months ago had been used as a night club catering to white patronage only. As the old Paseo Hall it has been the scene of many a gay party.

It wasn't a dance crowd. It was a throng that absorbed the swing and rhythm from Harland Leonard's Kansas City Rockets and later on from Kansas City's premier maestro, Bennie Moten himself and the band. The floor show from the New Harlem Night Club under the direction of S.H. Dudley Jr. was a happy interlude. One of the features of the entertainment was tap dancing on skates. Just an eyeful of the bevy of brownskin beauties was worth the price

of admission. Deacon Moore and his orchestra now fill-
ing an engagement at the Muehlebach Hotel was present.
He was asked to play but said he preferred to listen to the
Moten swing instead. It was a great party.

Source: *Kansas City Call*, March 15, 1935, 11.

Source: *Kansas City Call*, May 11, 1934, 13.

The Rise of the Cherry Blossom and Transition of Paseo Hall

By the early 1930s, a new kind of entertainment venue was challenging the dance halls in the black community. Modeled after the nightclubs of Harlem, the Kansas City nightclubs featured some dancing, but also stage acts, in a more elaborate setting. One of the first and most illustrious to open was the Cherry Blossom, in April 1933. Moving into the old Eblon Theater near 18th and Vine, it featured "an oriental motif, chromium posts containing gold-plated ropes" and a stage with a "Japanese god placed at the rear, overlooking the dancers. Japanese dragons and monsters are placed at various spots."[7]

---

[7] "Cherry Blossom in Eblon Theater to Stage First Class Floor Show," *Kansas City Call*, April 7, 1933, 6.

Three months after the Cherry Blossom opened, the Paseo Hall was closed for renovations to be transformed into the Harlem Night (sometimes spelled "Nite") Club. After a few weeks, the owners set a whites-only policy, and the black community thus lost the centerpiece of its dance culture.

George E. Lee opened the Cherry Blossom, but Moten took over in July, with Count Basie writing the show for the dancers and entertainers. Soon, Moten saw a better financial opportunity performing for whites at the newly- Christened Harlem Nightclub. When Moten demanded that his Orchestra take the job, his musicians revolted and voted him out of the band, replacing his leadership with Count Basie.[8]

800 Pleasure Seekers at Trouveur Cabaret Party

Eight hundred pleasure seekers jammed the Cherry Blossom supper club Monday night and danced several hours for "sweet charity." The occasion was the seventh annual cabaret party of the ever-popular Trouveur club. The capacity of the spacious club was taxed before midnight. Hundreds who came afterwards were unable to gain admittance. Every available inch of space was filled including the balcony.

Count Basie's new orchestra was at its best. The crowd gave it a tremendous ovation. Miss Lucretia Williams of Milwaukee, a new entertainer, got a big hand from the spectators. She has personality, sings well, and puts over her dance routine in fine fashion.

A classy floor show presented by performers from Vanity Fair, downtown night club, was loudly applauded. Jenkins and Jenkins, a brother and sister dance team, was outstanding.

The attendance was swelled by several out of town folk.

Thirty-five per cent of the proceeds from the affair will be given to charity....

Former cabaret parties have been given at Paseo Hall, now the Harlem Night Club.

Source: *Kansas City Call*, October 6, 1933, 4b

---

[8]Driggs and Haddix, *Kansas City Jazz: From Ragtime to Bebop*, pp. 121-124.

Two New Floor Attractions on at the Cherry Blossom

Kansas City's premier night club, the Cherry Blossom, has come into its own again by booking for its two floor shows some of the finest entertainers in the Middle West. This policy is in keeping with the announcement by Mr. and Mrs. E.D. Franks, new owners, that only the best attractions would be engaged.

Joe Stephen and Ollie Blackwell, vaudeville and night club headliners, will feature their new novelty "Slave Dance," which has never failed to click with cabaret crowds.

A big night is planned for Thursday, February 33 [sic], George Washington's birthday.

Another special attraction is Miss Pearl Madison direct from Milwaukee, who will thrill Cherry Blossom patrons with the newest and spiciest fan dance. Miss Madison has appeared in Kansas City before and has a large following. She is a singer and dancer extraordinary and will no doubt be welcomed by those who have seen her perform before.

And no other celebrity than Count Basie and his crew of genial, talented bandsmen will be on hand nightly to dispense dance rhythm as only he and his bunch can. Dance lovers need no introduction to this popular orchestra.

The newly-decorated cabaret bids fair to be more attractive than ever. A. Buford, manager, and Jimmy Ruffin, ever-smiling master of ceremonies, are back at their posts
....

Source: *Kansas City Call*, February 16, 1934, 11.

Abandoned by his band, Moten joined forces with Lee, who was also struggling with the downturn of the Depression, and the Moten-Lee Orchestra got the gig at the Harlem Night Club. And while cabaret-style venues were popping up all over the place, the Labor Temple, and a new dance hall, the Roseland Ballroom, continued to hold dances such as the annual Musician's Ball to benefit Local 627:

9 Bands Will Play for K.C. Dance Lovers

Floor Show From Harlem Nite Club to Perform; Doors Open at 8 p. m.

The annual musician's ball will hold forth Monday night, May 14 at Labor Temple, Fourteenth and Woodland Avenue. It will not only be a "battle of bands" but will be one of the greatest musical feats in the entire history of Kansas City.

Nine bands will furnish the music. The Bennie Moten-George Lee combination from the Harlem Nite club and the entire floor show from that cabaret will open the evening's activities at 9 o'clock. They will be followed in order by Clarence Love and his orchestra, Thamon Hayes and his band, Count Basie and his orchestra, Paul Bands and his orchestra, Tommy Douglas's orchestra, Andy Kirk and His Twelve Clouds of Joy. The guest artists will be Grant Moore and his famous orchestra from Minneapolis.

Each year it is the custom of the local musicians to introduce to Kansas City's dance lovers a new band. This year is no exception. Jimmy Keith and his band, the ninth band which will take part in Monday night's festivities will be "formally" introduced to the public. The young men of this band live in the two Kansas Cities and are very anxious to make good. And they're red hot too. They intend to give the older, seasoned veterans of the musical worlds a hot run for popularity....

Preceding the parade on Sunday there will be a smoker at the Musicians Local for members and friends of the musicians.

Source: *Kansas City Call*, May 11, 1934, 13.

Visits from Other Bands

In addition to the many bands and musicians that made Kansas City their home, the town also regularly played host to orchestras from the east, Chicago, and the west. The reputations of these bands preceded them, as they could be heard on the radio, and their recordings could be purchased at a music store owned by Bennie Moten and Thamon Hayes. The visiting band members stayed at the black-owned Street Hotel, on the corner of 18th and Paseo, three blocks from Paseo Hall. The novelty of an appearance by famous orchestra always brought the crowds and the commentary in the *Call*.

I have chosen to include articles pertaining to the appearances by the Duke Ellington Orchestra, Louis Armstrong, and Ada Brown for the detailed information they provide. The Ellington article illustrates the reputation developed from his broadcasts at the Cotton Club, and while the audience for this performance was black, there were white club managers and radio announcers present to convey the event to interested dancers on the other side of town. The Armstrong and Brown articles go into detail about each artist's background and include brief interviews. Ada Brown was not as famous as Ellington and Armstrong, but she was a Kansas City native returning home. In fact, she sang with the Bennie Moten Orchestra for their first recording session in 1923:

Kansas City Falls on Face before Onslaught of New York Jungle Band

Well, McKinney's Cotton Pickers have been out here, Fletcher Henderson, and a lot of the other big boys, but Kansas City had its first chance to hear Duke Ellington Monday night over at Paseo Hall. And with a paid admission of 2,105 at seventy-five cents per head, it would seem that Kansas City was anxious to hear the famous Cotton Club band on its first trip out of New York in five years.

Everybody was there-all the people that usually go to dances and hundreds of others who never go. White faces were there in abundance, among them the manager and radio man from the Pla-Mor and officials from El Torreon.[9] The boxes and balcony were full of listeners, and a solid phalanx of spectators twenty deep turned perspiring but marveling faces up at the boys from New York who could do such amazing tricks with their instruments. People were jammed into every available and unavailable cranny at the east end of the hall where the band played; they even stood precariously balanced in the windows.

And how that band could play! To say simply that every man was an artist is to state the facts very drably. Each man could do more tricks without effort than the average orchestra man could do after weeks of practice. And the whole effect was that infectious throbbing tom-tom music which has made Duke Ellington's band famous from New York to San Francisco and from Minnesota to Mississippi.

---

[9]Both were white dance halls.

A jungle band playing weird, wild jungle music. There is none other like it in the country.

The fans couldn't half express their liking for the unusual effects. They clapped and stamped and whistled and yelled out loud. Sonny Greer, the drummer, got more individual applause than any other man in the band. The trumpeter, the clarinet player, and the solemn gentleman who plucked the strings of the bass viol all got their share of cheers, as for that matter did all the men. And in the center of them all, the Duke swayed and rocked at the piano, spurring on all his henchmen to greater and greater efforts with a look here and a glance there, and a nod the other place.

Everyone agreed that it was a remarkable band. One man, manager of a local theater who himself has been an orchestra man and who has heard bands black and white that have come to Kansas City in the past ten years, said that without any question Ellington had the best band he had ever heard in the flesh. Praise was lavish from all quarters. And not the least of it came from the gallery of awe-inspired maidens who ganged the platform, cooed up into the faces of the musicians, and fairly sighed their unashamed adoration.

Ellington's band shows why it has been a feature at the Cotton Club in New York over a period of years. It has melody, rhythm (of a strange, distinctive sort), arrangements, and marvelous executional technique. It left Kansas City with an excellent opinion of the town, and left the townspeople with an excellent opinion of it. Here's success to their coming venture in pictures with Amos 'n' Andy.[10]

Source: *Kansas City Call*, August 1, 1930, 9.

Lou Armstrong Scores Heavily in Dance Here

A cornet player basking in the limelight of fame; the eyes of scores trained intently upon his figure as notes, sometimes weird, sometimes spritely, sometimes soft, sometimes loud, emanated from the mouth of the cornet—blended as only the expert touch of a master could accomplish.

---

[10] The movie was *Check and Double-Check*, which also featured Bing Crosby.

Louis Armstrong, world famous cornetist, and his band played at Paseo Hall Tuesday, May 2, as captivated dance fans and music lovers looked on.

What an impression this king of trumpeters made on his hearers Tuesday night!! They applauded his every effort, raved over his marvelous playing, [and] were fascinated by his personality.

A Chap with Talent

And does that fellow Lou Armstrong deserve such plaudits! In every sense of the word he was great. The success of his band wafts around on the wings of his ability as, first of all, a cornet player and secondly, a bandstand comedian who can make the crowd laugh as well as dance.

One of the biggest hits Armstrong scored Tuesday night was his blowing 200 short notes on his instrument without a pause. At the termination of this act, he immediately accomplished another feat said to be the most difficult in this realm of music, that of reaching high C in a clear and clean cut tone.

Lou Armstrong's band is good. The crowd enjoyed it immensely as a whole. But the noted trumpeter himself was the show, the thing that went over biggest.

During intermission, Armstrong had just a few minutes rest in which to recompose himself. We found him a very likeable person, pleasant and unaffected, despite the large number of honors tossed daily in his direction.

He was born in New Orleans, home of the rhythm, where he spent his early life. Later he went to St. Louis. It was there that the idea of becoming a musician, the type we read about in story books, became indelibly stamped in his mind. The idea seemed so attractive that its constant beating into his consciousness refused to let him rest until it was put into practical form.

He went to Chicago where he organized a band. Even then it could be easily seen that Armstrong had strong possibilities as a trumpeter. Those who predicted he would become famous someday can now pat themselves on the back.

Europe has seen Armstrong. Dear ol' London went wild over his playing. Overnight his fame came into being. The idea that once had been an obsession had become a reality.

Armstrong has had his present band approximately three years. They have traveled from coast to coast. Three motion picture shorts have been made by the aggregation. More are in the offing.

A Long, Long Grind

"I imagine it must have taken quite a bit of practice to reach the stage of perfection in trumpeting you have attained," this scribe directed at him.

"With the great amount of playing we have to do each week, a person has little time for practicing," was the comeback. I hardly think he needs it. He can get too much of the real thing in actual playing every night.

There's food for thought. But getting back to the dance, the numbers which appeared to gain the greatest favor with the crowd Tuesday night were "Tiger Rag," "You Can Depend on Me," and the everlasting "St. Louis Blues."

We would venture to say that practically half of the persons present chose to stand around the orchestra and enjoy Mr. Armstrong's playing and humorous antics in preference to dancing.

The band left immediately after the dance for St. Louis for a one-night stand. Following that, the unit took a jaunt into Memphis for three engagements. Monday night, it played in Omaha. Last Saturday night, Des Moines got a taste of the typical Armstrong music.

There will be other good bands to visit Kansas City in the future. That goes without saying. But just one little fact remains. Lou Armstrong has already visited.

Source: *Kansas City Call*, May 12, 1933, 2.

It Took Ada Brown Only a Short Time to Succeed

The summer of 1932 Ada Brown left Kansas City, where she had spent her vacation for New York to go in rehearsal with the one only Bill Robinson. The summer of 1933 Ada Brown returns to Kansas City, her hometown, playing with the said Bill Robinson, and oh what an Ada!

To say that "Ada," as everyone calls her, was glad to be home is just expressing it mildly. The smile with which she greeted her audience at the mid-night show at a downtown theater last Thursday night, June 15, will long be remembered.

"Am I glad to be home," she said. "Oh girl, it's nice but I am dead. Only one night have I gone to bed and then I told them it was either stop or drop."

One of Four Generations

The "them" Ada spoke of is her family. Over on the Kansas side she has a mother, Mrs. Anna Frazier, a daughter, Mrs. Gladys Leake, and a granddaughter, Ada Jean Leake, four generations of them, all made happy by her success as a crooner of blues and happier yet because she was home.

Sitting in her dressing room in the theater, she was a tired woman. For eight years she has been doing "big time." Most of that time she has been a single act on the R.K.O. circuit with Harry Swanagan, also a Kansas Citian.

With the more than 200 pounds of flesh she carries so well, being back with friends, the four shows a day, the many curtain calls and the encores she responds to, the fancy steps with an incidental snake hip movement she throws in, there is small wonder she was hardly able to make the last night.

Began by Playing the Piano

Ada Brown (Mrs. Brown to me, as I knew her when she began her theatrical aspirations) started her career with an engagement at the Lincoln Theater as a pianist in Harry Dillard's orchestra. It was there she began to sing. Singing choruses of songs accompanying silent pictures resulted in Ada's being where she is today, a co-star with the world's greatest dance.

Always Wanted to Do Things

Her early work took her on a trip to Texas and Oklahoma where talk of her smooth melodious voice had traveled. She returned to Kansas City, to her home and her husband and started work here again, entertaining and playing.

But Ada was restless. She reasoned that somewhere in the world others might like to hear the voice her home town people raved about. So it wasn't long before she took to the highway that leads to names in bright lights. Ada's name was soon in bright lights and she has been traveling since. She went away with Harry and she returns each year with him.

Many friends say Ada could not have succeeded so quickly had it not been for the sympathetic accompanying of Harry Swanagan. Harry is a large part of her success and vice-versa. He plays a big part in the show, and always will as long as he can use his hands, for he is a pianist of no mean ability, or as some express it, "his fingers just talk right back at her."

First Time Seen on Big Time

The mid-night show arrangement for Negroes at the theater gave friends an opportunity to see her work on the big time, as Negroes are not admitted in the theater otherwise.

Last summer, while she and Harry were back on their vacation, both appeared in a benefit show at the New Center Theater for Wheatley-Provident Hospital.

So "our Ada" left Kansas City Friday nights, after "Father" Bill [Bojangles] Robinson had made arrangements for her to ride in a private compartment. She goes east again for what, she did not know. What new laurels will come, we must wait to learn, but we do know that Baptist minister's daughters have a way of doing things, and Ada's days for such are not over. C.S.W.

Source: *Kansas City Call,* June 23, 1933, 7.

The Depression Comes to Black Kansas City

The essays in this chapter to this point give the impression that jazz and dancing continued to thrive during the Great Depression in Kansas City. But these essays mask some truths. The support for jazz from the men's and women's social and political organizations that was seen in the previous chapter falls substantially, especially by 1932. Instead, support more and more came from business interests with ties to the Pendergast machine—cabarets that were privately owned and served alcohol, instead of from dance halls, like the Paseo, that could be rented by an organization for an evening. The vice district of 12th and Vine boomed as well, and all of these new venues were attended by whites, who in the early 1930s were not impacted by the economic catastrophe nearly to the same extent as the city's blacks.

A few statistics take from Charles E. Coulter's book, *Take Up the Black Man's Burden: Kansas City's African American Communities, 1865-1939* will place our next examples into perspective.[11] Using census statistics and statistics from the Kansas City Urban League, Coulter finds declines for black employment opportunities in all sectors, especially in railroads, stock houses, packinghouses, and stone quarries. In 1920, 80.5 percent of the black male population was working; by 1930 that number was 72.7. In analyzing these statistics Coulter concludes "it is obvious that black men were finding fewer work opportunities and that more black women were being forced to move into the workplace in order to sustain their families."[12]

The *Call* covered nothing relating to Wall Street or the subsequent loss of jobs among its readership. Wall Street belonged to a different world, and focusing on job losses would not have sold newspapers. But from time to time C.F. Franklin used his editorial page to encourage his readers through these hard times. In the first essay, we see his take on the corrupt influence that politics held over the local police force. The vice resorts were located in black neighborhoods, and the politicians expected the police not to control the criminals, but to extort kickbacks from them. There is a poignancy in this essay, for although it is hopeful that these actions would end, as the Depression strengthened, graft and corruption would worsen in the black neighborhoods of Kansas City:

Killing the Graft

---

[11](Columbia: University of Missouri Press, 2006).
[12]Coulter, *Take up the Black Man's Burden*, pp. 273-274.

The police commissioners...announced that no campaign contributions are to be levied on their men. Because the police departments in Missouri are directed by appointees of the Governor, the custom has grown up of playing politics with the police. The change in Kansas City conditions is revolutionary and is the last full measure of proof that police duty, not party service, is the test for the Kansas City policeman....

Stopping campaign contributions by policemen breaks the grip of the underworld on the officials in charge of law enforcement. So long as an officer was expected to contribute funds to the party in power, his own initiative, and sometimes direct orders from superiors, made him a collector from the rackets which prey upon the community. The next step, as Chicago shows, was gangsters actually in police uniform....

Because Negroes have the least financial and political weight, ties between the police and the racketeers endanger us most, of all the elements that make up the city's population. As is typical of the American city, our residence district in Kansas City suffers the contamination of white vice resorts. In addition our own racketeers very naturally bid for protection, and the double burden is too much if the police are more interested in getting money than in safeguarding the public. The good citizen who has only his vote with which to win the attention of public officials, under the old system, has been hopelessly displaced by the racketeer with his campaign gifts and herd of followers. It is these who have brought to the whole race the reputation of being voters easily and cheaply bought, more anxious for degrading amusement than for justice and their rights. The new rule of the police department stops this barter and clears the way for the decent, home-loving majority to work and get their due.

Source: *Kansas City Call*, January 10, 1930, 6.

One of the first indications in the *Call* of economic hardship comes in this essay, a year after the market crash. Charitable organizations in black Kansas City were very active and effective up until the Depression, but as things became worse, C.F. Franklin's pleas to those who could help became more forceful:

Charity's Call is Yours

The 1930 charity drive is almost upon us. It comes at a time when needs bid fair to exceed anything this city has ever experienced and unfortunately amid general conditions which will put limits upon previous contributors. Among Negroes charity—its gathering and its bestowal—has more importance than the average of the city. We are of the laboring class and therefore among the hardest hit by present industrial conditions. This coming winter our group will have more than usual need of outside help. It must come from the money we help to raise in the charity drive.

Source: *Kansas City Call*, October 8, 1930, 8.

If 1930 was a difficult year for black Kansas Citians, 1931 was worse. Still, Franklin tried to keep his readership focused on the positive:

A Better New Year

The year 1932 will be better for everybody than 1931. It could hardly be worse. Two things have combined to give us hope for the future. Our acceptance of conditions as a long hard pull in which we all must have a part is the major, and the natural ability of men to readjust themselves is the minor factor. Bad as this time has been, our fathers knew worse. We have talked about hardships with everyone getting food and shelter somehow. Just because it was possible for a day laborer to buy silk shirts at $10 in the high price era that followed the World War, and because investments measured in dollars were shooting skyward two years ago, we forgot that those were not the normal conditions.

There is some responsibility on each of us if we would hasten the day when there will be work for all who wish it and at a fair wage. Each theorist has his own pet scheme, but they all agree that it is a cooperative job. One thing we know, the lesson of thrift has a bigger number who are letter perfect in it now than when a new and more alluring job was just around the corner.

We are going to have higher taxes, a burden we must carry. We are going to get employment at a lower average wage. We are not going to quit wanting what we bought when times were good. The net result of these demands and conditions is a wiser use of money, which is another way of saying we will come out of the Depression better off.

Source: *Kansas City Call*, January 1, 1932, 6.

As this essay implies, by 1933 unemployment in black Kansas City was between 20 and 30 percent. Still, traditions such as the Wheatley-Provident Fashion Show went on. Franklin found in that event the opportunity for his readers to overcome economic hardship, as they had overcome so many hardships in the past:

Keeping Fat, Thank You!

Kansas City has been in need of the reassurance which the fashion show of this week gives. Times are hard, no doubt about it. Men unemployed are many. But after all, the most of us are at work and are living about as we are accustomed to do. Because misfortunes make an interesting topic, the public's attention gets fixed on the hole in the doughnut, and it acts as though there was nothing surrounding the hole.

Six thousand well-dressed Negroes paying admission to a style show, over one-tenth of the total Negro population of Greater Kansas City, make very evident that the great majority of us are above want and living normal lives.

We give unmistakable proof that we are going about our business as usual. What if ten or twenty or thirty per cent are not working? The rest, the great majority are. They are not only working, but they are demonstrating that ability which has always characterized Negroes—they are keeping fat on what would mean deprivation if they were not the world's best managers. Black-eyed peas do not sound so aristocratic as mushrooms, but they are mighty filling!

Source: *Kansas City Call*, April 21, 1933, 6b.

The Death of Bennie Moten

Bennie Moten continued to lead a band at the white Harlem Night Club, eventually being joined by Count Basie. At the end of 1934, the nightclub closed, and Moten reunited some of his former band-mates. The old Paseo Hall reopened for blacks in the wake of the demise of the Harlem Night Club, and the Moten Orchestra performed with Bennie in the lead one last time for the Musicians Annual Ball on March 11.[13] After this dance, the band went to Denver, while Moten stayed in Kansas City for a tonsillectomy at the Wheatley Provident Hospital. He did not survive the operation, and his death dominated the *Call*'s pages for two weeks:

Moten, Band Leader, Dies

Removal of Tonsils Fatal to Musician

Dance Orchestra Head was Dean of Bandmen in Southwest

Bennie Moten, nationally known dance orchestra leader, died Tuesday morning at Wheatley Provident hospital following an operation for the removal of his tonsils. He had not been confined to his bed before entering the hospital the night before the operation.

The 41-year old rotund band leader was a favorite among both white and colored dance fans from coast to coast and was famous for his "stomp" rhythm that had wide appeal.

Born in Kansas City, MO, November 13 1893, he was graduated from Attucks school and attended Lincoln High school but did not finish. He chose music as his career and began early in his profession as a musician.

Charter Member of Local

He was a charter member of the Kansas City Musicians Local No. 627 and as a boy played valve trombone in Dan Blackburn's band.

Later he organized his own orchestra with three instruments. He secured engagements in local theaters and played dance engagements in Kansas City and nearby

---

[13]"Musician's Ball Monday at Paseo Hall; 7 Red Hot Bands," *Kansas City Call*, March 8, 1935, 13-b.

towns. As his orchestra grew his popularity spread. He was director and played piano. Bennie also was the composer of several dance hits.

On tours east Bennie Moten's orchestra attracted large crowds in New York, Philadelphia, Baltimore, Chicago, Cleveland and other well-known amusement centers. His orchestra made several recordings for Victor and Brunswick phonograph records. His band was usually billed as Bennie Moten and His Victor Recording Orchestra. In Kansas City he is considered the dean of orchestra leaders, as his band is the first large dance orchestra to originate in this section. Many musicians who are now playing in large and well-known eastern orchestras got their start with the Moten organization.

Featured over NBC

When the orchestra played in Cincinnati a few years ago it was featured nightly over the National Broadcasting Company's network. He became popular with radio listeners instantly. Two years ago, when a national circulated newspaper conducted a popularity poll to determine the most popular band, Bennie Moten's outfit stood high on the list.

Last week his orchestra left for Denver to fill an engagement at the Rainbow Gardens. Bennie was to have joined them after he had recovered sufficiently from the operation....

Source: *Kansas City Call*, April 5, 1935, 1.

Thousands at Funeral for Bennie Moten

Church filled long before Hour of Service; Throng Waits Outside

Thousands of both races from all walks of life filled every available space in the Centennial M.E. Church auditorium here Saturday and overflowed far out into the street during the last rites for Bennie Moten, beloved and widely known orchestra leader.

This was not the usual morbid funeral crowd that attended out of sheer curiosity. They all were friends of the musician who shared the family's sorrow at his passing. Bennie was 41 years old.

But in that brief span he had achieved more than some men who live out their full three score and 10 years. He was well known as a composer also.

Composed Several Hits

Probably the best known of Bennie's compositions are his "Moten Stomp," and the "Kansas City Stomp." Other of his compositions include "It's Hard to Laugh or Cry," "Lafayette Stomp," "New Tulsa Blues," and many other blues novelties.

The body lay in state in its silver couch casket from 12 noon until 2 p.m. A steady stream of men, women, and children filed past the bier for the final look at the man who built up one of the finest dance orchestras in the country. By 11 o'clock the balcony was virtually filled and ushers were seating persons in the wings of the main auditorium. The center section had been reserved for relatives, close friends and associates. Four patrolmen and two motorcycle traffic policemen were assigned by Captain Thomas J. Sullivan to keep the close-knit crowd moving orderly and to direct traffic.

Bandmen Form Guard

At intervals of 15 minutes each, two members of Harlan Leonard's Kansas City Rockets, several of whom had been members of Moten's orchestra, stood at attention on guard in their uniform at each end of the coffin.

Floral pieces were banked high about the rostrum. Outside the church a brass band composed of members of the Musicians Local No. 627 played well-known hymns.

At 2 o'clock the stentorian voice of the Rev. A. L. Reynolds intoned "I am the resurrection and the life…" as he led the procession down the aisle. At his side was the Rev. F. Jesse Peck, pastor of Ward Chapel A.M.E. Church. The relatives of the dead man followed. The widow, Mrs. Crable Moten and her 8-year-old daughter, Zella Mae were assisted to their seats by T.R. Watkins, funeral director.

Lawrence Keys played "Nearer, My God to Thee" softly on the organ. With voices that seemed muted the Centennial choir sang "Abide with Me." The Rev. G. B. Hancock, pastor of Mason Memorial M.E. Church of Kansas City, KA, prayed. Miss Margaret Davis sang "Precious Lord, Take My Hand."

Reads From Job

The Rev. R. A. Page, assistant pastor of Pleasant Green Baptist Church, read 22 verses from the fourteenth chapter of the Book of Job. The choir sang "Take Your Burdens to the Lord and Leave Them There." Miss Catherine Washington read telegrams and condolences from all parts of the country. Mrs. Blanche Watts read condolences from Centennial M.E. Church. The Rev. L.L. Boswell of the Metropolitan Spiritual Church sang "The Old Rugged Cross."

With simple dignity, the Rev. Mr. Reynolds spoke on the value of a good name.

"There's wealth in a good name," he said. "Bennie Moten, a Kansas City boy, born in an humble home, began his musical career at four years of age. He touched men in every walk of life in his work. He touched them at the bottom and at the top, but kept his manhood and his good name. He was both brave and courageous.

"Bennie Moten was a master builder of men in a symphonic whole.

"Men served Bennie Moten because he had that something that drew them to him and because they loved to serve him."

The local musician's union, of which Moten was a charter member, then took charge of the services.   Condolences from Local 627 were read by Harry Dillard. William Sanders sang "My Buddy," accompanied by Emile

Williams. The string ensemble from Shaw's Little Symphony Orchestra played Grieg's "Aase's Death." Benediction was pronounced.

The procession left the church headed west on Nineteenth Street to Vine, then north on Vine to Eighteenth. At Eighteenth Street it turned east to Woodland Avenue. Two motorcycle patrolmen formed a police escort, clearing traffic for the procession. Many who were unable to gain entrance into the church formed a line on both sides of the street for blocks to view the procession as it passed. Many who stood on the sidewalks as the funeral cortège crawled by wept openly.

Following the motorcycle policemen the band played a mournful funeral dirge. The procession slipped into the traffic lanes at Fifteenth Street and quickened its pace as it headed for Highland cemetery. Watkins Brothers had charge. It was the largest funeral Kansas City had witnessed in 20 years.

Source: *Kansas City Call*, April 12, 1935, 1.

Moten's death was not the end of jazz in Kansas City, of course. There were many other bands, including new leaders such as Jay McShann, and it is very possible that a 14-year-old Charlie Parker watched the funeral procession. Until the fall of Pendergast in the late 1930s, the jazz life of Kansas City remained vibrant. But for a variety of reasons previously mentioned, mainly the fact that jazz now belonged less and less to the black community, and more and more to those who operated within the context of the Pendergast machine, the *Call*'s coverage of musical events declines around this time. Yet, for the determined, there are still many items to discover in the *Call* regarding Basie, McShann, and Charlie Parker. However, in my attempt to address the *Call*'s coverage of this time period, this is a good place to conclude the chapter.

Chapter 7:
Jazz on the Chicago Stroll, 1916-1929

This book concludes with two chapters presenting material from the *Chicago Defender*, the African American newspaper with the widest distribution in the country in the 1910s and '20s. Its founder and chief editor, Robert S. Abbott, was deeply committed to the advancement of African Americans, and the newspaper's role in promoting Chicago as a destination for the Great Migration, and its inclusion of essays by Langston Hughes, Gwendolyn Brooks, and Willard Motley is well-known. It played a vital role in the African American cultural and artistic advancements arising all across the country during this period.[1]

These chapters cover the period 1916-1929. These thirteen years were an important period for black entertainment in the city, as the influx of the Great Migration and the vice associated with Prohibition met on the South Side. However, two chapters are not nearly enough space to cover the vibrant and diverse musical and theatrical activities of Chicago at this time. Fortunately, a collection of the *Defender's* advertisements for music and theater events during this period has been compiled by Franz Hoffmann in his series *Jazz Advertised, 1910-1967: A Documentation.*[2]

Chapter 7 will primarily examine activities on "The Stroll," the name

---

[1]For more on Robert Mott and the achievements of the *Chicago Defender*, see Ethan Michaeli, *The Defender: How the Legendary Black Newspaper changed America* (Boston: Houghton Mifflin Harcourt, 2016), Charles A. Simmons, *The African American Press: A History of News Coverage During National Crises: With Special Reference to Four Black Newspapers, 1827-1965* (Jefferson, NC: McFarland & Co, 2005), and, particularly for his discussion of representation of "art" music in the *Defender*, Lawrence Schenbeck, "Music, Gender, and 'Uplift' in the *Chicago Defender*, 1927-1937." *The Musical Quarterly* (Autumn, 1997): 344-370.

[2](Berlin: F. Hoffman, 1980-1997). Volume 7 of this series focuses exclusively on pictorial advertisements in the *Defender*.

given to the area of South State Street between 27th and 35th Street in Chicago's South Side. This was the strip of cabarets and cafes famous for the ragtime, jazz, and blues musicians who came to the city with the Great Migration, making it a center of black culture. The chapter will not be a comprehensive discussion of all of the musicians and the venues where they played. Rather, the focus will be on the *Defender*'s coverage of the city's black musical life, with the aim of illustrating the themes and issues that Abbott and other *Defender* writers found important.[3]

The first essay is actually a reprint by the *Defender* of an article that originally appeared a few weeks earlier in the progressive *New York Sun*. Almost since the initial appearance of the word "jass" in Chicago in 1916 musicians and scholars have attempted to define its origins. Thus, it is interesting to read contemporary hypotheses about the music's history, and the *Defender*'s endorsement of such hypotheses, at a time when the word and the music ran all through the South Side. In leading up to a discussion of New Orleans the interviewee describes a wide diversity of musical sources, including religious music from Africa, Native American rhythms, Turkish music, minstrel comedy, the importance of the 1893 Chicago Exposition. There were special musical effects, and an evolution from the trick saxophone to muted brass, and from syncopation to stop-time rhythm. Perhaps the final sentence of the essay captures a bit of the sentiment of the "jazz age."

Jazz Born in Africa, U.S., and India

Melodies Mixed with Tom Toms and Underworld Hilarity Produce It

In an uptown [Harlem] music store which has catered to theatrical and orchestral trade for a half a century, is a white-haired clerk who specializes in selling musical in-struments and has sold a shipload of assorted harmony

---

[3]There are several extensive studies on Chicago Jazz which focus on the cabarets and cafes of the South Side, and the musicians and bands who performed in them. William Howland Kenney's *Chicago Jazz: A Cultural History, 1904-1930* (NY: Oxford University Press, 1993), and Burton W. Peretti's *The Creation of Jazz: Music, Race, and Culture in Urban America* (Urbana: University of Illinois Press, 1994) have greatly informed the thinking in this chapter, and the choice of material. Lawrence Gushee and Harry Carr's article "How the Creole Band Came to Be," *Black Music Research Journal* 8 (1988): 83-100, and Gene Anderson's "The Genesis of King Oliver's Creole Jazz Band," *American Music* (Autumn, 1994): 283-303 are important examinations of these two bands, and provide insight into the ways in which bands traveled north, organized themselves, and ultimately created a Chicago jazz community.

and noise devices in his time. He can name instruments of all nations and he is an expert on jazz although he hardly looks it, with his dignified demeanor and his fatherly air, says the *New York Sun*:

"I have read, heard, and talked a great deal about jazz since the craze swept the country," he said the other day. "I prefer classical and dignified music, of course, but it is my business to know about jazz, and I am not fussy when it comes to turning quick profit for the firm.

"There is much about jazz that has never been printed. For instance, the early American minstrels realized dimly that there was an age of barbaric musical splendor to come, and they attempted jazz. The Negroes, from whom we really get much of our music, brought quaint religious chants with them from Africa, and for their gayer moments they evolved syncopated themes done on the old banjo which were not unlike our present day jazz.

"Into this, out of the air one might say in this age of radio, came the Indian tom-tom chants which sort of melted into the general musical idea. Turkish music, which made a raging hit at Chicago during the Colombian exposition in 1893, added momentum, and then the white and Negro hilarity from the Tenderloins of San Francisco, Norfolk, Cairo, Ill. And other points, including New Orleans, also became scrambled with the other rhythmic noises and the resulting omelet was the present day jazz.

"The first jazz instrument in this country was a pair of sawed-off cow ribs. Then two pairs, later manufactured for the minstrel trade out of ebony and other woods and known as rattle bones. The playing of these bones, or rather the drumming of them, is now virtually a lost art, but there was a day when all Negro musicians drummed with them to banjo melodies and produced what are now known as jazz effects.

"Some of the musical compositions jazzed at an early day were the height of syncopation. I recall one known as 'The Darkey's Dream,' with a tempo quite as exhilarating as any of the jazz numbers of the present.

"Then came such compositions as 'The Forge in the Forest' and 'Barnyard Echoes,' which were known as descriptive numbers.[4] These called for various effects, such as anvil, bells, chimes, animal calls, and the like. These were operated by the drummer and from time to time new 'traps' were invented for the drummer, and his was the job to jazz up the overture or the incidental numbers.

"With the saxophone, at first a trick instrument, and later a recognized orchestra instrument, jazz came into its own. Some soul for jazz was inspired to bring the banjo into the orchestra, and then jazz jazzed as it had never jazzed before. Syncopation led to stop-time and stop-time to saxophone jazzing, for at the stops in stop-time the saxophonist began carrying forward a harmonious offshoot to the real melody, blending back later into the main theme.

"Then the brass was muted and all jazz need was sufficient space for the drummer to crash everything he had within reach and we evolved into what the world insists upon as the daily or rather nightly musical fare of the present day.

"Jazz is the Tabasco that makes the musical oyster palatable. We have to have it."

Source: *Chicago Defender*, July 8, 1922, 8.

The Cabarets, King Oliver and Louis Armstrong

The first mention of the phrase "jass" in the Defender was an advertisement for a theatrical show, "Estella Harris and her Jass Entertainers," who appeared at Chicago's Grand Theater beginning in October 1916.[5] Music called "jass" or "jazz" from this point forward was a featured part of both Chicago's live theatrical entertainment and the music accompanying silent films. Advertisements for such shows appeared weekly in the *Defender*; there are far too many to be discussed in great detail in this chapter. But the paper also covered the music in the South Side cabarets, and a reading of these pieces offers a glimpse inside this world, shaped by new music from southern musicians, the interplay between entrepreneurs and gangsters, and the biases of *Defender* owner Robert S. Abbott.

---

[4]The exact reference of "Barnyard Echoes" is difficult to determine, but "The Darkey's Dream" was composed by G. L. Lansing in 1890. This song, and "The Forge in the Forest" were recorded in the early 1900s by Arthur Pryor, a former Sousa trombonist, and his band.

[5]Tony Langston, "The Grand," *Chicago Defender*, October 7, 1916, 4.

From about 1914 to 1929 the area on South State Street known as "The Stroll" was lined with cafes that offered dance music, and cabarets which also offered a floor show. Among the most popular were the Royal Gardens (later renamed the Lincoln Gardens) and the Dreamland Café. As will be seen later, the Dreamland Café held a special place for Abbott, whose paper privileged those establishments that he considered to be offering "high-class" entertainment. Here is the *Defender's* first extensive essay with the mention of the words "jass" and "creole" in conjunction with a cabaret:

Opens with Creole Jass Band at 11 o'clock Each Night

At the Pekin Dancing Pavilion the same high-class entertainment is given nightly, beginning at 11 o'clock sharp, with Emanuel Perry's full Creole Jass Band furnishing the music. In entertainers and song birds, no place in town can excel this house. [With] Carolyn Williams, Ethel James, Rita Scott, and Cora Allen, with Tony Jackson at the piano, at night at the Pekin is a treat. Remember that until further notice the dancing commences at 11 sharp, with the full orchestra. Mr. Wallace Tyler announces that the private club... will be open to members on June 15.

Source: *Chicago Defender*, May 25, 1918, 6.

By July 1919, Joe Oliver had arrived in Chicago and begun his stay there by splitting time between the bands at the Royal Gardens and the Dreamland Café.[6] He remained in Chicago until the summer of 1921, when the Royal Gardens and Dreamland temporarily closed. Oliver returned in the summer of 1922, when his name first appeared in the Defender with this small excerpt:[7]

Oliver's Band

King Oliver's Creole Jazz Band played an engagement last week at beautiful Castle Gardens, one of the leading cabarets in the Loop, and made a great impression. Among the audience were representatives from every leading orchestra in Chicago, and they were enthusiastic over the work of King and his group. A return engagement was played early the present week.

---

[6] Anderson, "The Genesis of King Oliver's Creole Jazz Band," p. 288.

[7] For more on the tumultuous spring and summer of 1921, when many of "The Stroll's" clubs closed or changed hands, see Ted Vincent, "The Community that Gave Jazz to Chicago," *Black Music Research Journal* (Spring, 1992): 43-55.

Source: *Chicago Defender*, August 5, 1922, 6.

Until the summer of 1923, only brief mentions of Oliver appear in the *Defender*. However, on April 5 of that year his Creole Jazz Band, with pianist Lil Hardin and Louis Armstrong, made the first of their legendary recordings for Okeh Records. From this point, coverage of Oliver in the *Defender* grows substantially, in conjunction with the spreading popularity of the group brought on by these recordings, which perhaps led to larger crowds at the Lincoln Gardens:

King Oliver's Jazz Band

King Oliver's Jazz Band, which plays every night in Lincoln Gardens [formerly the Royal Gardens], is now making records for Okeh. King Oliver's band is considered to be the finest Negro jazz band that ever came out of New Orleans. The band has been playing in Lincoln Gardens for the past six years, which is a tribute to its popularity.

Source: *Chicago Defender*, August 11, 1923, 7.

Lincoln Gardens

Lincoln Gardens on E. 31st St. seems to have taken on new life and the nightly attendance has grown to close to capacity. The fact that King Oliver's Creole Jazz band furnishes the music at the handsome resort, no doubt has a great deal to do with its present popularity. An additional feature, however, is the $5,000 Ball of Fire, a European novelty which reflects a series of colored lights upon the dancers. It is one of only three in the United States and Bud Redd, the manager, went to an enormous expense to secure this one. Correct dancing is insisted upon at the Lincoln and Department rules are enforced to the letter by King Jones, who has charge of the floor.

Source: *Chicago Defender*, September 1, 1923, 8.

The Oliver Band recorded in April, June, and October 1923. Here is a review of two records made on June 22:

King Oliver's Band

King Oliver's Jazz band, the razziest, jazziest band you ever heard, made another record for Okeh. "High Society Rag," which is on one side of the record, is a rag version of an old Sousa march that has been played for years by jazz bands at fairs and circuses throughout the South. Every southerner is familiar with the air, but not every person is familiar with the style in which it is played. For pure, out and out, unadulterated jazz, King Oliver's Jazz Band has them all beat. On the other side of the record is "Snake Rag," which is just about the jazziest thing imaginable, and then some.

Source: *Chicago Defender,* October 6, 1923, 8.

Indeed, the height of Oliver's career was the period 1923-28. With the Lincoln Gardens as his base, he expanded his band, performing for large crowds, including other entertainers, and occasionally toured with the group:

King Oliver

King Oliver and his New Orleans Jazz Orchestra are having a very successful engagement at Lincoln Gardens, 459 E. 35th St., after an extended tour of the Orpheum circuit. This aggregation is a wonderful one, and the manner in which they discourse the dance and entertaining music at popular Lincoln accounts to a large extent for the large attendance which it enjoy nightly. Every Wednesday is "theatrical night," and performers and their friends will find special and appropriate features arranged for them on that evening each week. Bud Redd, the manager, keeps everything "jam-up" for his patrons.

Source: *Chicago Defender,* June 28, 1924, 6.

Lincoln Gardens

Lincoln Gardens, which is still under the management of Bud Redd, is proving to be a most popular place of amusement. The fact that it is open but three nights each week and that it is prospering shows that Mrs. Majors, the owner, has the right idea. Our readers all know that the location is at 459 E. 31st St. but they don't know that King Oliver and his New Orleans Jazz band are still furnishing the singing and dancing strains which have been popular in the handsome place for years. Wednesday night is "professional" night each week. On that night a theatrical group from one of the theaters are special guests, and they usually "put on" something worthwhile. Saturday and Sunday night's special attractions are presented, and the crowds have been numbering as high as 1,200 on these nights. Give the old Lincoln Gardens the once-over next time you are out. Your will certainly enjoy yourself, as class sticks out all over the handsome place.

Source: *Chicago Defender*, October 11, 1924, 8.

In November 1924 Oliver was hired for the Plantation Café by Dave Peyton, a longtime Chicago musician and bandleader, and the subject of this book's final chapter. The Plantation often held or sponsored charity events with extravagant entertainment. In June 1926 a benefit for the American Federation of Musicians Local 208 was held at the Chicago Coliseum, one of the city's largest indoor venues. The event featured a revue called "A Night in Old Japan," which was currently playing at the Plantation, accompanied by "the Dean of Orchestra Leaders," Joe Oliver:

"King" Joe Oliver Will be there to Thrill Crowd

One of the extraordinary features of the evening's entertainment will be the accompaniment of the Plantation Revue, which will open the show, by the dean of orchestra leaders, Joe "King" Oliver, and his Plantation Serenaders.

Joe and his gang will be on hand when the show is opened, promptly at 9 p.m., to play for the extraordinary act. And only the King and his men could do real justice to this difficult job.

Joe Oliver's name is as well-known in the city of New Orleans, the town of jazz, as is that of the famous Mississippi River. He has a world of imitators, but not one who can equal his celebrated performance on the trumpet. Joe's rubber lip is famous from coast to coast, he having filled engagements in the past at some of the foremost dance palaces and cafes in the country.

Many Imitators

It is no uncommon sight nightly to see orchestra men from all over the city carefully studying some of Joe's characteristic breaks on the old clarinet in the hope that they will be able to go home and practice up to the perfection this "king" has reached.

A Real Good Fellow

Notwithstanding all of his tremendous popularity and success, the "King's" head has not expanded one little bit over its normal growth and he is the friend and good fellow to all who know him, and that seems to be just about everybody in the Windy City, because Joe's list of acquaintances reads like the city directory.

Great credit is also due the men of Joe's organization, because one seldom sees the equal of a group of such truly fine and well-trained musicians in one unit. Each one has been selected only after a third-degree test, all Joe's own, and when a man passes this test it can safely be said that he ranks with the finest in the country.

Undoubtedly Joe will have time to play one or two dancing selections before he will have to depart from the Coliseum to take up his regular duties for that night at the café, and if so, , brother and sister, be there, that's all.

Source: *Chicago Defender*, June 12, 1926, 6.

Louis Armstrong joined his mentor Joe Oliver in Chicago in August 1922. As an unknown second cornetist, his talent was not immediately recognized by the *Defender*. Armstrong's first appearance in the newspaper was the announcement of his marriage to the pianist in the band, Lil Hardin, in February, 1924. Attending the wedding were bandmates Warren (Baby) Dodds, Bill Johnson, Joe Oliver and his wife Ruby, plus fellow New Orleans musicians Johnny Dodds and Tommy Ladnier:

Miss Lillian Hardin is Bride of Louis Armstrong

Miss Lillian Hardin, daughter of Mrs. Dempsey Miller, 3310 Giles Ave., was married to Louis Armstrong of New Orleans, LA. They gave their reception at the beautiful Ideal Tearoom 2218 S. Michigan Ave. on Thursday evening, Feb. 7. The bride was beautifully attired in a Parisian gown of white crepe elaborately beaded in rhinestones and silver beads and Miss Lucille Saunders, a lifelong chum of the bride, who was her bridesmaid, wore orchid chiffon with silver trimmings.

Oscar Young's seven-piece orchestra furnished music for the occasion. Mr. and Mrs. Armstrong are both members of King Oliver's Creole band, who are recording for the Gennett, Okeh, and Columbia records.   They will leave on Feb. 22 for an extended tour on big time. The guests present were: Misses Lucille Saunders, Mae Gilbert, Laura Watson, Clara Gunn, Anna Ecton, Ruby Oliver, Myrtle Villavasso, Pauline Kinner, Laura Rawlyns, Messrs. Arthur Rockford, William Spratley, Louis Bustill, Val Harvey, James Hollins, Clarence Lee, Willie Saunders, Fred Hall, Warren Dodds, John Dodds, Bill Johnson, Lawrence Guidry, Dr. Owen Williams, Mr. and Mrs William Gunn, John Miller, Willie King, Joseph Oliver, Tom Ladinier, Raymond Whitsett, and Capt. A Pitts. The couple received many beautiful presents.

Source: *Chicago Defender*, February 14, 1924, 9.

A few months after their marriage, Lil encouraged Louis to leave Oliver and join Fletcher Henderson in New York City. They were there until late 1925 when they moved back to Chicago. Armstrong's subsequent engagements at the Vendome with Erskine Tate and the Dreamland are casually mentioned by fellow cornetist Dave Peyton in his *Defender* column "The Musical Bunch." But although Peyton was musically conservative, by 1927 even he had to admit to the level of Armstrong's talent:

> ... Louis Armstrong has closed his engagement at the Vendome Theater as a feature player in the orchestra there. Louis is in much demand, already having been offered many lucrative positions. Louis is the king of jazz cornetists. He knows how to humor his instrument: he com-

mands it, he plays "hot" and "sweet," and it soaks into the listener. There is but one "Louis."

Source: *Chicago Defender*, April 23, 1927, 6.

In early 1929, Armstrong realized that the era of the Chicago cabarets was coming to a close. He signed with a new manager, Tommy Rockwell, who secured his departure from Chicago for New York City. Armstrong's return to NYC began at the Savoy Ballroom, with a standing-room-only crowd that was reported back to his fans in Chicago:

Louis Armstrong Takes New York by Storm

New York, March 22—The people of New York City packed the Savoy Ballroom last Saturday and Sunday nights to hear Louis Armstrong, the world's greatest cornetist, who came here at great expense. Crowds were lined up for blocks trying to get in to see this famous musician and hear his inimitable style of playing. He was well supported by Louis Russell and his orchestra, a permanent Savoy attraction.

Mr. Buchanan, manager of the Savoy, gave a banquet the last night Mr. Armstrong appeared and invited all musicians of the city. T. Rockwell, President of Okeh Record Company, of which Mr. Armstrong is all exclusive artist, in his speech, acclaimed him as the greatest artist of his profession. Fletcher Henderson was master of ceremonies. Speeches were made by Jimmie Harris, Chick Webb, and Bennie Carter, all famous New York musicians. Never before in its history has New York lauded an individual in the music profession as it did Mr. Armstrong, who well deserves the name "King of Jazz." He became exhausted from autographing photos for the throng of admiring fans.

Source: *Chicago Defender*, March 23, 1929, 4.

The Dreamland Café

The Dreamland was by far the most frequently discussed venue in the *Defender*, indicating its importance and the belief of its owner Robert Abbott that it was a proper demonstration of the black entrepreneurial spirit.

Like several other venues in the city, it was open to performers and customers of all races. It was first opened in 1914, and then purchased, refur-
bished, and reopened in May 1917 by Billy Bottoms, an African American
real estate investor who, in Mott's view, was doing grand work for the
"Race:"

New Ideas

There is no more progressive young business man in the
city of Chicago than popular Will Bottoms, proprietor of
the Dreamland Café. Mr. Bottoms, or "Bill," as he is fa-
miliarly called by his legion of friends, has done more to
make The Stroll the amusement center than any of our
cabaret men, and as a consequence more interest is dis-
played in what he is doing and what he intends to do than
would ordinarily be expected. When Bill took the famous
Dreamland Hall over and transformed it into the finest
place of its kind in the world, owned and operated by and
for our people, many were skeptical and predicted a short
stay for him, thinking that he had "bit off more than he
could chew." But they reasoned without the man; success
has crowned his every effort and he has introduced many
novel forms of entertainment. And now comes another
idea that places him in the pioneer position. He has introduced real vaudeville in The Dreamland and done away
with more of the entertaining crew. In doing this he has
picked up an enormous amount of added expense, inasmuch as he has already and intends in the future to book
nothing but the very best acts procurable.

The current week and for the next week Mr. Bottoms has
Dan Wylie, the world's greatest skater, who is the real marvel of the age in his line. It is Mr. Wylie's first Chicago appearance, and his sensational work is creating a great deal
of comment. Next week will bring one of the finest novelty acts in vaudeville, direct from the big time circuits;
the Carson Trio, which showed a few weeks ago at the Ma-
jestic; a group of fine musicians, vocalists, and dancers,
that have been headliners all over the country and are
brought to the Stroll at enormous cost. Among the many
nations, the Russian dance is introduced, and many other
specialties never seen outside the higher grade vaudeville
theaters.

The fact that all acts used are being booked by Charles Van of the United Booking Offices, is a criterion of their class, and a line can be gained on the coming week's attractions by a glance at the photo-frames in front of the Dreamland Café at all times. The largest and finest cafes and cabaret rooms have adopted this form of entertainment, and they use mixed bills, many of the Race's performers playing them along with their regular vaudeville work. In this manner we will be able to see our own acts as well as the others as fast as they can be lined up for an engagement. Drop in at any time and see the "New Idea" in operation.

Source: *Chicago Defender*, February 2, 1918, 4.

According to Anderson, during the autumn of 1919, Joe Oliver split time between the Dreamland and its rival, the Royal Gardens. By the end of 1919, the Dreamland was struggling, necessitating the investment of its owner, Billy Bottoms, in another refurnishing and new acts. Bottoms replaced Oliver's band with Clarence Jone's Jolly Jazzing Jeopards, who presented a softer style than that of the New Orleans musicians. The Jazzy Jeopards only lasted at the Dreamland until April 1920, when Bottoms rehired Oliver. Renovations, both musical and architectural, continued for the rest of the year:[8]

Dreamland Café "Mecca" for Lovers of Amusement

The Dreamland Café, 3520 South State street, famous the country over for good order and up to date amusement, has recently added to its coterie of entertainers Miss Elnora Wilson, singer and danseuse, and Ollie Powell, a tenor singer of exceptional ability. Wm. Bottoms, the proprietor, has added an innovation that is entirely new—an elaborate oriental effect which gives the unique appellation of "Japland" to the Dreamland. This institution has justly acquired the reputation of being a place where the most delicate of taste and habits can go without fear of encountering boisterous conduct and fights such as have become so prevalent in other institutions of like nature.

The manifest good conduct upon the part of proprietor and patron makes it a desirable place for pleasure seekers to

---

[8]Anderson, "The Genesis of King Oliver's Creole Jazz Band," pp. 289-291.

attend. You are always surrounded with that element of safety which comes from a properly managed institution. The jazz orchestra is unsurpassed in its rendition of musical selections. In the effort to make the place habitable for the best element of pleasure seekers the management has spared neither pains nor money in consummating their program.

Source: *Chicago Defender*, February 14, 1920, 17.

The months-long remodeling of the Dreamland was completed in November 1920, and celebrated with a "Grand Opening." On the bandstand this night was King Oliver:

"Beauty Spot"

If Billy Bottoms should rename Dreamland and call it "The Beauty Spot," he would certainly be justified. In a recent issue we told all about how Bill was spending 15,000 simoleons — iron men — in remodeling and refurnishing, and those who have been fortunate enough to have gained admission to the place since the night of its reopening will surely agree with the writer, who has been everywhere, seen everything, and cogitated. It would be impossible to tell all about the different things the big sum expended has brought about; so many beautiful additions have been made and so many novelty ideas put into effect that it would take columns of newspaper measure to enumerate them. Possibly what will attract the most immediate attention is the new balcony which has been built entirely around the casino. It is of mahogany and is carpeted, furnished and lighted in exactly the same manner in which the main floor is, bringing the seating capacity up to over 500, making it the largest café on the south side. Another feature is the glass which has been installed in the center of the dance floor; under it is a light of 2,000 watts, and it takes more money to turn it on for a flash than it does to pay the entire electric light bill of the ordinary joy parlor; $3,000 is what was paid for the carpet which runs around the dance floor, and it looks like a shame for all those number 11s [men's shoe sizes] to be skidding all over it.

[Quoting Billy Bottoms] "It has been my ambition to give our people a place of amusement that will compare with

the best offered by the 'other' race. I have always maintained that they deserve it, and the people of Chicago are
justifying my ideas by a liberal patronage of Dreamland.
The fact that this latest renovating cost me a little over
$15,000 shows that I appreciate this splendid support. I
will always try to give the patrons the best entertainment
that money can secure, and they can at all times rest assured that Dreamland is one place that will demand a grade
of behavior by all which will make it a safe place to bring
wife, mother, sister, or daughter."

If there is one person in Chicago who deserves unreserved
support, it is Billy Bottoms. He has done more along the
line of furnishing a respectable place of amusement than
any one individual in the district. He deserves all the splendid success that he is having, and here's hoping that it continues.

Source: *Chicago Defender*, November 13, 1920, 4.

The Dreamland did indeed continue until 1928, featuring jazz lumi-
naries such as Cab Calloway, the Dodds brothers, Freddie Keppard, Doc
Cheatham, Ethel Waters, Alberta Hunter, and in 1925-26 a group led by
Lil Hardin and Louis Armstrong. But when Billy Bottoms relinquished
management duties in 1923, larger articles about the Dreamland in the
Defender ceased as well, again pointing to a close political and economic
relationship between Bottoms and Abbott:

Wickliffe's Band Still Jazz at Dreamland Café

Wickliffe's Ginger Band, fresh from a two-year's run in Milwaukee, the highest priced band now playing in the cafes
in the city of Chicago, is still the headliner at the Dreamland Café.... Jazz music can be had such as never before.
Wickliffe has always been a favorite here and the crowds
will continue to come to dance and to listen to his music.
On Sundays, starting at 7 o'clock, a popular concert pre-
cedes the regular entertainment.

Last Saturday, Armistice Day, 450 attended the breakfast
dance. The usual Thursday afternoon matinee is drawing
well. There will be a special matinee Thanksgiving afternoon. On Nov. 28 and 29, both afternoon and evening, Minor Haney of South American and J.H. (Bam) Simms will

play a billiard match.... On Nov. 23 the regular Thanksgiving afternoon matinee will be featured by the management acting as hosts to the members of the *Shuffle Along* company.[9]

Alberta Hunter is featuring "Don't Pan Me," "Downhearted Blues," and "A Woman Gets Tired of the Same Man All the Time." Ollie Powers, local lyric tenor, ably assisted by Miss Mae Alix, late of "Plantation Days," are nightly receiving their share of the applause.

The management announces that they are now prepared to take care of any clubs or parties wishing service in the food line. A capable chef, familiar with both Chinese and American dishes, has been secured and an appetizing bill of fare can be found on any table. For food, music, and entertainment, as well as courteous service, the Dreamland ranks first.

Source: *Chicago Defender*, November 18, 1922, 4.

New Entertainers and New Manager at Dreamland Café

Starting Monday night, Jan. 22, many new faces will be seen among the entertainers at the Dreamland Café, 3520 State Street, America's most beautiful place of entertainment. The most important change is that of Manger J. H. Corliss, old-time Chicagoan, [who] will assume that role and will attempt to give to the patrons the class of service obtained in the finest cafes in this country or abroad.

Ollie Power's Harmony Syncopators, an up-to-date aggregation of popular and capable musicians, headed by Glover Compton, king of the cabaret piano players; Clarence Lee, violinist extraordinary; Freddie Kapper [Freddie Keppard], the original jazz cornet player, and other musicians equally as popular. The musicians will be brought down on the main floor in place of playing in the balcony.

The list of entertainers will include Miss Alberta Hunter, blues singer of note; Ollie Powers, popular tenor; Mae Alix, Valada [Valaida] Snow, a newcomer, and Strappy Jones,

---

[9]The Broadway show by Noble Sissle and Eubie Blake, which had debuted the previous year, was currently playing nearby.

late of the Sunset. Last but not least is King Jones, the
celebrated announcer, who is with us once again. Tuesday
nights he will feature his Jazz Steppers. Monday night all
Chicagoans and their friends are invited to the opening
night of the new program. Will you join them? Remember
that this is the only cabaret in the city operated exclusively
by our Race. Don't forget the regular Thursday afternoon
matinee.

Source: *Chicago Defender*, January 20, 1923, 4.

The Cabarets and Corruption

Vice and corruption, including illegal liquor sales, gambling, and pros-
titution, were a part of The Stroll's cabaret scene. All club owners had
to negotiate these boundaries in order to operate. A "wide-open" policy
encouraged a particular kind of crowd and enabled the police and politicians to gain financially through kickbacks. But a too-lenient policy chased
away more affluent customers, occasionally attracted law enforcement,
and brought the wrath of the *Defender*.

In early 1920 a *Defender* columnist whose sobriquet was "Pink Tea, The
Dry Reporter" wrote a tongue-in-cheek series of articles about the Entertainer's Café, a venue that, as the name suggested, catered to musicians
and others who worked in the theater district. Bill "Bojangles" Robinson
was a frequent guest:

Flying Beer Bottles Disturb Shimmy-Shakers

(The Dry Reporter)

Talkin' 'bout throwing hand grenades, well, just to give
you a little idea of the art, ask anybody who happened to
be present at the Entertainer's Café, 209 East 35th street,
11 o'clock last Sunday night. If you couldn't duck, hike to
some secluded spot under a table, or locate the exit with a
60 miles-a-minute speed, pat yourself on the back for not
being there.

Everything was runnin' in good style until some waiter
rubbed the fur of Billy Robinson (Bojangles, we call 'im)
the wrong way. The music was in order; Izzy Shorr, the
proprietor, was happy; everybody shimmied until the critical moment. Critical, did we say; well, it grew fatal. Just

to disturb the harmony of things, the waiter assigned to look after the needs of Mr. Bojangles during his "high-lonesome" spied another party that looked to him a little bit more compensative; in fact, he had heard that they gave 10 cents more on the drink than "Bo" did.

He forthwith "railroaded" Mr. Bojangles & Co., and began to sell his services to the new arrivals. Presto! Change-fade out cabaret, in comes prize-fight:

Round 1—Bojangles sends straight left to waiter's jaw. Waiter sinks to floor, but comes back pop-eyed. Bojangles prepares for counter attack. Waiter seizes bottle, passes at Bojangles, but misses. Bojangles round.

Round 2—Spectators stampede place in attempt to effect exit. Fighting resumes. Bojangles confiscated all nearby bottles, glasses. Lays down barrage at waiter's head. Has plenty of room to act freely. Waiter "sells out," dashes for door and disappears. Bojangles round.

Round 3—Izzy, the proprietor, throws sponge in ring. Bojangles declared winner, but nobody there to hear the decision. Place cleared, coats missing, floor littered with broken beer bottles, and Izzy pleading with the "new champion" to be quiet and take his victory calmly. Curtain, please.

Source: *Chicago Defender*, January 24, 1920, 13.

Entertainer's "Private Stock" Raided by Revenue Officers

Although the Prohibition law went into effect on July 1, 1919, it required exactly seven months for Isadore Schorr, proprietor of the Entertainer's Café...to make certain that congress really meant business when it passed the law. 'Twas last Saturday night that Uncle Same decided to take a stroll into the above mentioned cabaret for the purpose of determining to what extent Mr. Schorr had been observing the latest addition to the Constitution of America, and to his surprise—but let Pink Tea, The Dry Reporter, tell it:

The clock had just struck 11, everyone was jazzin' to the strains of the "Kentucky Blues." As I sipped my cocktail, little did I think that I was soon to be forced to leave not only my glass but my overcoat as well. A couple of strange, innocent lookin' men drifted into the front door, but since all patrons of Entertainer's are innocent lookin' no one paid the least bit of attention to them. But soon these two gents were reinforced by about eight more—all innocent lookin'. One of these harmless lookin' gents cornered Mr. Izzy Schorr and held a private chat with him, during which time an expression of discomfort spread slowly over Izzy's face. Then came the command, "Everybody sit down!" The music stopped, the merrymakers ceased to jazz, and the search was on.

Empty, half-empty, and three-quarter-emptied flasks of old Kentucky's best were tossed under the tables by those who feared the wrath of an angry Uncle Sam. Silence reigned supreme as these men, who later proved to be internal revenue officers, wended their way among the tables, sniffing and smelling of the suspicious lookin' glasses sittin' around. Finally Izzy was coaxed into letting these gents from the department of justice have the key to his cellar. Then the fun began. In Mr. Schorr's cellarette it was discovered that old John Barleycorn, instead of being dead,was very much alive and in the best of health. Several gallons of the merry mucilage and firewater were removed amid tears and were taken down to the federal building along with the owner of the booze. As this official delegation left with their prisoners and loot the orchestra was heard to play, "They Got the Key to My Cellar."[10]

Source: *Chicago Defender*, February 14, 1920, 17.

Located on the *Defender*'s page 17, the previous two articles make for light reading. But a few months later, in July 1920, the newspaper took a much more serious stand on its front page:

Vice Runs Unchecked in 2nd Ward

Police Wink at Crime and Immorality in South Side Cabarets

---

[10]This could quite possibly be the song "Everybody Wants a Key to My Cellar," composed in 1919 by Ed Rose, Billy Baskette, and Lew Pollack and sung originally by Bert Williams. In the song, the protagonist has a secret stash of alchohol in his cellar, but made the mistake of telling his wife.

Whisky is Sold Openly

Vice conditions in certain parts of the Second Ward have at last attracted the attention of the police department, and certain cabarets are now closing at 1 o'clock. A careful observation of existing conditions justifies the assertion that the political leaders of the Second Ward are in no way responsible for the deplorable and immoral practices which have hitherto existed in the wee hours of the morning in some of these clubs and mad cabarets. It is strikingly strange that that they have just now attracted the attention of the police, but it's better late than never.

Shady Cabarets Named

Institutions like the Entertainers' Café, 35th and Indiana Avenue, where riots and near-riots are of frequent occurrence and where as late as Sunday morning a week ago three wagon loads of policemen were called from the Cottage Grove police station to quell a fight which is said to have nearly wrecked the place. Such an institution should not be closed at 1 o'clock, but should be closed permanently as a safeguard for the protection of young women and men of the community. Included in this list as being detrimental to the community are the Dreamland Café...the Pekin...the De Lux, and the Alverdor....

Liquor Sold Openly

It is difficult to understand how these all-night cabarets can run, selling whisky and other intoxicating drinks at will, without the heavy hand of the law falling upon them. It is, nevertheless true, however, that they are doing it with a boldness which defies all laws and semblance of decency and respectability.

Guarded by Power

The good people of the Second Ward cannot sit silently by and permit any authority, or reputed authority, to "farm out" the community to gamblers and disreputable cabaret proprietors. Who is this mighty power who is responsible for this? Upon "what meat doth he feed?" That he is able to turn the residential district of the Second Ward into a red light district remains a mystery.

Is Dumping Ground

No other section of the city, or group of people, would tolerate their community being used as a dumping ground for dissolute women and men of other races. Why should it be true of the Second Ward, our home? Why should this section of the city be made the locality of sport for white men and women of questionable character? Should this be the rendezvous for gunmen, murderers, and well-known members of the light-fingered brigade, as well as that type of men who are constitutionally opposed to work, and receive their succor from the ill-gotten gains of scarlet women?

Citizens Demand Action

We have in Cook County a state's attorney, elected by the people, whose sworn duty it is to conserve the interest of all the citizens, regardless of race or geographical location. We also have a chief of police, whose duty it is to enforce the law and ordinances. In addition thereto we have government authorities who are sworn to carry out the prohibition enactment, yet whisky and other drinks are still available in these cabarets and clubs, and no one acts. Who is responsible for the "immunity bath" these people seem to enjoy? Can cabarets run all night, gambling proceed unmolested, without someone giving the word? Answer, someone, and we want an answer by action.

Where Injury is Done

There is no justification of the police closing the Royal Gardens...at 1 o'clock [a.m.] and classing it as a cabaret, for the very good reason that this place has been carefully observed for several months and its conduct and management is above reproach. No strong drinks of any kind are permitted, nor is it frequented by women of questionable character. It is, in fact, the only high class amusement place where one might have no hesitancy in taking his family or friends. This institution is a credit to the community and a valuable asset to the community interest, in that during the past year over $7.000 has been raised through the good office of the proprietor, Virgil Williams, for worthy distribution among charitable organizations. Notorious dances, such as the "shimmie" and others of similar character, are strictly forbidden.

Source: *Chicago Defender*, July 10, 1920, 1.

The following week, again on page 1, the *Defender* pushed its battle against the clubs further. This article is even stronger than the first, emphasizing a "fight" with "no quarter." The article included a letter by Izadore Shore, whose Entertainer's Club had been singled out the week before. The writer also points a finger at the Pekin Café and the Dreamland, where supposedly illegal gambling was taking place:

Vice Lords Jeer at Police Rule

Dreamland, Pekin, Defy 1 O'Clock Closing Order Issued by Chief Garrity

Dive-Keepers Rush to Politicians for Aid

The fight launched by the *Chicago Defender* against gambling places and cabarets which go beyond the pale of decency will be kept up without stint or abatement until the conditions in the neighborhood complained of are improved. No quarter will be asked and none will be given. The morality for the community must be preserved at all hazards and those who are interested might as well understand that the *Defender* is not in the business of jollying gamblers and vice lords.

Politicians Warned

This is a fight to the finish at whatever cost, and no intimidation will be tolerated. Those who think that relief is forthcoming by appealing to politicians will find themselves sadly mistaken and the politician who has any regard for his future is warned to keep his hands off.

Paper Well-informed

The efforts of this paper to improve conditions in the Second ward were carefully and deliberately planned with a thorough knowledge of what is going on. Time and money have been spent in investigating conditions. Those who are willing that the community be demoralized and be made the home for the underworld element can array themselves on their side. The *Defender* is battling for those people who desire to protect their wives and daughters against the evil and sinister influences incidental to immoral community.

Race Issue Absent

There is no disposition on the part of the *Defender* in any way to interfere with the legal and legitimate business of anyone nor any desire to raise any race issue, either in business or otherwise, so long as the places are conducted in a respectable manner. Cabarets are not opposed as such, but are condemned when they become the rendezvous of a lawless element. Indecent and immoral dances must be eliminated if these places are to continue in operation. No "let-up" can be expected in this crusade until the proprietors put their houses in order....

Capt. Coughlin Notified

The attention of the commanding officers of the Third police precinct is again directed to the continual open gambling. The order to close the clubs has had but little effect. It appears that the gamblers have an understanding with someone who has been able to give the "word." Gambling on State Street and 35th Street car lines must be stopped. Professional gamblers are the cancers in any community.

They prey upon the working men and rob women and children of the support to which they are entitled out of the earning capacity of husbands and fathers.

Promises to be Good

That the onslaughts of the *Defender* are productive of results is proved by a communication received from Izidor Shore, proprietor of the Entertainers' Café, who says that he is willing to so conduct his place as to meet the approbation of law abiding citizens. This paper is willing to give him a chance. His letter is as follows:

Shore's Letter

"...I am willing to co-operate with the *Chicago Defender*, or any other newspapers, or any civic organizations, to improve conditions and to eliminate any objectionable conditions which may exist at the present time in my place of business. I will gladly entertain any suggestions from you as to the methods of improving any conditions which may prove objectionable.

"...I have in my employ about 100 of the Race members of the Second Ward, all who live and vote in the Second Ward. Ninety percent of these are married men with families and about 50 per cent of them are taxpayers in the Second Ward. The majority of these employees have been in my employ for some time past. They have been true and faithful and I certainly would not want to do anything that would prove detrimental to them, or that might throw them out of employment...."

Special Information

The tone of this letter indicates a change of heart and a willingness to pay some regard to the fitness of things. So much for Shore. The Dreamland , another conspicuous offender, and the Pekin have not indicated even a disposition to conduct [sic] respectable places. The Dreamland not only has a disorderly cabaret, but is said to conduct a flourishing crap game in the basement. This of course, may be important information to the commanding officers of the Third precinct police station, if so it is cheerfully given.

Source: *Chicago Defender*, July 17, 1920, 1.

The fates of the Pekin and the Dreamland illustrate the challenges faced by the cabaret owners. As we've seen, Billy Bottoms invested a large sum to refurbish the Dreamland for a "grand reopening" in November 1920. But the owners of the Pekin chose to maintain their policies. The Pekin closed permanently after this event:[11]

Deaths End Gun Battle in Pekin Café

Whiskey Ring Dispute Starts Reign of Terror in Café

Screaming women fled into the streets in hysterical terror to escape death when Hirsche Miller (white), ex-pugilist and west side politician, became involved in a gun battle with Detective Sergeants James (Pluck) Mulcahy and William (Spike) Hennessy, both white, in the Beaux Arts Club, an annex of the Pekin Café, 2700 State Street, Monday morning about 3 o'clock. When the smoke cleared away the officers were seriously wounded and later died in the hospital. Numerous theories as to the cause of the shooting have been investigated by the State's Attorney and Chief of Police Garrity, but none have been accepted as reliable. Attempts to connect the officers and Miller, along with the latter's partner "Nails" Morton, in an alleged whiskey ring which disregarded the split of money collected from South Side cabaret owners, have been made by special investigators from the State's Attorney's office.

Detectives Drunk

---

[11]The Pekin was opened in 1906 by Robert T. Motts, one of Chicago's first black entrepreneurs. It enjoyed a strong reputation in the late 1900s. After Motts' death in 1911, the reputation of the establishment declined. For more on the Pekin see Thomas Bauman, *The Pekin: The Rise and Fall of Chicago's First Black-Owned Theater* (Urbana: University of Illinois Press, 2014).

It was reported that Hennessy and Mulcahy entered the café under the influence of liquor, and were in close conversation with Miller and Morton before the shooting occurred. According to a statement from Mrs. Levenia "Salome" Baldwin...who was sitting near Morton when the detectives entered, Mulcahy received a signal from Miller, who held up two fingers [The article includes a photograph of Salome Baldwin]. Mulcahy paid scant attention to Miller and walked to the rear of the café where the bar is located. Miller followed. Mulcahy is said to have produced a $100 bill, which Robert S. Anderson, employee of the Pekin, asked permission to touch "just for good luck." Morton later joined in conversation with Mulcahy and after several words were passed the detective knocked Morton down.

Shooting Begins

When Morton was on the floor, Mulcahy attempted to kick him, and Miller drew a revolver and fired. Detective Hennessy rushed up and drew his gun, and the shooting became general. Chairs were overturned, mirrors broken, and the ceiling and walls were spattered with bullets. Morton and Miller made their escape through the rear of the place, and were apprehended several hours later. The report that the gun battle began over Detective Mulcahy's affection for "Salome" has been regarded as untrue, following a statement from the woman that she was not aware of the shooting until occupants of the place made a mad rush for the door. She declared she was in conversation with Dr. Gordon Jackson, who was seated with a party at the table next to her. Dr. Jackson was questioned by the police, but could give little information concerning the shooting.

Chief Investigating

Chief Garrity is investigating the case from the standpoint that the $100 produced by Mulcahy may lead to the fact that cafes where whiskey is permitted to be sold are paying protection money to officers. Hennessy and Mulcahy, it is said, were not on duty when the shooting occurred, having been relieved at 12 o'clock. Persons who were acquainted with the officers declared that they had frequently visited the Pekin, and that they were so well known by the management of the club that their appearance did not occasion the ringing of the "buzzer," which is a signal to "put the soft pedal" on the jazz music when the law is around.

Miller, who has confessed to slaying the two detectives, is thought to be the head of a booze ring. One of the stories which the State's Attorney is endeavoring to verify is to the effect that a South Side police lieutenant and three detective sergeants found a truckload of whiskey at a warehouse ready for shipment; that the lieutenant got $1000 to "forget the matter" and did not split. This transaction is thought to be connected with the shooting.

Pekin Manager Questioned

Wallace Tyler...manager of the Pekin, was placed under arrest Tuesday and questioned by Assistant State's Attorney Lowery. He denied having paid the police graft money, and said he couldn't account for the empty whiskey cases found in the basement of the building....

Is Well Patronized

The Pekin, which has been operating about five years under the title of the Beaux Arts Club, is not only patronized by characters from the old levee district, but white people from the most exclusive circles in the city. Movie actresses and stars from the downtown theaters are often seen there in the wee morning hours with white men high in the professional life here. Many of these people were present Monday morning when the detectives were slain, but have not been located by the police. Although operating when all other cafes were ordered to close at 1 o'clock and receiving crowds from other cabarets who are seeking to put a "finishing touch" on the night's gay time, the Peking [sic] management has, until the shooting, kept the place orderly. Chief Garrity has issued orders to close the club, pending a thorough investigation into the slaying.

History of Pekin

The old Pekin Theater, in which the club is housed, was
built by the late Robert Mott and was known as one of
the first theaters in America to be owned by a member
of our Race. Such celebrities as Prince Henry of Prussia,
Mrs. Potter Palmer and the Daughters of the Revolution
were entertained there.[12] A visit to Chicago was considered incomplete by prominent white people throughout
the county unless the Pekin was included in the itinerary.

Source: *Chicago Defender*, August 28, 1920, 1.

The Chicago Blues Women: Ada Brown and Al-berta Hunter

There was a strong connection between the dawn of the "race record"
industry and the Great Migration. African Americans who had recently
moved to northern cities like Chicago to take factory jobs now had buying
power, a phenomenon that the recording industry realized with the success
of Mamie Smith's early sides in 1920. By 1923 the recording of blues and
jazz musicians was well underway, and their products could be found in
music stores throughout Chicago. The *Defender* explained the history of
"race records" to its readership in late 1923:[13]

Fame and Fortune

"Blues" on Discs Making Race Composers Rich

Colored singing and playing artists are riding to fame and
fortune with the current popular demand for "blues" disc
recordings and because of the recognized fact that only a
Negro can do justice to the native indigo ditties such artists
are in great demand, says a recent issue of *Variety*.

---

[12]Mrs. Potter Palmer was Bertha Palmer, a philanthropist and socialite married to Potter
Palmer, a Chicago store owner and real estate developer.

[13]For more on the recording industry and "race records," see Paul Oliver, *Songsters and
Saints: Vocal Traditions on Race Records* (NY: Cambridge University Press, 1984).

Mamie Smith is generally credited with having started this demand on the Okeh records. Not only do these discs enjoy wide sales among the Colored Race, but have caught on with the Caucasians. As a result, practically every record making firm from the Victor down has augmented its catalogue with special "blues" recordings by Colored artists.

Victor created a special catalog with such artists as Moss and Frye, Lena Wilson, Eubie Blake, and [the] Shuffle Along Orchestra, Edna Hicks, Lizzie Miles, Rosa Henderson, Arthur Gibbs and his Colored Jazzers.

Columbia was among the first to follow the Okeh's precedent by featuring Edna Wilson, Johnny Dunn's Jazz Band, and Bessie Smith among others. The Vocalion records, marked by the conservative Aeolian Co., has also started a special Colored catalog with Ethel Waters, Viola McCoy, Fletcher Anderson [Henderson?] and his orchestra and Lena Wilson, among the artists.

Okeh, in addition to Miss Smith, has a galaxy of Colored performers in Sarah Martin, Clarence Williams, Eva Taylor (Mrs. Clarence Williams), Thomas Morris and jazz band, Alice Carter, Sheldon Brooks, et. al.

The minor companies also utilize these and other Colored artist's services now more than ever, with the Brunswick practically the only important company still passing up this field of endeavor.

As a result of this "blues" boom and demand, various Colored publishers are prospering. Perry Bradford and the Clarence Williams Music Co. are among the representative Negro music men cleaning up from mechanical royalties with the sheet music angle almost negligible and practically incidental. No attention to professional plugging is made, these publishers concentrating on the disk artists. Both have some of the Colored songstresses under contract and it is only natural that they record certain favored numbers.

The white publishers are getting on to this and also entering many, many "blues" in the market, one already having cashed in on the idea because of getting the jump on the proposition several months in advance with a strong "blues" catalog.

There are a few good white exponents of "blues" and novelty numbers like Sophie Tucker and Miss Patricola and
they figure importantly. Miss Patricola has been signed
by Vocalion after doing some exclusive work for Victor.[14]

Source: *Chicago Defender*, October 6, 1923, 8.

Alberta Hunter and Ada Brown were two of the most prominent of
the many female singers and musicians who worked in Chicago in the
1920s. The breakthrough for Hunter's career was her five-year stint at the
Dreamland , beginning in 1917. There she performed with a variety of
Chicago jazz musicians, including Joe Oliver. She recorded prolifically in
the 1920s, and co-wrote, with Lovie Austin, "Downhearted Blues," one of
Bessie Smith's most famous songs. Ada Brown was originally from Kansas
City, Kansas. She sang on three tracks, "Evil Blues," "Ill-Natured Blues,"
and "Break O'Day Blues," for the Bennie Moten Orchestra's first recording
session in 1923. She soon left for Chicago, where she gained further fame
singing for the theater. She was also a founding member of the Negro
Actors Guild of America in 1936.[15]

Alberta Hunter Goes Over the Top at Dreamland

Miss Alberta Hunter—or rather our Alberta Hunter—is just
cleaning up at the Dreamland Café...this week with her
rendition of "One Man Nan," and "Daddy, Your Mamma's
So Lonesome for You." Alberta has got them all beat when
it comes to singing ragtime. The owners of the Dreamland
say she is a world beater.

Visiting newspaper men and delegates to the National Negro League were in attendance Thursday night. The regular Thursday matinee is still drawing crowds.

Miss Lethia Hill in her dances still holds her own, and is
ably assisted by Margaret Ricks and Clara Lewis. Miss Ollie
Rickman, who has completely recovered from her recent

---

[14]Isabella Patricola (1886-1965), billed as "Miss Patricola," was a contralto vaudeville
singer who also recorded ragtime and novelty songs. For more on her see Frank Cullen,
Vaudeville Old and New: An Encyclopedia of Variety Performers in America Vol. 1 (NY: Routledge, 2004): 869.

[15]For more on Alberta Hunter, see Daphne Duval Harrison, *Black Pearls: Blues Queens of
the 1920s* (New Brunswick, NJ: Rutgers University Press, 1988). For more on Ada Brown see
Marc Rice, "Break O'Day Blues: The 1923 Recordings of the Bennie Moten Orchestra," *The
Musical Quarterly* (Summer, 2002): 282-306.

illness, gives us a touch of the classical side of life which finds many followers. Prof. Snow Fisher from Atlantic City has given up all intentions of returning home, as the many friends he has made here insist that he remain....

The Dreamland Orchestra, the best in the city, is causing dancers to appeal for encore after encore. The lighting effect and the beauty of the café, the artistic layout and the careful and polite service make it one of the best places to go for any evening or Thursday afternoon entertainment.

Source: *Chicago Defender*, January 28, 1922, 4.

Ada Brown

The Orpheum circuit star, Ada Brown is spending the holidays at home with her family. She remembered the Scribe [the author of this article] with a large box of Perfectos [cigars] that will keep him busy puffing until far beyond the holidays. Many thanks to this delineator of song and dance.

Ada Brown's rise in the show world has been spectacular. Coming to Chicago four years ago, she secured an opening at the Plantation Café, and under the guidance of the well-known producer Lawrence Deas, she rapidly got into form and registered herself an overnight success.

Hundreds of folks of the Nordic race became to know her at this place, booking agents gathered nightly to hear Ada sing, the offers for her services came thick and fast, and finally Maurice Greenwald, the man who owned and produced Plantation Days, the famous musical comedy production, gave her a contract. Today she is one of the biggest starts on the Orpheum circuit and has a route lined up that will carry her far into 1928. Harry Swannagan is her accompanist and in the act does a piano specialty that clicks with the high-brow Orpheum audiences. Ada Brown wishes all her friends, who have contributed to her unusual success, a Merry Christmas and a Happy New Year.

Source: *Chicago Defender*, December 24, 1927, 6.

Jazz Outside of the Cabarets

The Bud Billiken Parade and Picnic were the creation of *Defender* founder Robert S. Abbott. Bud Billiken was a comic strip character created by Abbott to develop a youth section for the newspaper. The parade and picnic sponsored by the*Defender* began in 1929. The oldest and largest African American parade in the United States, it is still held on the second Saturday in August:

Five Bands

5 Red Hot Orchestras Will Play at Bud Billiken's Picnic

Five of Chicago's greatest jazz bands are going to the South Side Saturday, Aug. 13, and play red-hot, low-down jazzy tunes for ol' Bud Billiken and his gang at the big Washington park jubilee.

What a program it's going to be, with Chicago's five jazz kings blaring, creening, and burning up the big band stand in Washington Park with red hot rhythm, the kind that will make you want to dance.

Sensational stars of the radio and records will be out to do their bit for the big Billiken jamboree.

The program of jazz to be dished out by the bands will be the finest you've ever heard, so come on folks' let's get busy.

Johnny Long and his Roaming Troubadours are the latest addition to the long string of jazz bands we have secured for the picnic. A Chicago boy, Johnny has one of the finest bands in the Middle West. His playing of "Between the Devil and the Deep Blue Sea" will set your heart afire.

Johnny came to the Windy City from Indianapolis and you know those Hoosiers have a style of jazz that's different.

Name Musicians

Johnny and his 12-piece band will take the stand during the late afternoon and will play while the little kiddies eat their ice cream....

Of course you'll be entertained at intervals during the day with jazz tunes from Bud Billiken's Original Tin Can band. Four boys who make music from a washboard, a box, tin cans, tub, and ukulele. You'll have to be there to enjoy their special style of music.

Holding the spotlight during the day will be the music from Earl Robert's Syncopators and Jack Ellis and his Wild Cats. Roberts, as you know, has a distinct style of jazz that has set all Chicago to talking. He played all the dances of the various social clubs last year and is a favorite among the members of the younger set.

Jack Ellis' Wild Cats

Jack Ellis will come to the Billiken picnic direct from the beautiful Villa de Luxe roadhouse where he is heard nightly in a program of jazz. Jack's Wild Cats will tear old man jazz into parts as they play the feature, that famous "Tiger Rag."

Mr. Ellis is a great lover of children and explained that he will be on hand all day during the outing. He is anxious to do his bit to make the picnic a success....

Dolly Hutchinson

Despite the fact that Dolly Hutchinson's 12 Spirits of Rhythm are to play out of town Saturday, Aug. 13, they will remain long enough to play some hi-low down melodies for Bud Billiken and his gang.

Dolly, as you perhaps know, is one of the greatest woman cornetists in the country and you'll surely miss a treat if you fail to hear her and the 12 boys in a program of red hot jazz. We are truly grateful to Dolly for her contribution.

Now, folk's let's get together and be ready to shake our feet at Bud Billiken's big picnic, 'cause we're planning a stomping down good program.

Source: *Chicago Defender*, August 13, 1932, 16.

The final two examples in this chapter point to the pressures that Chicago's black jazz musicians faced in the late 1920s. The first discusses a vote by the city's white musician's union, the Chicago Federation of Musicians, Local 10. The article touches upon the presence of jazz music to accompany movies in the silent era. But the tone of the essay is bitter, as the writer states firmly that jazz was created by African Americans, and that they are losing their hold on it to white competitors:

Vote to Continue Jazz Music in Movie Houses

The jazz that was created and spread throughout this country and the world by Race musicians is in this country to stay. The latest indication of this was given Monday when the Chicago Federation of Musicians, composed of 6000 members, voted to continue to play jazz music in the theaters at the request of hundreds of motion picture patrons.

Our musicians, who started this vogue in American music, have become satisfied with their creation and are sitting idly by and allowing white musicians to capitalize on their gift to the world. Many of these musicians who started the jazz age of music are without work, having been forced out by white musicians who are daily getting better in rendering this class of music. Musicians must not permit themselves to reach a point of satisfaction, but must continue to improve on the music they gave this country and the world.

Source: *Chicago Defender*, October 15, 1927, 2.

The final article reflects the state of the jazz business during the Depression not only in Chicago but in the rest of the country as well. By 1932 Chicago's cabaret scene was gone, and those musicians who could find work had to travel constantly to make a living. The days of a musician belonging to one particular city were over; the days of a jazz style being identified with a city were dwindling fast as well:

Bands Use Radio for Fame, Tour for Cash

Big Shots all Prefer Travel for Money

By Hilda See

Now and then you run into a red hot jazz orchestra con-
tenting itself with playing in one spot, theater or café, but
generally the fellows with the sellers prefer to be on the
road. "The real money is found in travel," one of the leaders of the orchestral world told this writer only a few days
ago.

Truly, the man who would name the outstanding orchestras among our group is a superman, but even the
most critical of critics will admit that   Duke Ellington,
Fletcher Henderson, Noble Sissle, McKinney's Cotton Pickers, Hardy Brothers, Jimmie Smith, Cab Calloway, Bennie
Moten, Louis Armstrong, and a few others hard to recall
just now, lead the field in money making at least.

All Travel

Now, gentlemen, try if you can to recall when either of
this group of top-notchers played an engagement at one
place or theater for more than a week's duration or two
weeks at the most, and you have one on us. Ellington's last
engagement of length was at the Cotton Club, New York,
as was Cab Calloway's. Fletcher Henderson also played a
stretch at one of New York's famous cafes, but that was
some time ago, and even then King Henderson spent early
evenings playing around New York at the various theaters.
Sissle is playing a hotel engagement, but that is about the
biggest thing New York has to offer, which makes it an
exception.

The same holds good in Chicago, where Walter Barnes,
Earl Hines, Eddie South, Jimmie Noone, Ralph Cooper,
Harley Parham, and a few others are bidding for national
recognition. They are all playing here now, but Ed Fox
[manager and owner of the Grand Terrace Cafe] is already
trying to get a spot for Hines that will keep him on the
road for a stretch. Hines, having a radio outlet, is perhaps the best known orchestra in these parts where the
outside world is considered, but Fox knows the Grand Terrace must send Earl on the road for that recognition and
money that Duke Ellington, the Cotton Pickers, Calloway,
and others are already pulling down.

The most talked of orchestra just now is Tiny Parham's Granada café bunch, which occupies a spot on radio station WBBM's "Around the Town" program. Either Parham or Hines stand a good chance of gaining fame on the road when the already arranged time comes for their departure. Yes, that pot of gold can be reached only through travel, and that is what two or three of our best bands are about to learn. Walter Barnes leaves early next month for a tour that should produce a part of that "pot of gold" he is seeking.

Source: *Chicago Defender*, February 6, 1932, 5.

Chapter 8:
The Writings of Dave Peyton in the *Defender*

The final chapter of the book presents selected writings from Dave Peyton (1885-1955), whose column, "The Musical Bunch," appeared in the *Chicago Defender* from September 1925 until September 1929. Peyton began his career in Chicago in 1908, playing in a trio with Wilbur Sweatman. Peyton was a pianist, songwriter, ("I Ain't Got Nobody," was among his most famous tunes), arranger, and the leader of several vaudeville orchestras. In the 1920s he was one of the city's best-known African American orchestra leaders. He had deep connections within Chicago's musical scene, and his essays in the *Defender* are the most detailed contemporary account of happenings on The Stroll. He is a primary source for any researcher of Chicago jazz.

But Peyton was quite opinionated, as befitting a newspaper columnist and a bandleader in a hyper- competitive field. His writings also illustrate the struggles between long-established musicians and the new arrivals from the South. His beliefs encapsulate the dynamic tension between European-influenced composition and technical performance, which was his background, and the emphasis on improvisation and unorthodox playing techniques, which characterized the new jazz music, and the New Orleans musicians in particular. In essay after essay, he extolled the virtues of European-influenced composition and formal musical training and admonished those musicians who he felt did not meet his exacting standards.

It is easy with just a brief overview of his writings to think of Peyton as an older, more conservative musician who felt threatened by newer styles of music which operated counter to the traditions he valued. But there is much to be gained from a close reading of his work. In his argu-

215

ments for proper training, correct technique, and the value of composition, Peyton's work illustrates a conflict between 19th and early 20th century African American musicians and composers—between those who strove to make music in the European tradition for an audience which felt that upward mobility meant the emulation of the dominant white class, and those younger black musicians and their audiences, who either preferred the new, exuberant dance rhythms, or felt that more Afro-centric art forms should take their place alongside those of Euro- Americans.

In reading Peyton's words, we gain some insight into important questions regarding Chicago's jazz history. How did the northern musicians feel about the newly arrived New Orleans players? How did African American musicians regard their own music history? How was black musical employment organized? When and how did black musicians begin to assert their demands for equality among the players in the white dominant class? What was the experience of a black musician who did not play jazz? And who were the important musicians and bandleaders who did not make it into the modern jazz canon? Peyton's writings are the work of just one opinionated person, albeit a person with considerable experience regarding the city's music scene. To the modern reader, who now understands the genius and importance of the New Orleans musicians, Peyton can seem overly conservative and out-of-touch with the changing trends around him. But his writings do provide some of the best-documented evidence of how jazz shaped musical life and opinion on the South Side during the 1920s.

Peyton and African American Music History

The first essays are further examples of how African Americans of the period saw their own history. Peyton begins immediately by reclaiming for blacks the slave songs that were appropriated by whites for their own commercial purposes. He suggests that the whites valued the songs' "weird melodies," but ultimately missed the connection between the songs and the slave experience, which resulted in melodies that were "poetic, quaint, and very plaintive, and are often full of soul-stirring dramatic power, with marked contrasts of fear and bliss."

Slave Songs

In the early part of 1867 several white writers, bent on commercializing our spiritual music, edited and published many of our original tunes. These people went among

our people in the guise of missionaries, stole their tunes and with their own imaginations augmented them and presented them in book form to the public. They did the best they could with the weird melodies but they missed the connecting link between native African music and that of the American slave music. The earlier songs seem to have preserved a kind of individuality, for while there were relations between the various plantations, slaves being sold from one to the other, their melodies seem to have been little affected by this bartering of human souls, many of them retaining their distinct features.

Sorrow Songs

The "sorrow songs" of the slaves are the oldest of the kind to survive. They are endowed with a strain of suggestive sadness and other moods and it takes no great mental acuteness to discover the yearning for relief from their surroundings, as well as the heart throbs when ties of home and family, no matter how simple nor how rude these may have been, were ruthlessly severed. Even the reading of the lyrics of these songs, mostly devoid of poetical treatment, conveys to the mind a pathos which, regardless of the source from which they emanated, makes its appeal to humanity at large.

In many of the "sorrow songs" there may easily be detected the doctrine of the fatalist giving place to the yearning after of things spiritual and the hope and faith of life to come. At moments, even in the most despairing of the "sorrow songs," there floats out a triumphant note, as if the veil of darkness suddenly had been rent and some fair world beyond had revealed itself to view. One of these inspirational characteristics is the repeating of lines in the song over and over again, especially in the refrains, which as a rule are short.

Spirituals

The present-day spirituals have evolutionized themselves from the slave songs and sorrow songs. They have been polished, but maintain their characteristic moods, which were created under intense excitement in a religious atmosphere; death, the Resurrection, and Satan being their favorite themes. Many of the early themes were extemporaneous outbursts of emotion while laboring under excitement, usually of a religious nature. Most of the spirituals were sung sitting down, but there were "running spirituals," shout songs, which were accompanied by all sorts of fantastic motions. These songs were emotionally enacted by those who had professed religion and had seen the Christ. These emotional spirituals served as aids to the mourners who occupied what they called the mourner's bench, and to this very day the practice prevails in many of the Baptist churches. Both the words and music of spiritual hymns are poetic, quaint, and very plaintive, and are often full of soul-stirring dramatic power, with marked contrasts of fear and bliss.

Source: *Chicago Defender*, November 17, 1928, 6.

This next essay reveals some of Peyton's musical prejudices. In his opinion, the first black orchestras "knew nothing of theory," and thus were "fake players." But "time brought development," and the first "legitimate orchestra" in the early 1870s. Ultimately he sees a kind of musical evolution, where musicians become more highly trained and skilled, and "are [currently] standing in rank with any in the world."

The First Race Orchestras

Directly after the Civil War there were many Race orchestras which knew nothing of theory. They could play the different instruments, but they knew not why and for what reason certain things were executed by themselves.

Most of them were fake players, not many of them could read music, and where one could read music he was hailed as a master.

Time brought development and in the early 1870s we had real musicians playing all of the instruments and capably reading music.

The first legitimate orchestra went to England with the original Georgia Minstrels in 1877. This aggregation produced such well known musicians as Bill Berry, George Freeman, and Henderson Smith.

During this period, all Race organizations were used on the big boats plying the Mississippi River. They were hired as porters and barbers, and during the evenings were used to entertain the passengers.

The real crack Race orchestra was formed in Chicago in 1882 by Billy Henderson, a violinist of unlimited talents. This orchestra played for the rich elite of Chicago. There were 10 men in Henderson's orchestra, all first class musicians. Occasionally, white men were used to assist them when a larger bunch was required.

Billy Henderson and his orchestra reigned supreme in the Middle West for many years. The famous Johnny Hand was a pal of Henderson and would often put their orchestras together at big affairs at such places as the First Regiment armory, at 16th St. and Michigan Blvd. This orchestra had the same kind of reputation that Paul Whiteman and his orchestra have today.

Coming on down the line, we hear of Henderson Smith and his orchestra, a well-trained group of players that were great favorites over the white orchestras in the Middle West.

Dink and Syl, Coperidge brothers of St. Louis, MO., made [trained] fine musicians and some of them are living today, standing high in the music profession.

Jim Hill of Nashville, TN had an orchestra made up of mandolins, guitars, violins, brass, and wood wind. They were employed at the famous Maxwell House in Nashville, playing for the Blooded Horse Association.

Our great statesman, Frederick Douglass, was a recognized violinist before the war. He used to play "call dances" by himself on the fiddle. He was such a master of the instrument that he didn't need any other assistance. He could play chords and carry the theme at the same time.

Today Race orchestras—and I mean Our Race orchestras— are standing in rank with any in the world. We have orchestras that can play anything from grand opera to jazz. Our musicians, most of them, have been taught by our own teachers. What is the matter with these orchestras,

Fletcher Henderson's, Leroy Smith's, Erskine Tate's, Garland Anderson's, and many others too numerous to mention? They rank today with any, and we should feel proud of the wonderful development of the Race in the world of music.

Source: *Chicago Defender*, May 29, 1926, 6.

Peyton and the Orchestra

In the early 20th century there were several types of ensembles that carried the designation of "orchestra." There was, of course, the purely symphonic orchestra which performed the European classics in large halls. But the ensembles that accompanied movies, dancing, and cabaret activities were called orchestras as well, and in fact, the repertories of each type featured some classical music to varying degrees. Thus, for virtually any professional ensemble, there was a spectrum between the "sweet" and the "hot," or music with lavish arrangements and music that was more heavily influenced by jazz timbres, rhythms, and improvisation.[1]

This essay provides a glimpse into the world of the theater orchestra and reveals again Peyton's prejudices against musicians who are not trained or do not perform to his standards. The first paragraphs discuss the challenges that the theater orchestras faced: for vaudeville venues, there were two completely different shows per week, and the musicians had to learn the shows with little rehearsal. The orchestras in moving picture theaters had more rehearsal time, but the leader had to match the music and even the instrumentation with the emotion of the film. In the final two paragraphs, Peyton acknowledges that some of the cabaret musicians are "first class" because they play "high-class dance music," but he is frustrated because "gutbucket" orchestras, which do not meet his standards of musicianship, are more popular:

Types of Orchestras

In the great big orchestra field are four classes—the picture house orchestra, the cabaret orchestra, the dance hall orchestra, and the dignified symphony orchestra. In the wide field of demand each of these orchestras get its share

---

[1] For more on the African American orchestras of Chicago in the 1920s, see Thomas J. Hennessey, *From Jazz to Swing: African-American Jazz Musicians and Their Music, 1890-1935* (Detroit: Wayne State University Press, 1994): 67-71.

of business, and if they are distinctive in their line they get the preference.

In my article this week I will try to give my readers a brief outline of how one class of orchestras compares with the other classes. In certain fields expert musicianship is required; in some fields the mediocre musician can probably fit the bill.

The Vaudeville Orchestra

The orchestra giving service in the vaudeville theater must be composed of first class musicians of the orchestra [if it] desires a reputation and a standing with the best orchestras to that line. Their task is harder; they must possess a rare amount of versatility; they must be quick to think, and, above all, must have the average intelligence.

It makes no difference whether the combination be large or small, the same tricks must be employed to fill the requirements. When the combination is small the men that compose it only work harder to get results. In America there are many vaudeville houses with the small orchestras of three, four, five, and six players, but on the larger circuits you will find the larger combinations.

The orchestra in the vaudeville houses never gets the opportunity to take the show music home and practice it. It comes to them on Monday or whatever the house opening day is, and they have one rehearsal of an hour or so and have to play for the matinee performance. If the music is not played the orchestra gets the scorn of the performers and the bawling out from the house manager.

Best Musicians Required

To handle the vaudeville orchestra the very best musicians should be employed. The so-called "ham" is out of his class in this line. You don't know when you will be called upon to play a grand opera score, as anything goes in a vaudeville house. I remember a few years ago when I was the leader in a vaudeville house playing big time acts of both races. An act came in by the name of Von Cello, a German musician of no mean ability. He played the entire overture of William Tell on the 'cello in presto tempo. The orchestra was wringing wet when the overture was finished, but they played it, and after it was over I was proud of my orchestra. What would have been the result if the orchestra had been made up of mediocre musicians? All of them were well-qualified in technique to accompany this master 'cellist.

The System

Ten or 15 years ago most all the variety houses changed their bills weekly, but competition caused them gradually to change the system by giving the patrons two or three changes a week, until today nearly all of the family houses throughout the country have adopted the split week policy, which requires the orchestra to rehearse for each change of show. Sometimes the actors are late arriving for rehearsal, which works a handicap on the orchestra having to play the act by requiring the orchestra to play without rehearsal, which is also an imposition. The listening public does not know and does not care who is to blame when the clash comes between actors and orchestra, due to the fact that neither had time to rehearse and understand each other.

The impression is made that the orchestra is bad, which is very unfair to the players, so you see the more capable the players are, less will be the troubles encountered in the vaudeville house. The orchestra in the vaudeville house has the hardest job and should receive great credit and praise. They deserve it if they are making good and are fully qualified.

The Picture House Orchestra

The orchestra in the picture house with its extensive library has the advantage over the vaudeville orchestra. They have plenty of opportunity to rehearse and prepare their programs. Nothing comes upon them without their having a chance to rehearse it before performances. They even have the opportunity to take the parts home to carefully study them, giving the mediocre player time to get the piece under his fingers. In most of our Race picture houses, mostly controlled by white capital, the Race orchestras discolor the atmosphere that should prevail in the picture house by not characterizing the photoplay, although having all the above mentioned advantages.

During a death scene flashed on the screen you are likely to hear the orchestra jazzing away on "Clap Hands, Here Comes Charlie." I blame the leader for this carelessness. He should watch his picture more closely and make his settings to harmonize.

Another bad feature in the picture house orchestra is the improper lineup of the instrumentation. The big brass tuba, banjo, and saxophones have no business in the legitimate picture orchestra during the showing of a dramatic screen play. The regular legitimate orchestral lineup should be employed, and the leaders should visit the larger Loop and outlying houses, see the system, and employ it in their theaters.

During orchestral specialties these instruments are all right for the jazz band expression, but only then. There is entirely too much "hokum" played in our Race picture houses. It only appeals to a certain riff-raff element who loudly clap hands when the orchestra stops, misleading the leader to believe that his efforts are winning the approval of the entire audience. It is only driving away the lovers of the photoplay drama to the large legitimate Loop houses, where the screen drama is characterized with appropriate music.

Polite syncopation, during a comedy or news reel picture dealing in the popular syncopated melodies is delightful to hear, but the awful, low-down, so-call blues should be eliminated entirely from the pit. On the stage they are all right when done by a feature jazz band.

The Cabaret Orchestra

Squeaks, squawks, moans, groans, and flutters are the standout features that make the cabaret orchestra popular. If these things are not in evidence the band does not hit with the crowd. In the cabaret orchestra the "ham" musician finds a comfortable birth. He doesn't have to stick to the score; a mistake can be counted as a "trick figure" and will be applauded by the crowd, and you can hear different ones saying all around you, "Ain't that boy hot?"

There are many legitimate, first class orchestras in these places that are made up of first class musicians, but as a rule most of them are unpopular because of the high class of dance music that the orchestras put out. The crowds seem to go where the "noise" is and I guess, after all, it is what the crowd says that counts. The "gut bucket orchestra" today is what the people want and the leader who is not versatile enough to give the crowd this kind of an orchestra will have to seek another musical field in the legitimate environment. The hip liquor toter wants sensational noise. They have no consciousness of what real music is, and if you don't give it to them they won't patronize your place, so that's that. Let the box office ring.

Source: *Chicago Defender*, September 3, 1927, 6.

In this later essay, one of his last, Peyton has come to terms with the popularity of jazz, but with a caveat. He emphasizes that the best orchestras that incorporate jazz features have the best, "schooled" musicians. For him, the best instrumental combination includes three saxophones, a violin, and both bass and tuba. Presumably, having the lowest brass and string instruments would allow for greater orchestral versatility. He also states that the modern dance arrangement is "ultra-symphonic," and that musicians need to practice on a regular basis:

The Modern Jazz Orchestras

The craze orchestra unit today is the modern jazz orchestra. Not only in this country, but in every civilized part of the world, has the jazz orchestra forged a place of distinctive recognition. In the best known jazz orchestras are to be found some of the finest timber musically. The schooled musicians, endowed with all the requirements of real musicianship, have harbored themselves in the jazz orchestra. One must be A-1 on his instrument to get in the first-class units today. The modern jazz orchestra offers no place for the faker or the mediocre musician.

Instrumentation

The proper instrumentation of the modern jazz orchestra, in order to get the best results, should be violin, bass, banjo, three saxophones, two cornets, tuba, trombone, drums, and piano. This 11-piece combination will enable the leader to most capably handle the modern jazz symphonic orchestra arrangement.

Of course it is much better if a leader can get a larger combination of players, but this roster is sufficient to handle the arrangement if every player is capable of carrying his part. Each player should have a slight knowledge of harmony and should by all means know the capabilities of his instrument, which gives them flexibility in playing. Creative figurations will come to them more easily. In the modern jazz orchestra you will find individuality. Most all of them have one feature man and in most cases it is a cornetist or saxophonist. These feature players generally take liberties in improvisation when it comes to their special stunt or on a hot chorus where the rest of the instrumentation is silent, except the accompanying instruments.

The Arrangement

The arrangement today for the dance orchestra is ultra-symphonic in construction. You encounter difficult figurations, which require astute technic to handle and in some forms of figurations one can see the gleam of operatic treatment. You do not get the easy orchestral scores of long ago, where the figurations were just "fillings" and all played along in the same mood and rhythm. Today we encounter the jazz cadence, the jazz break, the jazz obbligato, and all are developed in solo and sectional form. Then we encounter the heavy-dramatic introductions and codas, which require exceptional musicianship to handle. Players should take their parts home and work them out when they become difficult, and not hold back the ensemble rehearsal. It is no disgrace to be stuck with a little hard work, and practice on any particular spot on the part that is difficult will remedy the situation. But, practice is the key to a musician's success. Even after you have attained the heights in the profession you must practice hard each day to keep fit. The great musicians today, who are in the limelight, put in many hours each day in rehearsal. They lay their stress on finger gymnastics in order to have plenty of flexibility in manipulating with speed and accuracy.

Make up your minds to do this daily. It may come hard and monotonous in the beginning, but after a short while you will see the improvement in yourself, which will encourage you; then daily practice will become a part of your routine work and you will like it. New styles in arrangement are coming out every month from the aggressive music arrangers who are trying to get in front. Many tricks are inserted in the arrangement, although some are not theoretical, but with the proper acquirements in technique one can successfully handle the scores.

Source: *Chicago Defender*, May 18, 1929, 6.

Peyton's Views on Jazz

Peyton held very strong views regarding the new music that had taken hold on the South Side. He was not a "hot" player himself, and he demanded from his orchestras the ability to read music quickly, to execute complex scores, and to play with proper technique. But he did recognize the legitimacy of jazz history, and the achievements of its best players. Here he admonishes his readers, especially black musicians, to take the music back from their white competitors:

The Birth of Jazz

Thousands and thousands of music lovers have heard different stories about the origin of jazz music. Many writers have given their ideas about it, and all claim their stories are authoritative. Some have claimed that jazz had its beginning 1,000 years ago. Maybe so, but I am going to give my readers my idea about the birth of jazz music, as I see it after careful study of the situation.

As usual, the white man has taken credit for the birth of jazz and its development. He has never considered the rights of our own Race writers. He has selfishly taken the credit for everything in music. Nevertheless, that doesn't make it true...

The jazz music that the world is crazy about today had its birth in America and its originators were Race musicians...

I want to impress upon the reader's mind that to our own group belongs the credit for the birth of jazz, and we can justly claim it; it is indisputable. And we are also responsible for a great share of its development. How many times have I seen white musicians coming around where the Race orchestras were playing, trying to catch on, learn something, get the tricks, and our dumbest musicians giving it away to them. Today the white brother has it, because we gave it to him, and he is beating us commercializing it. Get wise, bunch, and hold your stuff in the future. There are bound to be new creations from our group in music, because we are naturally musical.

Source: *Chicago Defender*, February 4, 1927, 6.

Jazz musicians and orchestras competed with Peyton's own ensemble, and younger people seemed to be more attracted to them. He also had little tolerance for musicians who did not play to his standards. He must have been particularly frustrated when he wrote this essay, for it is one of his more caustic regarding jazz, or at least how he saw jazz on this particular day:

What Jazz Has Done

This writer has carefully studied the effects jazz music has had on the individual player and has concluded that it has done them no good from many angles. It is true that many musicians have made big money playing jazz, but from an artistic viewpoint they have done themselves no good.

Many [jazz] musicians have studied their music properly and have mastered technique. They have executed with rapidity, able to conquer the most difficult passages. They embarked upon the modern jazz playing, which must be played with all sorts of incorrect fingerings, thereby losing the methodical way of execution. Today many of the players who have suffered under this circumstance can hardly play standard music any more. It is pitiful, for the call is coming when real music and musicians will be in demand. Look at the picture theaters today; in the legitimate picture places music from the masters is played, [and a] fine caliber of musicianship is required for this work. This is only one of the things that jazz has done to cripple the legitimate musician.

The Jazz Crazed World

The world is jazz crazy. Europe, Asia, Africa, North and South America and even the far East Orient have all gone jazz wild. In China they have imported an American jazz band to play music there in the largest American hotel. This jazz band has been in China for three years and has been offered a five-year contract. All over the world the American jazz music has caught grip. In sentimental Europe no effort is made by the high-calibered musicians to learn this American music. They would rather import bands from this side to do the work. Many efforts have been made in England and France to influence the labor boards to forbid entry of the American jazz bands. It worked with the actors, but as yet no ruling has been made against the jazz musicians.

Jazz Appeals

This music, jazz, appeals to many emotions of the human being. It offers a lure of immorality to some and to others it is just a laugh fancy. Some it thrills, to some it makes toil easier, and to the younger dance folks it offers an entry to the road that leads to shame and destruction. There is a syncopated form of music that is delightful to the ear. It is the popular melodies artistically arranged by diligent music arrangers that have graduated from the jazz class. The dangerous jazz is the barbaric, filthy, discordant, wild, and shriek music, that should be eliminated from the public dance halls and should be disqualified by the decent element. This writer has several orchestras and it is only upon request from patrons that this sort of music is rendered, and then it is short and sweet.

Source: *Chicago Defender*, July 16, 1927, 6.

This final paragraph reveals Peyton's conflict with the new music. He understood the African American roots of jazz and reviled the white appropriation of any black music. Yet a good jazz musician must, for him, demonstrate an understanding of European-influenced harmony, melody, rhythm, and technique. He writes that the best jazz is not solely African in origin, but is "purely American," forged in a country where "crude rhythmic noise" could find "sweet melodic accompaniment." He also provides a long list of composers and musicians who he feels have met these criteria, giving the utmost respect to his former employer Wilbur Sweatman:

The Origin of Jazz

The origin of jazz music has been attributed to many sources and most writers claim that their reports are authoritative. Many writers have gone back as far as the beginning of the world, and they have been contradicted by the later day writers who claim the birth of jazz at later dates.

The story about jazz having its origin in Africa is imagination. Many claim the natives created it, first by beating intensely on the tom-tom in rhythmic fashion. This may or it may not be true, but if it is true there was sweet melodic accompaniment to the crude rhythmic noise. Today jazz music has developed into an institution. It is purely American, and this great country recognizes its great importance among its arts. Europe, too, has grasped the American jazz music. This so-called jazz music really was given birth in America and we are responsible for its creation.

About fifty years ago "ragtime" was born and from this music jazz has had its evolution. Scott Joplin was the greatest ragtime composer of his time. His "Maple Leaf Rag" was a masterpiece of technique and originality and for tone color and rhythm his euphonic sounds brought to the syncopated music world a new idea in syncopated composition.

Both of these numbers required artistic musicianship to handle them, as the technique was difficult and required fast fingering. Stage pianists loved them and played them as flash numbers. We now come along down the line to Will Marion Cook, who contributed *Clorindy*, which at that time set America wild with its creative syncopated figures, one of them especially, "Whose Dat Said Chicken in Dis Crowd?" which was one of the largest sellers of the day. Then J. Rosamond Johnson came along with his *Red Moon* score and until today we all remember such numbers as "The Big Red Shawl," "Sambo," and before these hits the immortal "Under the Bamboo Tree."

Ernest Hogan and Sam Lucas were also contributors to the syncopated music world, and their song numbers are in the standard album today. James Scott was also a brilliant ragtime composer who ably contributed to the evolution of syncopated music into our present day jazz music.

We come on down the line to Cecil Mack, Chris Smit, Jim Europe, Lucky Roberts, Maceo Pinkard, Spencer Williams, Clarence Williams, Joe Jordon, Eddie Haywood, [and] W. C. Handy, all of whom have done their part in the making of this scintillating jazz music.

The Instrumentalists

Now we will take a few moments with the instrumentalists, those who put syncopation before the public and who deserve as much credit as the composers because without them the works would have gained no publicity.

Ted Lewis, Isham Jones, Paul Biese, Rudy Wiedoff, Paul Spechet, [and] Ben Bernie were about the first along this line.[2] They came before Whiteman and we may call them the jazz trailblazers. They originated the weird, barbaric, musical expressions that attracted notice. It was all in the

---

[2]These musicians are discussed in Hentoff and McCarthy, *Jazz* (NY: Rinehart and Company, 1959).

orchestral arrangement. It was about this time that the saxophone was introduced in the modern orchestra. Its capabilities were unlimited in the production of freak musical expressions and today it is indispensable in the modern jazz orchestra.

Before the above mentioned musicians came into their fame, Wilber Sweatman was playing the clarinet in the Little Grand Theater in Chicago. In combination were three players, piano, clarinet, and drums. The elite of Chicago was the support of this unique little theater, about the only one in the neighborhood in 1905. Mr. Sweatman led the orchestra with his clarinet and made a great reputation for syncopating tunes on his instrument. This writer truly believes Wilbur Sweatman was the creator of jazz music. White musicians would come to this theater from far and near to hear this little freak orchestra He would moan his tones, shriek them, and all of a sudden in rhythm would rapidly play difficult figures in syncopated mood. This style of playing was adopted by the white musicians and I do not believe any of the authorities on jazz know of this period and of Mr. Sweatman's activities at that time. Nevertheless it is very true and this writer takes the responsibility of handing to Wilbur Sweatman the crown as the creator of real jazz music.

Today we have such well-known jazz players as Johnny Dunn, King Joe Oliver, Reuben Reeves, Tommy Ladiner [Landier], Louis Armstrong, William Green, Fess Williams, Darnell Howard, and many others. In conclusion I will say that we can justly claim the origin, the development, and perpetuation of jazz music and any other claim is erroneous.

Source: *Chicago Defender*, June 16, 1928, 6.

Ultimately Peyton came to realize that jazz was a musical force in the world and that the musicians who played it could be, to his standards, good musicians. In this essay, he concedes that jazz is popular, has a history as a part of the black experience, and can be played well if it is executed by well-organized and trained ensembles:

The Jazz-Crazed Public

Jazz music seems to hold a firm grip on the public, especially the dancing element, who will not patronize places of amusement where the "hot" jazz band is not the feature.

This word, jazz," seems not to be entirely understood by quite a few people. First, it is a coined word, created by some unknown person and belongs to the "slang" family of expressions.

Ragtime music, which swept the country a score of years or more, has evolutionized itself into the present-day music craze, and they call it "jazz." Ragtime carried its sweet melody flows, accompanied by brilliant harmonic embellishments, the theme or melody always predominating, and when developed for the orchestra, it was delightful to hear—smooth and mellow.

Discordant Jazz

Down on the levees and plantations of the sunny South was the real beginning of jazz. A group of singers and players would get together after sundown, when the day's toil was over, and harmonize.

They would pick some piece the group were familiar with, and each person would extemporaneously compose his own counterpart or variation to the melody. Rich and natural figures would come forth from the instruments: tones overblown, but effective in character, seemed to put a jovial spirit in the listener. It is this style of jazz playing that has developed itself into the jazz of today. The discordant style is still played by the leading orchestras of the country, but they are wise in not playing it too often. It is usually used as encore dance music.

Versatile Orchestra

The orchestra today that possesses versatility is the one which is in demand—one that is able to play "hokum" and first-class music. By first-class music I mean the modern popular dance arrangements compiled by the expert arranger, who puts it in the symphonic atmosphere. In the latter style there is no tome to fake. You must read your score accurately, because the brother next to you might suddenly come in with a solo break. With this music the faker has no chance. He must either get down off the band stand or stand the humiliation.

Popular Jazz

The style of jazz the public has gone wild about is that which Paul Whiteman, Vincent Lopez, the late James Reese Europe, Leroy Smith, and Fletcher Henderson's orchestra are putting out—beautiful melodies garnished with eccentric figurations, propelled by strict rhythm. The mushy, discordant music is on the wane and will very soon retreat to the realm of oblivion.

Of course the dance fans want it played during the evening, but it must not become monotonous. It is sandwiched in by the wide-awake orchestra leader. A few will loudly applaud this discordant stuff, making one think it is what the public wants.

I base my contention on the above facts from careful study of the situation. The successful orchestras have adopted the versatile way and they have created first-rankers by public opinion.

Picture Houses Use Jazz

The largest movie houses in the country are in the market for novelty jazz bands. They use them as crowd drawers and they seldom miss, especially if the band has a name. I have noticed that of all the attractions on the bill to receive entrance receptions, the jazz band always gets the heavier applause. If they put it over, the show is broken up, which goes to convince me that the masses want jazz in its polite formation and will pay money to hear it. In Chicago there was a well-known theater that was a losing proposition. Everything was tried out in the form of entertainment to put the house over, but it didn't hit. The house fell into the hands of new lessees who had been watching the trend of things at this house. They acquired the theater and immediately installed a jazz band, with an eccentric leader, and for the past year this house has been one of the best paying theaters in Chicago.

Russia Comes In

Russia, the Great Bear of Europe, has finally lowered the barriers against jazz. She has been an impregnable fortress against the invasion of jazz. No doubt some of our American tourists journeying in the Soviet have informed them of what they are missing, telling them of the pep and vigor that jazz puts onto one.

In a recent article this writer told of the refusal of Russia to admit into the country Sam Wooding's orchestra, with the Chocolate Kiddies show, an all-Race aggregation, who have made the old world sit up and take notice. They gave as the cause protection of the Russian grand opera, claiming they wanted no distraction of the people's mind from this art. The color of the show made no difference, so that's that. Now, a few months later, Russia—the government itself—has contracted with Frank Withers and his six-piece jazz band to play for the Russian people.

Now Russia is going to hear real jazz played by a real Race jazz band. The leader, Frank Withers, hails from Emporia, Kansas, and is one of the most eccentric trombone players in the world. He and his band have held Paris awed for the past five years with their novelty musical creations, and now they are called to Russia to show her how to get peppy. They are traveling with the Soviet Philharmonic Society to enliven the dull night life of Russia's biggest cities with the latest American jazz at $200 a night for the six-piece orchestra and will run for four months, with the government holding an option for a continued period.

The appearance of one of the musicians outside the Soviet foreign office, carrying a saxophone, excited great curiosity among the Russians, few of whom had ever seen either a member of our Race or a saxophone.

Jazz Music to Stay

So the reader will see the effect this "American jazz" has on the other big countries. England, France, Germany, Italy, and Spain have welcomed it and have contracted bands to stay and play it for them—a wonderful field for our Race musicians if they can bolster up enough courage to leave their haunts. A great opportunity awaits the hustling, leader-contractor. Pick up a bunch, rehearse them well, and make application to different consuls in Washington, telling them you want to go to their countries with your jazz band, or advertise in the national newspapers, whose addresses can be obtained from your town newspaper information department.

In America the symphonic jazz will live, and it requires real musicians to play it. It is now standard music with the American people, and I am proud to say that our Race are standout factors in its development.

Source: *Chicago Defender*, February 27, 1926, 6.

Peyton and the New Orleans Players

Peyton's style and personal beliefs concerning music contrasted markedly with those of the New Orleans players. The new arrivals to Chicago initially did not play his kind of orchestral jazz. But he recognized the energy of their new rhythms, and that several of them were highly talented, including cornetist Freddy Keppard and Joe Oliver, whose orchestra competed with his own. And by 1927 nobody could deny the musical supremacy of Louis Armstrong:

Creole Musicians

The original Creole Jazz Band found their way to Chicago in the year of 1914. They opened an engagement at the Grand Theater and were a distinct hit on the all-star vaudeville bill. How well do I remember that opening night, and at that time I predicted that the Creole style of playing music would soon grip the Middle West. This original combination worked their way to New York over the largest circuits in the country. They spread their weird, scintillating music all over Broadway and were signed as a feature attraction in a Broadway production called Town Topics. In the bunch were Freddie Keppard, now famous as a jazz cornetist; George Baquet, a wonderful musician and woodwind artist; Bill Johnson, the man who brought us the style of pizzicato bass playing; Jimmie Palo, a clever violinist, now deceased, Eddie Vincent, jazz trombonist, and Bill Williams.

These newcomers made their hit and at the same time brought on jealousy of the northern brother musicians. They could play sweet and jazz, and with it they played soft. The brother had been hanging away for many years around these parts and the advent of the Creole musicians in our midst was somewhat of an innovation.[3] Time went on and they made a huge success of music. Their Creole brothers down home, learning of this success, decided to come to the land of the free and plenty money. One by one they came north, most all of them top-notchers on their instruments, with the probable exception of one, Sydney Bechet, who did not know one note from another, but was a natural wizard on the clarinet, and proclaimed by the whites to be the greatest clarinetist in the game at that time. Then came along King Joe Oliver, whose name to-day brings pleasant memories. Joe located himself in the Royal Garden café and dance hall. With his little six-piece band he startled Chicago. White musicians from all over the city would gather at the Royal Gardens to hear King Joe blow those weird, soulful tunes. He was really a profitable asset to the place. Later on he brought the present king of jazz cornet player, Louis Armstrong. A green looking country boy, with big forehead, thin lips and robust physique, this newcomer brought us an entirely different style of playing than King Joe had given us. He was younger, had more power of delivery, and could send his stuff out with a knack. Today Louis Armstrong is in great demand. He could work day and night. He plays the early part of the evening in a theater and after theater hours he doubles in the night clubs.

---

[3]Throughout his writings Peyton uses the phrase " the brother" to refer to his primary readership, Chicago's black musicians. Here he means those musicians already in Chicago when the southerners arrived.

Better Dance Players

The Creole musicians are better dance players than the brother. They have a peculiar rhythm and they can play humorously. One of their great endowments is soft playing, which is the vogue today. The Creole musicians brought the style here and they should have credit for it. Their coming here has revolutionized the dance style. They are poor show players, but in dance work they reign supreme.

Meet Opposition

In Chicago and New York they met with opposition from the brother and at times things were very disagreeable for them, but they stuck together and attended to their own business and finally won out in the battle, until the brother locked arms and worked harmoniously with them. Today Creoles and the brother work together and nothing is thought of it. They are all one, and it is a wonderful thing, too.

Creole Stars

In Chicago are many of the famous Creole star players, who are fine musicians and feature musicians. They are Jimmie Noone, Emanuel Perez, Arthur (Bud) Scott, Freddie Keppard, Arthur Campbell, William Oray [almost certainly Edward "Kid" Ory], Joe Oliver, William Dutrey, Louis Armstrong, the Dodd brothers, and Simion brothers, Charles Elgar, and others who have helped largely in making Chicago one of the greatest dance orchestra fields in the world. More power to the Creole musicians and may the brother and them always work harmoniously together.

Source: *Chicago Defender*, November 19, 1927, 6.

Peyton Taking a Stand for Musicians

As we have seen, Peyton was conflicted concerning jazz as a whole, and the New Orleans musicians specifically. It's tempting to see those writings expressing disdain for the new music as a manifestation of a conservative, controlling ego. But I agree more with Eric Porter's assessment: "[Petyon's] sometimes schizophrenic attitude toward jazz was in part a product of his concerns about the employment opportunities available to African American musicians and the artistic limitations the music industry placed on these performers."[4] Whatever else may be thought about him, it is clear that Peyton was a strong advocate for his "brother" African American musicians. Often his writings regarding proper musicianship and conduct read more like instruction rather than admonition, preparing younger musicians to succeed in the racist world that employed them:

Our Musicians Shut Out

Many avenues in the great American orchestra field are closed to our Race musicians. The opportunities are very limited nowadays. The great curse of race prejudice is pitted against us, although we have the goods and can deliver them.

Some few of our orchestras have gotten under the barrier, but as a whole and considering the broad field that America offers for orchestras, we are poorly represented. The rottenest kind of white orchestra can get the best of jobs when they in no way compare with our crack Race orchestras. The barrier is lifted for them and is slammed down when the brother applies for the job.

In most places where our musicians are hired, they are forced to work cheaper, and this is mainly the reason that many of them are installed in some of the white amusement places. The union prices are alike for both races, but in order to get work some of our contractors, it is said, have taken the jobs at the employer's price.

Reports have reached this writer that the employers have shown convincing evidence that the white musicians also work cheaply, too. It is said that white musicians have

---

[4]Eric Porter, *What is This Thing Called Jazz?: African American Musicians as Artists, Critics, and Activists* (Berkeley: University of California Press, 2002): 34.

agreed to work cheaper than our bunch in order to get our bunch out of the jobs and get control themselves. Why is all of this knifing done? Simply because of prejudice and nothing else.

The saying of old is "art knows no color line." This may or it may not be true, but it is not applied to our group of musicians. The exhibitor who hires orchestras has made a canvass of the amusement managers, asking them not to hire our musicians. In Chicago, in one of the largest wards in the town, certain political pressure has been brought to bear in order to shut out our musicians in this ward, and so far they have succeeded.

The booking agents throughout the country tell their clients who apply to them for our musicians that we are uncivilized, flirts, and void of cleanliness, and they, the booking agents, advise their clients to use white musicians. With this unfairness to our musicians and the convincing argument of the booking agent, no trouble is encountered in turning the client away from the idea of hiring Race musicians. The battle against the brother is finally won.

Other Causes

Let us ask ourselves this question: "What is the direct cause of this situation? Are we ourselves to blame for this condition" In answer I will say "Yes, we are, bunch." We have been too negligent of our jobs. We have not carried ourselves just right. The white musicians may not be as good as we are in discipline, but their misbehavior passes by unnoticed. But when our musicians do anything, and it does not have to amount to much either, the whole world takes notice of it. That is why we have to be so careful of our conduct on the job. They give it to us for playing good music and would rather have us, but the booking agent lends an argument against us and we prove this argument by not doing the proper thing on the job.

We have orchestras holding a few responsible jobs in different parts of the country, and in looking up their history I find that they are all hitting the ball. They are all real musicians and in their organizations they have the proper kind of discipline. About ten years ago in New York the Race musicians held full sway. They were preferred mostly in the elite social circles. The Wannamakers, the Vanderbilts, and other millionaire families would not think of giving their affairs without the services of a Race orchestra and Race entertainers. Handsome salaries were paid them and for a few hours work nightly. It was a hard matter to get first class musicians to take a steady job by the week. They could make more money working only three nights and they had the rest of the week to hang around and have a good time. Things went along fine until crude conduct, disappointments, and other general misbehavior caused them to lose out and when the final curtain rang down on one of our greatest leaders, James Reese Europe, it was the finish.

James Europe held the ship together. He was a master musician and a natural born leader of men and was highly considered by the above named group of millionaires. At his passing the bunch went wild and lost their foothold and today the white musicians have the best class of work in the eastern metropolis. So what opportunities come our way now, bunch, let us make the best of them. Let us do our work and in time we, with our originality and natural ability, can redeem ourselves and regain the place we once held, and when we do let us not forget our past experiences and watch our step.

Do These Things

Stay away from the guests, eliminate smoking on the bandstand, do not indulge in unnecessary conversation on the bandstand, keep your uniforms in apple pie order, do not be afraid to practice your instrument often and when called for rehearsals by your leader, don't send up a wail because your orchestra practices too much. There is no such thing as "too much rehearsal." When on the job work and play when you are through. Follow this and you can't go wrong and at the same time we will get more work. Get the respect of our employers and sail on to the final goal of success.

Source: *Chicago Defender*, October 8, 1927, 6.

Peyton's advocacy for his fellow musicians extended to his union work. He was an officer and recruiter for the Black Musician's Local 208. Here he extols the virtues of the union, even stating that it is preferable to the white union, in which African Americans could not advance:

Organized Musicians

The organization of the Musicians Union of America has done much to standardize the profession. During the many years of its great activity in the American Federation of Labor it has become an important factor in the development of the country.

Our group of musicians have alone benefited wholly by the existence of this body. We work under the same conditions that the white musicians work, being paid the same salaries, working the same hours and, in fact, enjoying all the rights and privileges enjoyed by them, are applicable to our group.

It has given us the advantage of organization. It has given us our own officers, and we have learned the power of organization and its demand for things that are just and beneficial to the musician.

Musicians Recognized

In this country the Race musicians are recognized in body by the American Federation of Musicians, whose headquarters are in New York City. In some cities our group are members of the white locals and are eligible to join anywhere in the country. Of course, prejudice finds its birth in many places and acts as a barrier to our group, but in New York City, Detroit MI, Denver, CO and a few other cities there is one local and both races compose its membership. Today we have several locals in the federation that are officered by and composed of Race members, and are standout units in the great world of music. In most cases it is of our own choosing to have our own locals, but I don't want the reader to misunderstand me—we are welcome to join the white local, but for social reasons we would rather have our own headquarters.

Local No. 208, Chicago

One of the largest and most prosperous locals in the federation is in Chicago. It is local No. 208, with a membership of over seven hundred. This local has been spoken of in the national convention by [AFM] President Weber, who said it was one of the finest in the federation. This is wonderful when you think of the size of the Federation, and the President picks out our own to commend.

Our Own Officers

In the white local we have no chance to become officers, although we have the ability. The preponderance of the white vote would overwhelm any effort to elect a Race official, because of the majority vote of the white brother, so we benefit by having our own locals, because we have our own officials who get the inner workings of the federation and stand shoulder to shoulder in the national convention with the rest of them. Our locals are chartered by the American Federation of Labor and are given the same power of functioning as the white locals....

Advantages Gained

I can remember back 10 years, when $25 a week was considered a handsome salary for the musician, and it stayed in that class until our group began to see the power of their organization. The union was organized, but it was idle, its rooms were used more for a hangout by the old-time musicians. They seemed satisfied with conditions. The white theater owners in our own district offered what they thought you were worth for your services and got away with it.

But during this time the younger musicians came into power in the organization, primed with intellect and pride, injecting into the union modern ideas. In time things were shaped up and conditions and salaries increased, and today the musician is receiving handsome compensation for his work. Although it was forced, it goes to show the power of organization. To the brothers everywhere, I want to say, get into the union; it cannot do any harm. Do not let anyone scare you. If you live up to your oath after you get in, you will benefit, because your union will see to it that you are paid a living wage for your service....

Source: *Chicago Defender*, March 13, 1926, 6.

Peyton on Louis Armstrong

This chapter and this book conclude with a selection of Dave Peyton's essays concerning Louis Armstrong. Peyton began writing about Armstrong when the cornetist left the Fletcher Henderson Orchestra and New York City in November 1925 to return to the Dreamland and the Vendome Theaters in Chicago. Peyton's writings follow Armstrong through his time with Erskine Tate at the Vendome, to his joining Carroll Dickenson's Orchestra at the Sunset, his move to the new, elaborate Savoy Ballroom (Chicago), and end with Armstrong's final departure from Chicago and initial success in New York in August 1929.

Although Peyton is often criticized for his conservative views and domineering presence on the music scene, his writings on Armstrong, when taken together, reveal him to be sympathetic to, and even admiring of, the younger musician. If Peyton did take umbrage with lesser jazz improvisers and New Orleans musicians, and if he did feel threatened by them, he could not, and did not, deny the musical genius who was lighting up The Stroll:

Mr. Armstrong, the famous cornetist, will grace the first chair in the Dreamland Orchestra sometime this week. William Bottoms made him an unusual salary offer to return to Chicago. Mr. Armstrong has been the feature cornetist with the Famous Fletcher Henderson Orchestra in the East.

Source: *Chicago Defender*, November 7, 1925, 6.

...Louis Armstrong, the cornetist, has been engaged by Erskine Tate to play in the famous Vendome Theater Orchestra. Mr. Armstrong is a versatile artist, and will be an asset to this orchestra...

Source: *Chicago Defender*, December 12, 1925, 7.

...Louis Armstrong, the cornet player, was slated to join Joe Oliver's orchestra, but switched over to Carroll Dickerson's Sunset Café Orchestra at the last minute. Louis is in demand in the Windy City and there is a reason—he toots a wicked trumpet....

Source: *Chicago Defender*, April 14, 1926, 6.

...Louis Armstrong, the "iron lip cornet wonder," is the big feature in Carroll Dickerson's Sunset Orchestra, Chicago....

Source: *Chicago Defender*, June 5, 1926, 6.

...Louis Armstrong and his Hot Five broke up the big ball June 12 with their hot playing. Some jazz band! I tell 'em so!

Source: *Chicago Defender*, June 19. 1926, 6.

Carroll Dickerson and his fine orchestra are turning things over at the Sunset Café, Chicago. Carroll has the best dance band in Chicago, and aside from this they can play a show and real concert music. Louis Armstrong is a feature in the band and lately Cecil Irvin has been added. Earl Hines, one of the cleverest pianists in the country, spanks the ivories. Other members of the band are all first-class, versatile musicians, and under the capable leadership of Carroll they are a standout unit in the west. This organization has injected new life into the Sunset since their installation, and the cause of the large nightly crowds is partly Carroll Dickerson's Orchestra...

Source: *Chicago Defender*, July 3, 1926, 6.

Louis Armstrong, the world's greatest jazz cornetist, will sever his connection with the Vendome Theater Orchestra April 17. Louis is in such great demand for his original style of playing that greater compensation is offered him on the outside. He will be a great loss to the Vendome Orchestra as a feature man. In Chicago Louis has a strong following that may have a telling effect on the business at the Vendome....

Source: *Chicago Defender*, April 9, 1927. 6.

Our jazz cornet king, Louis Armstrong, has edited two books that will add much to the development of jazz music in America. Louis has penned in book form some of his eccentric styles of playing. This will come as good news to those who have long admired this little giant of jazz! He has a book on "Jazz Breaks." One hundred to select from that can be adapted to most any piece of music. The book contains jazz endings, jazz connections, and jazz breaks. The other book contains 100 "Jazz Hot Tunes," builds on the Louis Armstrong style of playing The Melrose Music Co. is publishing both books for Louis who is all smiles nowadays, riding around in his brand new Hupmobile 8. The writer admires the exceptional ability of Louis as a "stand-out player." He will always be an important asset in anybody's orchestra. The public is wild about him for his individuality, a regular fellow at all times. By himself, in a regular orchestra, under a real leader, let him alone. I say so.

Source: *Chicago Defender*, April 16, 1927, 6.

...The famed jazz cornetist, Louis Armstrong, is featured with the Carroll Dickerson Orchestra in Chicago's Savoy Ballroom. Louis has the gang with him and when he gets through with his cyclonic jazz figures, he stops the ball. Louis is the only musician I know of who really stops the ball, just as an actor stops the show....

Source: *Chicago Defender*, April 28, 1928, 6.

..."Pouring oil" is an expression created by the musicians in Chicago. By that they mean some band has played better than the other. Last Saturday night at the Savoy Ballroom in Chicago three orchestras played: Clarence Black and his gang, Carroll Dickerson and his gang, and Erskine Tate and his gang....

A note was handed to the house orchestras by Mr. Fagin, asking them to join in and play the "Savoy Blues," with [the Clarence Black Orchestra]. This was wonderful. The three bands, consisting of 37 players, rocked the beautiful ballroom with their scintillating music. It was Louis Armstrong, a member of Carroll Dickerson's orchestra, whom this writer has termed the "Jazz Master," who saved the hour. As the boys would say, Louie poured plenty of oil and it soaked in it too. The crowd gathered around him and wildly cheered for more and more. Louie really poured oil last Saturday night and Carroll Dickerson was proud as a peacock of his robust jazz master, Louis Armstrong....

Source: *Chicago Defender*, May 5, 1928, 6.

One of my most valued friends is King Menelik, who is none other than the great Louis Armstrong, the jazz cornet wizard, who has slaughtered all of the ofay jazz demons appearing at the Savoy recently. Louis doesn't get "hot" until this writer gives him a look and yells, "Go get him, Louie," and then the war is on. There is only one King Menelik....[5]

Source: *Chicago Defender*, July 14, 1928, 6.

The famous cornetist, Louis Armstrong, is taking a much-needed vacation this week in Idlewild, Mich. The Savoy Ballroom, where Louis works in Carroll Dickerson's orchestra, was last this week without King Menelik, whom

---

[5]In several essays around this time, Peyton calls Armstrong "King Menelik," referring to Menelik II, who ruled Ethiopia from 1844-1913, chased out Italian invaders, and expanded the Ethiopian empire.

this writer thinks is the greatest novelty jazz cornetist in the game. He has an individuality in playing his cornet that wins. Mr. Menelik has no peer anywhere in the world when it comes to jazz cornet playing....

Source: *Chicago Defender*, August 4, 1928, 6.

...The name of the orchestra that has taken New York by storm is none other than our own Louis Armstrong and his Recording Orchestra, of the Savoy Ballroom, Chicago. The boys are intact just as they left the Windy City. The only change is the name of the band. Carroll Dickerson is the leader as of yore, but the New York exhibitors thought that the name should be changed owing to the tremendous popularity of the famous cornetist, Louis Armstrong.

Hence the change in name. The unit opens in Connie's Inn on June 24 for an indefinite run. The boys all shoot regards to the gang back home in Chicago, and Sutie (Zutty Singleton), the dapper drummer, says "It's just too bad Jim...."

Source: *Chicago Defender*, June 22, 1929, 6.

...Chicago's own Louis Armstrong and his orchestra are the current rage in New York. They have taken the city by storm. They have things their own way and to this writer they are playing better than ever before. Louis is doubling himself at the Hudson Theater, where he is a feature in the Hot Chocolate Show orchestra, and after the theater he is with his own unit, playing at Connie's Inn, a popular night club....

Source: *Chicago Defender*, August 10, 1929, 7.

Index

249

About the Author

Marc Rice is Professor of Musicology at Truman State University and is the Area Chair of the Perspectives of Music program. He has extensively published on gender and race issues concerning jazz in the Midwest. His work can be found in the journals *American Music, Musical Quarterly*, the forthcoming *Encyclopedia of African American Music*, and the *Grove Encyclopedia of American Music*. He has also conducted fieldwork in Louisiana, tracing the Cajun music revival, and is currently researching the implications of the new media on musical production and consumption. He teaches the music history sequence for music majors, graduate courses on early music and music and improvisation, as well as courses on jazz history, the music of Louisiana, and music and political protest.